D0234846

ROBERT PLANT

LED ZEPPELIN
JIMMY PAGE
&
THE SOLO YEARS

Published in 2008 by
INDEPENDENT MUSIC PRESS
Independent Music Press is an imprint of I.M. P. Publishing Limited
This Work is Copyright © I. M. P. Publishing Ltd 2008

Robert Plant
Led Zeppelin, Jimmy Page & The Solo Years
by Neil Daniels

All Rights Reserved

This book is sold subject to the condition that it shall not,
by way of trade or otherwise, be lent, re-sold, hired out or otherwise
circulated without the publisher's prior consent in any form of binding
or cover other than that which it is published and without
a similar condition being imposed on the subsequent purchaser.

No part of this publication may be reproduced, stored in
a retrieval system, or transmitted in any form or by any means,
electronic, mechanical, photocopying, recording or otherwise,
without the prior permission of the copyright owner.

British Library Cataloguing-in-Publication Data.
A catalogue for this book is available from The British Library.

ISBN 0-9552822-7-6 and 978-0-9552822-7-0

Cover Design by Fresh Lemon.
Edited by Martin Roach.

Printed in the UK.

Independent Music Press
P.O. Box 69,
Church Stretton, Shropshire
SY6 6WZ

Visit us on the web at: www.impbooks.com
and www.myspace.com/independentmusicpress

For a free catalogue, e-mail us at: info@impbooks.com
Fax: 01694 720049

ROBERT PLANT

LED ZEPPELIN
JIMMY PAGE
&
THE SOLO YEARS

by Neil Daniels

Independent Music Press

CONTENTS

ACKNOWLEDGEMENTS

First and foremost I'd like to thank Martin Roach for asking me to write this book in the first place and I must extend my hand to the staff at Independent Music Press.

In many ways, this book is a complementary companion piece to my first book – *The Story Of Judas Priest: Defenders Of The Faith* – because the earlier careers of both artists overlap in obvious ways: Robert Plant and Judas Priest come from the same area of England and both artists began gigging in the same era prior to finding success in the 1970s, onwards.

For this biography I have occasionally repeated quotes from interviews I conducted in 2006 for that Judas Priest book; I spoke to various former members of Judas Priest, namely, guitarist Ernie Chataway, bassist Bruno Stapenhill, drummer John Ellis and singer Al Atkins. I have also used some fresh quotes from Al too. I'd also like to thank Jim Simpson (Big Bear Records) for his time during the period I spent researching my book on Judas Priest; his stories on the Midlands music scene in the 1960s proved more than helpful for this book too; likewise many thanks to Pete Boot.

I'd like to thank the following musicians, fans and acquaintances of Robert Plant/Led Zeppelin for their time with interviews: Al Atkins (ex-Judas Priest,) Frankie Banali (Quiet Riot,) Ernie Chataway (ex-Judas Priest,) Michael Davis (MC5,) Kevin DuBrow (Quiet Riot,) John Ellis (ex-Judas Priest,) Tony Harnell (Starbreaker,) Simon Phillips (Toto,) Don Powell (Slade,) Brian 'Bruno' Stapenhill (ex-Judas Priest,) Mark Stein (Vanilla Fudge,) Marc Storace (Krokus,) Joe Lynn Turner (ex-Rainbow/Deep Purple) and Midge Ure (ex-Ultravox).

I'd like to pass on my thanks to those musicians and producers who have previously worked with Robert Plant and helped the author gain an insight into Plant's working methods: Moya Brennan, Andy Edwards, Chris Hughes, Tim Jarvis, Tim Palmer, Hossam Razmy, Innes Sibun, Mark Stanway and Dave Weckl.

I'd like to say a small thank you to John Oakley for his little anecdote about Plant in his pre-Led Zeppelin days and thank you to journalist Deborah Frost for her article. I'd also like to thank Bruce Mee, my editor at *Fireworks*, for giving me his extensive collection of rock magazines from the 1980s and a big thank you to author/journalist John Tucker for offering advice, guidance and support throughout the hectic writing of this book.

Thank you to my friend Robert McKenna (*Spark*) for designing and setting up my website *www.neildaniels.com*, which proved invaluable in terms of pre publicity for this book. Thanks to my family and friends and to my partner, Emma Kilgannon.

The next round is on me people!

For John and Mary (R.I.P.). Thanks for three years of hospitality.

INTRODUCTION:
A LIFE IN MUSIC

*"I'm relentless ... I've got a career which
doesn't just lean on one period."*
Robert Plant speaking to *Classic Rock* in 2004

This is not a book about Led Zeppelin. This is a book about Robert Plant. The man who has more nicknames than probably any other rock star: there's the unimaginative 'Planty', the mundane 'Percy' and the iconic 'The Golden God'. In an interview with author and *Spin* magazine writer Chuck Klosterman, Plant said, surprisingly, that he'd never read the famed Led Zeppelin unofficial bio *Hammer Of The Gods* but "... the only thing I read was the 'After Zeppelin' part, because I was so eager to get on with music and stop living in a dream state."

Evidently, Plant himself wants the world to understand and appreciate his solo music and what better way than in a book? After all, there have been books on Jimmy Page, John Bonham and even manger Peter Grant, but never Mr. Plant.

Robert Plant's interesting and eccentric solo career has long been overshadowed by the mighty Led Zep – a band surely worthy of the title of "the world's first and most dangerous rock and roll band." They were implausibly creative, brilliant and flawed all at the same time. But Zep's career came to an abrupt and highly publicised end on September 24, 1980 when John Bonham was found dead. How could they go on without him? The fact is that they couldn't and they knew it, so they wisely went their separate ways.

On December 4, 1980, an official (albeit ambiguous) statement by the remaining members of the band – Jimmy Page, Robert Plant and John Paul Jones – and their infamous manager Peter Grant was issued declaring the end of the band; Led Zeppelin was over ...

More so than any other member of Led Zeppelin, Plant in particular found it extremely difficult to be creative and thirsty for music after the unfortunate death of his close friend, band mate and fellow Midlander. After some thought, Plant started with a clean slate and began jamming with an ad hoc R&B covers outfit called The Honeydrippers. The project gave him some degree of confidence to pursue a solo career that came with the superlative *Pictures At Eleven* in 1982 and, from then on, began a deeply fascinating albeit at times inconsistent series of solo albums that continue to be made right up until the time of writing. The interesting thing about Robert Plant's career post-Led Zeppelin is that you never know what he is going to do next and it's that kind of creative spark and willingness to explore new musical avenues that is a fundamental part of his enduring legacy. Although some critics harshly accuse him of being pretentious and self-important, others admire his passion for creating different sounds and landscapes.

He went solo on his own terms. He didn't tour straight away and for years he refused to play any Led Zeppelin songs – the former probably out of confidence and the latter due to a desire to mark out his own territory. He downright refused to play 'Stairway To Heaven' – a song he has disliked for a long time – on the grounds that he could not, and indeed still can't, relate to its mystical, undecipherable lyrics. Yet in the late 1980s, armed with a new band, he had a change of heart, gave in to demand, his inner voice, and began playing Zep tunes albeit with different arrangements; he famously tweaked them 'here and there' to make himself more interested in his old material. Importantly, Plant has also had a few solo hit singles in his time and is happy with the format – intriguing really, when you think that Led Zeppelin refused point blank to release any of their songs as singles in Britain[1] (although record company politics saw singles released abroad against the band's wishes).

His solo commercial success has always been famously unpredictable; he also worked with Jimmy on the extravagant Page & Plant project, and has guested on numerous occasions and gone through numerous line-ups for his own solo tours and records. Yet there's always a hint of former glories. One journalist, writing in *The Music Box*, said of Plant's solo work: "He also appeared to be paralysed by his attempts to hold onto the past while slipping into the present."

The biggest problem was that the Robert Plant of the 1970s was emphatically not the Robert Plant of the 1980s and he never wanted to go back to his old self, so he had to play around with the structures of those Zep songs years later. Explaining in *Classic Rock* magazine in September 2003 why he continuously recoils from Led Zeppelin's mass profile and popularity, he said: "It's like: 'Oh, get out of the way! There he is again!' I've seen so many third-party images of myself from another time that I just drift past it … I don't care about it. It isn't boosting my ego. It's just something that happened that was marvelous. I'm quite detached from it in a way."

However, both careers, both men, both Robert Plants, the two separate lives, finally merged in the late 1980s, thus creating a blistering unification of highly-imaginative and unique songs.

It is important to note that there have been a few one-off Led Zeppelin 'reunions' after John Bonham's death and repetitive rumours of a full-blown world tour are persistently circulating in the press, on internet forums and amongst anoraks, especially in the wake of the December 2007 reunion gig in London.

Robert Plant has made a fascinating solo career against all the odds. His solo albums may not match the enormous record sales of Sir Paul McCartney or Rod Stewart, but he is content with himself as a singer-songwriter-performer without playing to the American charts the way the aforementioned Rod Stewart has with his kitsch *American Classics* series of albums, or invading the classical charts the way McCartney has – Plant knows his boundaries and he'll stay well within those confines … usually.

That's not to say Plant hasn't made a few wrong turns here and there. En route to solo stardom he has made the odd mistake. It is certainly believable that in the 1980s he disregarded his love of the blues and folk music for a sound that was drowned in synthesisers and glossy production (which is similar to the route Phil Collins and Eric Clapton took). Yet, even then, there was always a random hint of Zeppelin – the tinges of blues and folk music.

In recent years as a solo artist, Plant has received glowing reviews for his studio work and in particular his live performances from just about every quarter of the notoriously tough British music press, gaining strong reviews in top quality music magazines as well as high-brow broad-sheet newspapers. He has also won awards and accolades outside of the Led Zeppelin camp while he receives due praise for his charity work and his commitment to aiding various causes in Africa (which in many ways is his 'spiritual homeland').

He yearns to discover new lands but his working-class background in the Midlands is still important to him. In fact, as a keen lover of both dogs and cats, he even named two of his cats Tipton and Dudley[2] so he would not forget his Black Country roots.

Robert Plant's solo career has allowed him to be his own boss, like a magician who can conjure any potion he wants to, a writer who can let his imagination run free when pen is put to paper. Plant is no longer creatively linked to Jimmy Page or John Paul Jones. Plant's solo career post-Led Zeppelin deserves to be re-evaluated and so this book attempts to do just that when so many books on Led Zeppelin have whisked through his career as an afterthought.

As Led Zeppelin continue to hold a God-like status ('Hammer Of The Gods', 'Rock Gods', 'Guitar Gods', 'Golden God', etc) in the world of popular music, Plant's career is, to many, unfairly lagging somewhat behind. So here is the author's attempt to offer a serious and critical overview of Plant's life after Led Zeppelin. Of course, it is almost impossible and also rather silly not to mention anything that came before 1982's *Picture At Eleven* because Led Zeppelin, and before it the Band Of Joy, are still an integral part of Plant's music. So this biography offers a hop through his childhood, a skip through the bands of his pre-Led Zeppelin days and a small jump through Plant's role in

Led Zeppelin before strolling through the core of the book with his solo career.

As with any rock biography, the author hopes that the reader will want to re-visit those albums and appreciate the career of a man who continues to offer his uniquely powerful voice to a large and enthusiastic audience; a man who is as important to classic rock as his idol Robert Johnson is to the blues.

Listening to his albums, one will hear that Plant has tried various styles and therefore lived a life in *music*, not just rock music: blues, jazz, pop, rock, ballads, world music, art rock and (although he refuses to label Led Zeppelin as such) heavy metal. Songs such as 'Communication Breakdown' and 'Rock And Roll' laid the blueprint for what we now know as heavy metal – for many, the group created the genre. Practically every band in Zeppelin's wake has paid tribute in one way or another to them, and in particular their album, *Led Zeppelin IV*.

Plant's extensive retrospective box set *Nine Lives* is a perfect example of his diversity whilst also proving that Led Zeppelin still, in some way, has an effect on his music. Plant continues to challenge himself (and the listener). Speaking about his switch to folk music with the short-lived project, Priory Of Brion, he told *Folk Roots Magazine* in 2000: "Someone like Elton John ought to step out and do this. Van Morrison has got it right in a way. He does gigs when he feels like it and when he does them you don't know what you're going to get. One minute he's got Lonnie Donnegan and Chris Barber with him. Then he's got Mick Green from the Pirates or whoever. He can do rockabilly night or jump blues night and I think that's great."

★   ★   ★

This is the first book on the subject of Robert Plant and as such it has been challenging in more ways than one. Whereas the pool of books on Led Zeppelin have concentrated on the band's hedonistic and highly controversial past, this book will deliberately avoid much of Plant's personal life and concentrate on his music. Exactly what was his role in Led Zeppelin? Plant has had a fair share of tragedy in his life: he was temporarily paralysed after a serious car accident (which also involved his then-wife Maureen) on the Greek island of Rhodes in the mid-1970s, but the worst was yet to come when his son, Karac, died from serious respiratory problems in 1977. His world was left shattered but he survived those periods of unhappiness, absorbing himself in music. Those unfortunate times are cemented in history, they happened when Led Zeppelin was dominating stadiums around the world, creating mischief wherever they went.

A solo Plant has proved himself to be far more sustainable and intriguing than Led Zeppelin's Jimmy Page, as writer Mick Wall correctly stated in *Classic Rock* in January, 2007: "There's no denying that Robert Plant is the sole surviving member of the band who has made the better fist of doing exactly that: surviving."

The chances are extremely low that Plant will 'tell all' in an autobiography because he prefers to look ahead to the future rather than burying himself in the past. Yet Jimmy Page has hinted at writing his memoirs as he told *Classic Rock* in November, 2004: "So there's a good book to be written, and I'm thinking about writing it."

What this particular book attempts to do is to compile all the details of Robert Plant's life after Led Zeppelin; to try to make some sense out of it, to find out what makes the man tick. What is it that causes him to keep going? After all, he can afford never to work again. While his former colleagues Jimmy Page and John Paul Jones enjoy the sanctuary of their respective English countryside mansions, only working at sporadic times, Plant enjoys the time-consuming process of album after album, tour after tour, interview after interview, proving his undying passion for creating new music.

Led Zeppelin, Jimmy Page & The Solo Years will hopefully explain why Robert Plant's career after Led Zeppelin is as exciting, important and pertinent as any other contemporary rock artist, young or old. The man himself spoke to *Folk Roots Magazine* in mid-2000 about his life: "I've had a fantastic career, although I don't really like that term. I prefer to call it a life in music and I've ridden so many waves of fashion and critical acclaim and lack of acclaim and acceptability and rejection."

Therefore, this book is a celebration of his fantastic career.

Neil Daniels
October, 2007.

A BLACK COUNTRY BOY
1948-1968

*"I didn't invent any of the processes that I've used.
So basically I've been a voyeur and a
traveller through all these curious developments."*
Robert Plant speaking to *Classic Rock* when promoting his
critically acclaimed compilation *Sixty Six To Timbuktu*

Robert Plant's first ever solo music DVD was released in the autumn of 2006. Filmed for the American music programme, *Soundstage* (hence the title: *Soundstage Presents Robert Plant And The Strange Sensation*) and recorded at Soundstage Studios in Chicago on September 15, 2005, Plant and his band of expert multi-instrumentalist musicians performed in front of a relatively small crowd, churning out a short set-list of new material from their latest album the *Mighty ReArranger*. While Zeppelin's rock songs were made to be sung to an audience of many, many thousands, Plant's songs are emphatically not, so it is apt that the set is in front of a small audience of probably just several hundred people. The group Strange Sensation is a bigger entity than Led Zeppelin but only in its membership: guitarists Justin Adams and Skin Tyson, keyboard player John Baggot, drummer Clive Deamer and bassist Billy Fuller.

Amongst some new tracks, they also played a total of five Led Zeppelin tracks (out of the nine songs performed). It was a world away from the insanely large crowds Led Zeppelin had performed to in some of the world's greatest stadiums and arenas, yet here, on this DVD, Plant appears more content and comfortable than ever ...

The drum thump and tribal beats of the first song begin proceedings as Plant, dressed in designer black trousers and shirt, strolls onto the modest

17

stage to an enthusiastic applause from the dedicated American audience. The song is 'No Quarter' – a Zeppelin track from 1973's revered *Houses Of The Holy* opus, later made famous as the title of the 1994 Page & Plant album *No Quarter: Jimmy Page And Robert Plant Unledded*. It doesn't sound like a typical Zeppelin track, it's not fully-charged rock and roll and consequently the Soundstage audience is not quite sure how to take to it. Plant stands behind the microphone, the euphoria calms down with polite claps greeting the music, rather than the head-banging of Led Zep's yesteryear. Plant clearly revels in the new arrangements of the old Zeppelin tracks, which he hand-picked himself for the live set. The manner in which those songs have been re-imagined is the reason why he does not shy away from singing them anymore. His professional collaboration with The Strange Sensation, which began after the abrupt end of his pub folk-rock outfit Priory Of Brion in 2000, has created a new phase in his illustrious and diverse career.

As for his appearance and particularly his facial looks, the observant camera takes every opportunity to give close-ups and sporadic glances at this ageing rock icon. Plant – a man in his late fifties – hardly shows his age; he is not too far away from being registered as a pensioner in Britain, which currently stands at 65. Like David Bowie and the indestructible Lemmy of Motörhead, Plant's age is irrelevant – nobody cares about age in rock music. The camera shows that he has deep wrinkles but each one must tell a tale from the many facets of his truly extraordinary life. He is still slim and in great shape. Over three decades ago, the young singer (Plant refers to his career in Led Zeppelin in third person) would have exposed his slender chest to thousands of screaming fans; here, he keeps his clothes on but can't escape from making cheeky dance moves and ever-so slightly sexually provocative gyrations. Perhaps the American melodic rock singer and Led Zeppelin fan Tony Harnell says it better: "I think he's a rare talent with a beautiful energy live. He just seems like a cool guy that you want to hang out with. He makes you want to support his music and artistry forever because he just looks so happy doing it and is still so damn good at it."

For the most part, Plant may be interested in world music and folk but he has not forgotten about his roots in rock and roll, which is proven on the DVD's second track, 'Shine It All Around.' It's a heavy, funk-filled song from the *Mighty ReArranger* and when Plant nods to his band, signalling them to begin, the bass-led groove of the track kicks in. It's quite a heavy number with strong guitars and a sturdy bounce; Plant refuses to show his age as he dominates the stage, showing energy and charisma that is undeniable. 'Black Dog' from 1971's groundbreaking *Led Zeppelin VI has* also been tampered with, but as it's one of the more famous and popular songs in the Zeppelin arsenal, it gets a fiery applause. Plant allows the audience to jump in and sing with him, much to their delight – he even seems to be enjoying it himself.

The camera shows a strong female presence, many of them attractive and surprisingly young, so clearly Plant has not lost his appeal to the opposite sex. Arguably, the 'Golden God' is still a 'Sex God'. Finally, after 'Black Dog' ends, he calmly greets the audience: "Good evening everybody … Very nice and intimate here tonight."

The politically-motivated song 'Freedom Fries' from the *Mighty ReArranger* erupts and when it finishes, he speaks for a moment; the audience are quiet and attentive.

Introducing the Zeppelin song 'Four Sticks' from 1971's *Led Zeppelin IV,* Plant looks at the crowd, seeming oddly uncomfortable, and when he speaks his slight unease is obvious. He says, "I'd like to dedicate this to my old friend John [Bonham] who passed away twenty five years ago this year, September – there ya go, mate."

He looks up and probably has some silent thoughts before he starts singing …

'Tin Pan Valley' is a retrospective song from the *Mighty ReArranger;* it begins casually before the lights clash and collide and the band picks up speed and dimension. The final crescendo is a ferocious medley of drums, bass, guitars and keyboards. Then Plant and his band return to Zeppelin's back catalogue with 'Gallows Pole' from 1970's *Led Zeppelin III* and later made popular in the 1990s on the Page & Plant live album *No Quarter.* It's refreshing to hear these old songs given a new lease of life even if they are – by definition – not true to the original studio versions. Indeed, Zeppelin never played those songs rigidly either and famously experimented with structures, so Plant's latterday re-workings are entirely apt. Plant and The Strange Sensation add a world music texture to those old classics, making them just a little more intriguing although one cannot help but wish Plant would shed his inhibitions and blast into 'Rock And Roll' the way Zeppelin would have played it.

Plant is sweating by this point – it's only a short DVD, around fifty minutes – but even with his bouts of energy and excitement, he doesn't look too fatigued. 'The Enchanter', another song from 2005's *Might ReArranger*, is greeted with glee and strong applause. But it's the final song on the DVD that truly gets everybody going. At first it's unrecognisable but when the guitar riff finally explodes the fans get into full-on head-banging Zeppelin mode as 'Whole Lotta Love' is unleashed. Plant shows signs of his former self – the charismatic and iconic rock star from the 1970s – as he takes the microphone off the stand and grooves with the music, showing off his famous stage manoeuvres and gestures. But it's his voice which is remarkable; it can change speeds, tones and textures. It is contradictory: unique and forceful, melodic and strong, rugged and delicate.

Before we get to the intricate details of his life and work it is important to understand where the man, the artist, the imaginer, is now …

Led Zeppelin still plays an integral part of his life and always will, but Plant – himself 'The Mighty ReArranger' as it were – will arrange and rearrange those classic tunes to keep himself interested in his former band, an undying entity which will never leave him and forever haunt him. Paradoxically, his former band has become his muse but also his enemy. He wants people to be interested in what he has to say now with his solo work rather than any talk of a Led Zeppelin reunion. It's ironic that as the author revises this paragraph in October 2007, there has been a flurry of activity on the internet and in the press about the Led Zeppelin reunion (with Jason Bonham on drums) that will take place in December at London's O2 Arena to commemorate Ahmet Ertegun, the founder of Atlantic Records who died in 2006. However, in June 2007, when Plant was in Athens, Greece to play a gig at the three day Rockwave Festival, the one-off Led Zeppelin concert was just a rumour that had blown up into gigantic proportions. He spoke at a press conference, saying, "If there was one, then there wouldn't be enough doctors to support it!"

As evident on the Soundstage DVD, Plant certainly doesn't need a doctor to perform brilliantly, he is still fighting fit – indeed, he is probably healthier and happier than he has ever been in his life.

But who is Robert Plant?

And where did it all begin?

★   ★   ★

It was during the usual round of dull and repetitive interviews midway through 2006 that Robert Plant's mind began to wander. A journalist was scheduled to speak to him for a retrospective piece about his solo career after Led Zeppelin and in particular his forthcoming DVD with his band The Strange Sensation, but the questions kept veering towards Led Zeppelin: *"So will there be a reunion?" "How often do you speak to Jimmy Page?" "Why don't you sing 'Stairway To Heaven' anymore?"* Plant was generous, offering polite but short answers although he was surely thinking, *"Oh, bugger off will you! Stop talking about bloody Led Zeppelin – it's in the past!"*

Indeed, Plant was probably day-dreaming about his beloved football team – Wolverhampton Wanderers. It was getting close to the 2006-2007 season and the first fixture against Plymouth Argyle. A lot had happened in the club recently: ex-Sunderland manager Mick McCarthy was hired to take care of the team, replacing controversial ex-England manager Glenn Hoddle. Prior to the start of the season, twelve major players had left the club and two directors in the boardroom had also departed.

Regardless of what was happening in the world of popular music, Robert Plant always thought about his home in the West Midlands ...

Robert Anthony Plant was born on August 20, 1948 in West Bromwich – the heart of the West Midlands. It became increasingly obvious to his parents that Plant was a clever and creative child who would end up mingling with the local bohemians at some point in his life. Before his death from a heart attack in 1995, Led Zeppelin manager Peter Grant gave what would be his last interview with *Kerrang!* in 1990. He was asked by rock journalist Paul Henderson, "How do you see each of Jimmy, Robert, John and Bonzo in terms of individual personality?" Grant replied: "Robert was a tremendous showman, and well-suited to his star sign, Leo – I'll leave you to read the rest of it!"

In that respect, if you believe anything in astrology then you'll understand that Leos are lions, kings of the jungle. Further traits of Plant's star sign – the fifth sign of the Zodiac – include generosity, creativity and romance. They are entertaining, humorous and honest people. They are calm people who have an abundance of pride and dignity. Indeed, Plant joins an important group of artists in the hierarchy of show business and popular culture that includes Peter O'Toole, Robert Redford and Andy Warhol – all Leos.

Plant was born at just the right time. He belongs to a particular breed of post-war, Midlands-born rockers who dominated the 1960s music scene in that large industrial region. This scene is popularly known as Brum Beat, which featured a whole generation of rock artists who ultimately shaped the way that this massively controversial genre evolved; eventually it turned into heavy metal with more than a little help from earth-shattering Midlands bands like Black Sabbath and later Judas Priest. Alongside Robert Plant, other Midlands rock artists born and bred in the immediate post-war years include ex-Judas Priest singer and co-founder Allan Atkins, Black Sabbath guitarist and mastermind Tony Iommi, Plant's future collaborator and best friend, John Bonham, Steve Winwood and Magnum's Bob Catley. The Brum Beat period is an integral part of Plant's life for many reasons and will be discussed at length later in this chapter.

Although Plant was born in the tough working-class confines of West Bromwich, in the borough of Sandwell – the centre of the industrial region known as the Black Country – he was actually raised in nearby Kidderminster, a far prettier area in the leafy county of Worcestershire. Some sources have suggested he was raised in Halesowen in the borough of Dudley, West Midlands but it is commonly understood that Kidderminster was his childhood home.[4]

To understood Plant and his future motivations, it is important to describe, briefly, his home town: Kidderminster is a rural community, which lies in the Wyre Forest district of Worcestershire, some twenty miles south-west of Birmingham's large city centre and close to the English/Welsh border. Those who live in the northern towns of Worcestershire such as Kidderminster and Bromsgrove are commonly understood to have a distinctive Birmingham dialect, known in the UK as a 'Brummie accent.' In fact, the Black Country – as opposed to Birmingham – has its own accent which is less nasal and grating. Plant's geography of childhood has given him more of the latter rather than, as is so often misconstrued, a Brummie accent.

Having said that, these days Plant seems to have lost much of his thick Midlands dialect, although he still slips out those distinctive tones during interviews sometimes. Indeed, having a regional accent is almost essential for any British rock star. Other famous residents born in the Midlands such as Ozzy Osbourne, former Slade front man Noddy Holder and Judas Priest's Rob Halford, have lost very little of their accent. Historically, the nasal accent of the Brummie and its sister dialect from the Black Country has provided much material for comedians over the years, eager to mock any public figure with an odd accent. Americans have openly declared their love of British rock star accents as immortalised in such classic music-related comedies as *This Is Spinal Tap*, *Wayne's World* and *Rock Star*; no doubt somewhere along the line the screenwriters had Plant in mind.

Robert Plant's family was distinctly middle-class. Unlike many local residents in the West Midlands during the 1950s, the Plant family did not struggle for money. His father, who was also named Robert, was an RAF veteran so he had a comfortable Government pension; they certainly weren't rich but they had enough cash in the bank to afford hot meals everyday and pay utility bills whereas a lot of families in the region struggled to get by after the heinous and inhumane attacks on Britain instigated by Adolf Hitler and the Nazis during World War II. Knowing there was a meal on the table each night was, for many people in the post-War Midlands, a luxury they did not enjoy.

Robert Plant Senior was aware of his son's creativity and artistic notions from an early age; his teachers at primary school also knew he was different from the other boys. He was told by his stern, military trained father – a civil engineer at that point who also played in a local brass band – to register at King Edward VI Grammar School in Stourbridge in the West Midlands. His mother was behind her husband every step of the way, wanting only the best for their beloved son.

At thirteen-years-old, Plant was still relatively young when he made his first steps into the fabulous world of record collecting. His first musical interest was undoubtedly Elvis Presley and he also enjoyed the sounds of American rock 'n' roll stars like Jerry Lee Lewis and Carl Perkins, whose creative peak was primarily in the 1950s; in the 1960s, they were largely seen as relics of the past who had slid down from their creative zenith.

When Plant first became interested in rockabilly,[5] Elvis' music career was not doing too well; after being honourably discharged from the army on March 2, 1960, he made a series of embarrassing albeit successful Hollywood movies which did nothing for his credibility except to diminish it. Carl Perkins was also suffering – he left Sun Records and signed to Columbia in 1958 but he made the unwise decision of 'going country' by adopting the Nashville Country sound, whilst struggling to battle an addiction to alcohol. Jerry Lee Lewis also had trouble in the early 1960s: he signed to Smash Records in 1963 after his contract with Sun ended but he failed to match the successful sales he had enjoyed during the previous decade. As Bill Haley entered the 1960s, he too suffered from a massive commercial decline despite being a live favourite in some parts of the world. Other iconic 1950s rock and roll stars who struggled to sell records in the next decade included Little Richard who left the music business to preach gospel after having been warned of his eternal damnation in a prophetic vision. Buddy Holly died tragically in 1959 in an aircraft accident, which also killed fellow rock and roll stars Ritchie Valens and The Big Bopper. The past, one way or another, was being brutally dismissed.

The young Plant also enjoyed the music of other revered artists who were signed to the Memphis-based label Sun Records such as Johnny Cash and Roy Orbison who have famously battled their own demons and personal addictions.

Plant discovered how to sing from the blues masters like Robert Johnson and Sonny Boy Williamson; he learned that singing was not just about carrying a note but *telling a story* and making an indelible impression on the listener. Through his love of Johnson, Plant learned about other blues artists such as Charley Patton, Willie Brown, Son House and Lonnie Johnson.

Despite missing out on the 1950s rock and roll scene as it actually happened, Plant had years of music to catch up with; he was revelling in the back catalogue of those aforementioned artists. There was a selection of 1950s singles that really got Plant's zest for music flowing; amongst them was 'Hound Dog' by Elvis Presley, Chuck Berry's 'Maybelline' and 'Great Balls Of Fire' by Jerry Lee Lewis.

However, well into his teenage years, Plant quickly became obsessive and deeply inspired by the blues – an impressively mature preference for one so young. The blues was simply too much to take for the mostly bourgeoisie population of rural Kidderminster and other parts of middle-class and rural Worcestershire at that time, so while it may have been ignored by many elder Brits it certainly grabbed Plant's post-war generation with robust gusto. Contrary to popular understanding, Plant's parents were not totally against their only son's newly discovered interests even though they did not particularly enjoy and thus understand the music he vehemently adored. Their tastes lingered toward classical music and easy listening while their son craved for something more dangerous. Speaking to writer Sylvie Simmons of *The Guardian* in 2005, Plant enthused: "My parents cut the plug off the record player … I think it was after they heard 'I Like It Like That' by Chris Kenner seventeen times in one hour … he [Robert Plant Senior] didn't get much bluer than Johnny Mathis. I think he found Robert Johnson too dark."

Despite Robert Plant Senior's apparent lukewarm response to his son's evolving musical tastes, he regularly drove his eager young boy down to the Seven Stars Blues Club in Stourbridge and, later, a place called Mothers Club in Birmingham which opened in 1968 (although the latter was known more as a 'progressive' type club) to hear some real blues played live. "My own childhood was a pretty black and white world – colour arrived later – but at least I was able to be exposed to different kinds of music. I could go to Birmingham Town Hall when I was fourteen to see Son House," Plant later told *Uncut*'s editor Allan Jones.

Although the likes of Elvis still played a fundamental role in his search for wisdom and inspiration through music, it was the sounds of hardened black men from the poor southern US states that held him under a trance like some kind of mystical spell. His favourite blues singers included Skip James who died the year Led Zeppelin released their first two albums. The delta blues singer and guitarist Bukka White and the Tennessee-born blues musician Sleepy John Estes were also early inspirations. Plant equally devoured records by such blues legends as B.B. King, Muddy Waters, John Lee Hooker and Big Joe Williams. Yet there were a few earnest blues artists that eluded his attention for quite some time as he told writer Barney Hoskyns in 2003 for the piece, 'Stairway To Snowdonia: Rapping With Robert Plant': "It probably took thirty years of my life before I even had time for Wynonie Harris or Roy Brown or even Big Joe Turner. In fact, especially Big Joe Turner. Because I thought the productions were all big and a bit smooth, and I thought the brass parts … were just a little bit hackneyed."

In the early 1960s, when Plant was a teenager, the blues thrived in the Midlands and indeed the rest of Britain although the hotspots where primarily Birmingham and London. The black American artists who told tales about the hardships of living in deprived southern states had a profound influence on working-class kids in a war-torn, industrialised Britain.

Blues music and blues musicians told stories of what is was like to be descendants of slaves, brought from the mass landscapes of Africa against their will, to work – literally – for nothing in an extremely wealthy western country. They were treated like second class citizens by rich white folk because of their race, and through sheer anger and frustration black men began to pick up guitars and write songs, venting their fury at the injustices they faced on a daily basis. Music offered a creative outlet for them and eventually the blues found its way over to Britain where a generation of white kids born in the immediate post-war years loved every second of it. Robert Plant, of course, was one of these willing kids. He later told *The Guardian* about his early blues-loving years: "When I was at school, I had a paper round to earn money and I bought the Robert Johnson release that came out on Philips, the original first album with the gatefold sleeve with a picture of a sharecropper's shack on the front. When I heard 'Preaching Blues' and 'Last Fair Deal Gone Down' – I was probably a year or so behind Keith [Richards] and Mick [Jagger] – but I went, 'This is it.'"

In 1960s Britain, black men came from America to tell their tales of woe and white kids picked up guitars and sang their own stories of daily hardships and frustrations. But exactly how did the blues, a style of music that was not even popular in its native United States, reach British shores thus influencing a generation of aspiring artists like Robert Plant?

It happened through a number of means: primarily it was down to US Army servicemen who arrived in rainy Britain at cities like Liverpool and Southampton and other major ports. With them, they carried pall malls, magazines with pictures of attractive burlesque dancers, tatty paperbacks worth a couple of cents, faded black and white pictures of home and loved ones, and scratched blues records, known then as 78s. Eventually those records landed in the eager hands of record collectors, broadcasters, musicians and, most importantly, people at the BBC. The BBC aired radio shows about the blues, broadcasting songs by such masters as Muddy Waters, T-Bone Walker, 'Blind' Lemon Jefferson, the twelve-stringed guitarist Ledbetter and the legendary collaborators Sonny Terry and Brownie McGhee. It is thought by many that songs by those artists (and others) played via crackly radio broadcasts helped people to get though the horrendous Nazi bombings on Britain.

Within the large catalogue of blues singers that energised Plant, it was emphatically Robert Johnson who had the biggest impact on the adolescent Robert.[6] Years later, he spoke to *Musician Magazine* in 1991 about his admiration for Johnson: "I was absolutely astounded. I'd never heard anything so seductive. It's the way the voice and the steel strings intertwine; they weave through so much pain and anticipated pleasure. I was really struck by 'Goin' Down To Friar's Point/If I Be Rockin' To My End!' from *Trawling Riverside Blues* – the joy, the abandon with which Johnson looks forward to things! ... Johnson has followed me everywhere. The anguish, the desolation in Johnson's music is beautiful. It's the most remarkable and beautiful currency for an entertainer to feel and sing like that. He is a huge musical force in my life; he's been a touchstone, really. Robert Johnson has followed me everywhere."

Even in the twenty first century, Robert Johnson continues to inspire and intrigue Robert Plant – as well as countless other successful artists – so it is important to briefly consider his life: born in Mississippi in 1911 (or 1913 as some sources suggest), Robert Johnson's life and premature death at twenty seven has given birth to copious amounts of mythology and fable of an apparent Faustian pact with Satan: it has been told through the decades since his death in August, 1938 that he willingly sold his soul to the Devil at a crossroads (purportedly where Highway 49 and 61 conjoin in Clarksdale, Mississippi) with the Delta in sight, in exchange for mastery of the guitar. Indeed, local legend has it that in those depressed and deprived times in the Deep South, one could become a master bluesman by going to the crossroads with a guitar in hand at midnight where you would be approached by a mysterious figure (the Devil himself?) who would take the guitar from you, tune it and hand it back. The deed is then effectively accomplished – you would become a fully-fledged bluesman and a legend in your own right.

Equally controversial has been the exact cause of Johnson's death; although the main theory is that he was poisoned to death by the jealous husband of a woman he was seen having a fling with one night at a club. He died having made only twenty nine songs; several contain lyrics about the Devil and hell: 'Hellhound On My Trail' being one of his most notorious compositions. He is considered to be one of the all-time great guitarists.

★ ★ ★

By the time Plant reached the troublesome age of fifteen, he had become well versed in music, with a developing and broad knowledge; he relished his regular adoption of new trends and images such as the stoned hippie, the stylish Mod and the intellectual Beatnik, whichever took his fancy. He studied and even mimicked the moves of such great performers as Elvis Presley and Jerry Lee Lewis, like an aspiring thespian who looks at himself in the mirror. Plant would often gyrate and swing his hips at home in the privacy of his bedroom, close to his carefully catalogued collection of vinyl. He'd take a brush and use it as a microphone whilst singing and dancing to 'Jailhouse Rock.' It was a prudent decision to copy the moves of the young, slim Elvis. Singing alone in his bedroom would not satisfy his yearning for performance for very long, however; it was time for him to put what he had learned in private into practice in front of an audience …

* * *

John Oakley, back then a budding rock star from the Midlands, recounted an anecdote about the vociferous young Robert Plant during correspondence with the author: "It was 1963. I was twenty one and the lead singer in a group called The Bluetones," remembers Oakley. "My brother Trevor Oakley was twenty three [and] he was the drummer. We were from Tipton. The guitarist was Tony Pearson from Wordsley, he was eighteen and attended Wolverhampton Grammar School. The bass player was Frank Dudley; he was fifteen and lived in Wollaston. As a group we played chart covers of that time. We played local towns such as Stourbridge, Bromsgrove, Kidderminster, Wolverhampton, etc. On one occasion we played Stourbridge Town Hall and Frank told a school mate if he waited at the stage door and helped us in with the gear, he could get in for free. Frank's mate was Rob Plant, so in a sense we had Robert Plant acting as roadie for us that night. We worked with him later on when he formed a group. He was singing and playing blues harmonica; stuff like Muddy Waters and Sonny Boy Williamson. I remember Frank saying. 'He'll never get anywhere playing that rubbish.' It just shows, eh? The rest is history!"

As told in countless Led Zeppelin biographies including the infamous *Hammer Of The Gods* by Stephen Davis, two of Plant's earliest bands were the Delta Blues Band and the Sounds Of Blue between 1963-1964, when he was still in education. The latter group featured multi-instrumentalist Chris Wood who later played in Steve Winwood's influential 1960s blues-inspired rock band Traffic. However, it was the Delta Blues Band – his first proper venture into blues playing – that really showed local blues fans just how good a singer Plant actually was.

It was at the popular Seven Stars Blues Club in Stourbridge that Plant could regularly be heard wailing, screaming and screeching to songs like 'Got My Mojo Working' which was made famous in 1957 by the revered bluesman Muddy Waters. The Delta Blues Band was even given a club residency there, an honour that was rarely bestowed on most amateur blues bands. Plant found a real life mentor in Terry Foster, a local eight-string blues guitarist who was also in the Delta Blues Band. Foster had a fiery temperament and was a magnificent guitar player who took the impressionable teenage Plant under his wing. What struck Plant most about Terry Foster was the fact that he played the guitar in a way that was reminiscent of Big Joe Williams.

It has become a cliché that the school reports of successful artists – whether they are musicians, writers or actors – warn parents that their son/daughter is, in fact, intelligent; however, they could do so much better if they had an ounce more determination and more discipline, etc, etc.

Plant was a child who was bright but not really interested in a life in academia; he'd run home from school each day just so he could play his favourite records. It was jam sessions at places like the Seven Stars Blues Club that Plant looked forward to, not his next test result and a pat on the back from his teacher. So at the tender age of fifteen, Plant had some tough decisions to make, which would ultimately affect the course of his life and consequently have a fundamental impact on those around him.

His parents wanted their only son to settle into a secure office job, so he began training classes in chartered accountancy at Kidderminster College. However, he found the rudiments of the training so utterly boring that he soon quit and returned to an academic institution to acquire some O-levels. After several months of disinterest in college work, he packed the whole lot in. No 'secure' job for this Midlands boy, then. Instead, he began a musical journey of unparalleled success and unimaginable adventures that would literally take him, in due course, the length and breadth of the entire world, a Shakespeare-esque drama troubled with tragedy, depression and loss but also love, humour and creativity. Talk about crossroads.

★ ★ ★

At sixteen, Plant's hair was already shoulder-length. He was concerned about his parent's reaction toward his bohemian demeanour and his taste for what they perceived as odd American music, literally decades old. It was around this time in the early 1960s that the aforementioned Brum Beat was already in full swing and Plant was heavily involved in that exhilarating period of music. Yet Plant was so eager to learn from the true blues masters that he probably didn't realise just *how much* was happening around him on a musical level.

Original Judas Priest singer Al Atkins, who was also born in Robert Plant's home town in the late 1940s, remembers that era well enough, over four decades later; speaking to the author, he enthused: "Oh, it was brilliant. There was lots of bands coming out … it was a great scene in those times. The music was great! We had the Liverpool beat boom and then we had the Birmingham beat boom … that's when lots of us first started …"

Brum Beat was a reaction to the Mersey Sound of the North West. Did Robert Plant give a damn about The Beatles and the Merseybeat bands? In two words: not really.

The Beatles have been written about more than any band in history, enough to make a library of their own; suffice to say the Liverpool band were – are – fundamental to popular music and indeed popular culture in general. The huge success that they achieved was a great cause of interest for record companies who looked to Liverpool for ideas – thus a flurry of bands and solo singers in the Merseyside district dominated the British pop charts in the early 1960s, particularly around 1962-1965. Despite Plant's general disinterest, some context is needed.

A local magazine called *Mersey Beat*, which was dedicated to championing Liverpool pop artists, was published by a chap named Bill Harry, a close friend of John Lennon's; besides The Beatles, other Liverpool groups and singers from the Merseybeat era[7] included stars such as Cilla Black, Gerry and The Pacemakers and The Searchers. The success of The Beatles also gave star-struck kids throughout the rest of Britain enough of a confidence boost and impetus to learn an instrument, write songs and form a band. However, those Merseyside bands were far too fluffy and commercial, lacking the grit of American blues, for his eccentric and sophisticated tastes. Speaking to *Entertainment Weekly* in 2002, Plant said: "I was always amazed that Herman's Hermits and Gerry and The Pacemakers, all that rubbish of the so-called British Invasion in the 1960s, had such an effect on people."

The Beatles released the single 'Love Me Do' in 1962 when Plant was just an eager teen and as the success of The Beatles grew to unprecedented heights, Robert Plant was steadily learning his craft, studying the blues and moving from band to band in the West Midlands. The Mersey Sound meant very little to Robert Plant. Despite its contemporaneous success, it was not a direct influence on him.

It was, however, integral for Plant to learn as much about the live blues scene as possible; as well as devouring imported American records like a Buddhist monk studies sacred texts, he also made visits to as many blues festivals and gigs as possible, even if it meant travelling long distances around England. Plant's future best friend, Kevyn Gammond – also a fellow blues fan who joined the Band Of Joy in 1967 alongside Plant – remembers those days vividly as he told a journalist during an interview in 1992 sourced on *www.led-zeppelin.org*: "Everybody from Robert Johnson to Muddy Waters to Howling Wolf, all of our heroes. We [British blues fans] used to get these package tours with all these people on then, it was amazing! I used to go up to Lightnin' Hopkins and say, 'Can I have your autograph?' and he would sell me his hankie for 50p or whatever. Incredible really, so we used to get, once or twice a year the whole package show coming over [to England]."

It was especially inspiring when the gigs he attended were by American artists, although he did enjoy amateur British blues bands too. According to the *Hammer Of The Gods*, he even got to meet Sonny Boy Williamson backstage at a gig in Birmingham in 1965 when the over-zealous teenager allegedly stole one of Williamson's bass harmonicas.

As Plant approached the age of seventeen, he was moving from one demoralising job to the next and had already left home, which would have a detrimental affect on his relationship with his parents. After waving goodbye to the Delta Blues Band and the Sounds Of Blue, he joined the aptly titled The Crawling King Snakes. The name came from the John Lee Hooker song, one of Plant's many idols. The band set about gigging as much as possible and played to broad audiences because they had a more commercial sound than Plant's previous endeavours. Their crowds included rockers, soul fans, Mods, R&B admirers, you name it; they just wanted any gig, like most ambitious bands aspiring to make an indelible impact in the music world.

While the guitarist Terry Foster of the Delta Blues Band had been a major influence on the impressionable teenage Plant, there was one man who briefly joined The Crawling King Snakes on drums, attempting to mimic his idol Keith Moon of The Who. The man's name was John Bonham and he would go on to to become Robert Plant's soul mate.

Born on May 31, 1948 in Worcestershire, John Henry Bonham was known as Bonzo to his mates. His previous bands had been Terry Webb and The Spiders, The Blue Star Trio, The Senators and A Way Of Life. All of them are now largely forgotten. Bonham was flat-broke and needed the cash so when the opportunity came to join The Crawling King Snakes – a band that paid – he jumped at the chance. Little did they know at the time but when Plant and the likable Bonzo struck up an immediate rapport and became instant friends, the seeds were now being sown for one of the greatest rock bands in history. As quoted in a 2003 issue of *Classic Rock*, Plant remembers his first encounter with John Bonham: "John came up to me and said, 'You're alright, but you're only half as good a singer as I am a drummer.'"

At this point, Plant was struggling financially – he did not even have a proper home of his own; consequently, he used to sleep over at John Bonham's house whenever the drummer could allow him. They would chill out and give their favourite records a spin, dreaming of success just like every other band in the Midlands …

Merseybeat is well chronicled. Brum Beat was similarly the centre of attention for bands and music lovers in and around the vicinity of Birmingham and it lasted throughout much of the 1960s. It was a period of energetic activity, sweaty euphoria and steaming creativity. American rock and roll was a fundamental influence on both the Merseybeat and Brum Beat bands, or groups as they were commonly known in those days. But what made the Brum Beat bands stand out from the Merseyside bands was their love and passion for the blues. Plant moved from one blues-rock-pop outfit to another throughout the decade, all the time garnering more and more experience.

In 1965 when Plant was in the pop-orientated group The Crawling King Snakes with John Bonham, there seemed to be a band playing in every pub and social club in the Midlands. Laurie Hornsby – author of the indispensable guide to the era *Brum Rocked On!* – writes, "as a result of the output of American rock 'n' roll and rhythm and blues artists, musical seeds were scattered in youthful abandon around the city of Birmingham in the hope that someday these seeds would produce a harvest of sorts."

Birmingham and its surrounding boroughs produced literally dozens of groups in a relatively short space of time before the whole scene imploded. Hornsby continues in *Brum Rocked On!*: "The Applejacks, the Rockin' Berries, the Fortunes, Spencer Davis Group, The Move, Locomotive and The Moody Blues all achieved Top Ten chart positions on the national hit parade, waving the flag for the city of Birmingham."

As the Midlands was full of aspiring rock and roll artists, there had to be plenty of venues for them to play: Birmingham Town Hall, the Golden Eagle public house, The George pub, The Crown, The Grand Hotel, Rubery Social Club, Mothers Club, Seven Stars Blues Club, Las Vegas Coffee Bar, The Golden Eagle and Digbeth Civic Hall were just a small sample of local venues that saw performances by singers and musicians such as singer Al Atkins, guitarist Dave 'Clem' Clempson and drummer Bev Bevan, as well as bands like the Locomotive, the Steve Gibbons Band, The Move, the Moody Blues and The Bakerloo Bluesline. Robert Plant and John Bonham constantly made appearances at various clubs and pubs in the area. Other popular venues of the day included the Plaza Ballrooms, Old Hill, the Adelphi and Rialto in Birmingham as well as the Adelphi and the Gala Hall in West Bromwich. Colleges and university campuses also opened up their doors to the aspiring bands and singers from the Midlands.

Heavy metal singer Al Atkins, who was in several semi-professional Midlands blues rock outfits during the 1960s prior to forming Judas Priest in 1969, recalls that Plant often used a particular venue called Holy Joe's in Wednesbury for rehearsals: "There was loads of bands that use to rehearse there [such as] Trapeze, Slade, Robert Plant, there was me ..."

Holy Joe's was a very popular rehearsal space. Erstwhile Judas Priest drummer John Ellis recalls: "It was an old school run by a vicar. We use to call him Holy Joe. He loved to drink and he used to collect all the money off the bands who were practising there. I think there were eight or ten rooms or something. He used to nip up to the old pub just on the top of the road on the corner. And he used to come back worse for wear. Sometimes he used to let people practice in his front room to earn extra cash."

Jim Simpson of Big Bear Records was a prominent figure in the Birmingham music scene during the 1960s and ran a blues-themed night at The Crown public house called Henry's Blues House, which was named after an Afghan Hound.[8] He vividly remembers that busy period in music; speaking to the author, he recalled: "There were lots of pop bands around … the earlier pubs of that decade had put on five or six nights a week of live pop music … The boom, I think, was [the] early 1960s and mid-1960s. I use to work for a magazine called *Midland Beat,* and we did a band register once … it went from Norwich down to Bristol and up to Sheffield and as far south, as, certainly Oxford … there was about five and a half thousand bands [that] we registered!"

Designed to promote and review local Midlands-based bands, *Midland Beat* was first published in the autumn of 1963; it was evidently influenced by the enormous success of Bill Harry's music paper *Mersey Beat*. During the mid-1960s, there were so many bands in the region it was like living in a small village and *Midland Beat* was crammed with duly band advertisements and requests by the dozen.

Pete Boot, who was in the West Bromwich band Blue Condition with Al Atkins and later the Welsh outfit Budgie, explains: "Back in those early days, everybody knew everybody and nobody knew anybody, but they all knew somebody who played in a band, just friends making music."

Musicians and singers in the Midlands went from one band to another and Robert Plant was no exception: in the mid-1960s, he'd already been in the Delta Blues Band, Sounds Of Blue, The Crawling King Snakes and later the Tennessee Teens. Like a lone cowboy in the Wild West, drifting from job to job, he also found time to jam with other, lesser known, Birmingham rhythm and blues inspired outfits such as the New Memphis Bluesbreakers, the Black State Moan and The Banned from Stourbridge. Although the Midlands was a hive of talent, buzzing with activity, at the same time it was a tumultuous period with little money on offer and so Plant often found himself in financial dire straits.

A bass player from West Bromwich named Brian Stapenhill – Bruno to his mates – formed various bands in the area during the 1960s with his best friend Al Atkins; those bands included The Bitta Sweet and Sugar Stack and it was often the case that they would cross paths with Plant and Bonham during their time together in The King Crawling Snakes, and later, the Band Of Joy. Speaking to the author, Stapenhill speaks retrospectively about the period: "We all use to use the same pub in West Brom above Woolworths, the Duke Bar above Wooly's," he reminisces. "Bonham use to go in and we use to go in and Planty, you'd sort of exchange what was happening in the music world [with them] and that. It was only a small room and it was always full of musos and people like that, it was all right."

Al Atkins remembers what it was like when there were just so many bands forming and folding. Speaking from experience, he can clearly evoke a picture of the hectic band lifestyle led by the likes of Robert Plant and himself: "My band mate Bruno and myself would get a band together about every year back then," recalls Atkins. "We would rehearse and hit the road for about twelve months, if it didn't seem to be working out we would pack it in and restart with a new line-up and a new name. So you could say The Reaction was 1963, The Bitta Sweet was 1964/65, Blue Condition in '66, Sugar Stack in '67, Jug '68, and finally Judas Priest in '69. The 1960s was a busy period for Black Country bands."

Plant's exhaustive curriculum vitae was no different from that of Atkins. Plant was relentlessly cutting his teeth in the Black Country blues club scene; by the end of 1965, The Crawling King Snakes had folded – their style of pop music led to their quick demise. Plant joined a small band called the Tennessee Teens on their request – the band had been playing at the Palette Club in Fulda, Germany and upon their return were in desperate need of a talented singer.

During this fertile gigging phase of his early career, Plant struggled to make ends meet with a series of mind-numbing and tedious day jobs; he even had a brief day job working for the American retail store Woolworths at their site in Halesowen, near Dudley. It was the dream of enjoying success with music that helped him through the drudgery of a series of dull and depressing vocations. Al Atkins also seems to recall Plant having to move house quite a bit: "This would be 1965-66, when Plant joined the Tennessee Teens." This group was a Walsall-based three-piece outfit that was more focused on Tamala-Motown and soul, rather than more commercial pop sound of The Crawling King Snakes. Shortly after, they changed their name to Listen.

Listen comprised of lead guitarist John Crutchley, bassist Geoff Thompson and drummer Roger Beamer. After playing a storming gig at the Plaza Ballroom in Birmingham, the band was approached by a city talent scout on behalf of a major record label. Listen's first officially released single 'You Better Run', a cover of The Young Rascals song, was issued in November, 1966.

Don Powell, drummer in The N' Betweens (later renamed Slade) remembers: "Back in 1966, The N' Betweens released 'You Better Run' by The Young Rascals. Listen – the band with Robert Plant as singer – released a record of the same song, at the same time. Theirs was augmented by brass (a much better record, I thought!) but neither records had any success, except ours was a Number 1 in Wolverhampton for six weeks!"

Prior to changing their name to simply The Rascals in 1968, the American band had a degree of success in the singles charts with their fusion of soul and rock and roll, exactly the type of music the Tennessee Teens/Listen had modelled their sound on. Their first release as The Rascals was the hit-album *Time Peace: The Rascals Greatest Hits* in 1968, which achieved strong sales: it featured their original version of 'You Better Run.'

Plant was growing more confident as a songwriter and even co-wrote the B-side to 'You Better Run' called 'Everybody's Gotta Say.' Plant spoke to writer Barney Hoskyns in October, 2003 about his first recording session: "Coming out of that studio at the end of that session, I've never been so relieved in my life. It was like 'Christ, I did it.'"

Suffice to say, 'You Better Run' and its sibling 'Everybody's Gotta Say' was definitely not a hit, although in November, 1966 it lasted one week in the lower echelons of the *NME* Top 50 but quickly faded into obscurity after its hasty release. The label persuaded Plant to sound more like a contemporary pop star than the young gravel-voiced blues rocker he clearly was. Despite his impressive work-ethic and thirst for performance, it was evident that his career was not entirely going to plan.

Undeterred and under the tutelage of music publisher Eddie Kassner and talent scout Danny Kessler, Plant recorded and released two further solo singles for CBS. Initially, to fulfil his three-single contract with CBS, Plant had thoughts of re-recording 'Incense' by The Anglos but CBS had other ideas and got him to record 'Our Song' – a cover of the Italian number 'La Musica e' Finita' – with the B-side 'Laughin', Cryin', Laughin'' as well as 'Long Time Coming' with the B-side 'I've Got A Secret.' They were released in early 1967 but both failed to make any impact in the UK singles charts. Plant also found his picture in the popular music weekly, *New Musical Express*. CBS's plans to mould Plant into a model of Tom Jones and Engelbert Humperdinck failed to take off in the direction they'd initially hoped; the label even got Plant to cut his hair. A similar fate befell the leading British blues singer, Long John Baldery[9] who released a Humperdinck-type pop single in 1967 called 'Let The Heartaches Begin.' Although it was a Number 1 hit in Britain, blues purists were angered by Baldry's perceived treachery of the genre; this was the man, who along with Alexis Korner, Chris Barber and Cyril Davis, aided the careers of The Rolling Stones, Rod Stewart, Eric Clapton and later Elton John, amongst others. So why the hell was he singing a cheesy pop song? Blues can be an unforgiving master.

Despite its considerable regional appeal, many of the Brum Beat bands did not achieve the type of monstrous success that bands from Liverpool had been overwhelmed with. Yet something was rumbling in the British music scene that would be artistic, intelligent and – eventually – huge in America and implausibly endurable from around 1965 onwards: British rhythm and blues.

The global success of The Beatles and other pop groups undeniably brought British music to the world's attention; Americans loved it and the

'British Invasion' saw many UK bands hit the States like a hurricane. However, a new sound was being nurtured back in the UK; a sound that merged influences from American rock and roll with the blues.

American rock and roll was in decline, so there was a void to be filled by many budding electric guitarists and rock singers who were less influenced by the clean-cut, wholesome image of The Beatles and more influenced by the blues and such players as Buddy Guy.

Jeff Beck spoke to *Classic Rock* in October, 1999 about that period in British music: "There was no real danger anymore. Overnight, everybody was named Johnny This or Johnny That, and they were all singing this terrible V-neck-sweater music. So it was like, 'What are you bastards doing with my music? I'm not going to have that taken away!' So I think we decided we just wanted to take it back."

This new sound was far harder than The Beatles and grittier than The Shadows. As Robert Plant was growing up and playing in mid-1960s, outfits like Listen, he was hearing this new style of music, wishing he could be that successful and popular whilst still being committed to the music he adored.

British rhythm and blues was the blues played by thirsty young white men for a young British audience in need of something home-grown and darker than what had previously been on offer. In the process, the new genre turned young British listeners onto southern American blues by updating it for a contemporary audience. It also proved to be so successful in the States throughout the 1960s (and right up to the present day) that previously myopic, white Americans also began to learn about their heritage, which many had initially refused to embrace. So it was the Brits who effectively gave them lessons on how to play the music they invented; bands like The Kinks turned up the volume and played it a little heavier. Former Rainbow and Deep Purple singer Joe Lynn Turner confessed to the author that he is a great fan of 1960s British rock bands: "The British invasion set the stage and that got America ready for something different," he says. "[Those bands] took the Mississippi Delta blues, which originated in America, and put their own spin on it; their own electric arrangement, which was brilliant."

A focal point in the thriving British rhythm and blues scene – and a band which Robert Plant admired – was The Who. Their first two singles, 'I'm The Face' and 'I Can't Explain', was heavier, bluesy and more rugged than any of The Beatles' early pop recordings. But it was their seminal 1965 single, 'My Generation' which grabbed a generation of male music listeners by the testicles and did not let go.

Plant spoke to writer John Hutchinson of *Record Magazine* in 1983 about his varied musical tastes: "I used to listen to what were, in England, the more obscure American hits – a lot of New Orleans rock, what you

might call R&B for whites … Although it wasn't Robert Johnson or Blind
Willie McTell, it was still very poignant, and had a remarkable effect on
how I wanted to sing … I wanted to get some shrieking into my music,
so that took me vocally more into the guttural American approach to
singing, which I suppose people like myself, Robert Palmer to an extent,
and definitely Lennon and McCartney got into. We all had a kind of edge
on our voices that comes from American R&B."

Other British blues-driven bands that began life in the mid-1960s
included The Kinks, The Animals, the Rolling Stones and, of course, The
Yardbirds, all rising to incredible heights of success. But those bands were
based in London[10], a glamorous city that seemed too far away from the
daily activity in Robert Plant's life in the industrial confines of England's
central city.

While Robert Plant was gigging anywhere and everywhere he could,
British rhythm and blues – led by such titans as The Who, The Kinks and
Cream – was quickly emerging from the city streets onto the radios and
television before world domination finally occurred towards 1970; the
swinging capital, once a dark and dirty environment, looked more
colourful than ever before. Mini-skirts were worn by every desirable
woman and men took an unprecedented interest in the latest fashion
trends. The city was literally bursting with great blues guitar players such
as the legendary John Mayall and his already revered protégés, Eric
Clapton and Jeff Beck. There was also one young lad named Jimmy Page
who ended up doing session work and producing records in the big city
for artists such as Eric Clapton, Chris Farlowe, Nico and John Mayall.

This was all a far cry from Plant's own fairly stunted momentum. Listen
had not exactly gone to plan. After the failure of the CBS singles, Robert
Plant joined the Band Of Joy sometime toward the end of 1966, which
was also the year he met an attractive Asian woman from Walsall named
Maureen Wilson, who later became his first wife. It is a story which has
been told by Plant many times and retold by writers, fans and just about
everybody else who follows his career: Robert Plant and Maureen Wilson
met each other at a George Fame concert in 1966 and the pair soon
became inseparable. It has often been said that the couple took up
residence in Walsall where the band Listen came from, yet West Bromwich
singer Al Atkins seems to recall that Plant went to "live with his girlfriend
Maureen in Trinity Road, West Bromwich." Trinity Road is known for
housing Indian and Caribbean immigrants.

Whichever tale is true, it is believed that the pair lived in a cramped and
poorly equipped house in a poor, working-class area, typical of the period
when families were still suffering, financially, from the effects of World War II.
It was at this time in 1966, when living with Maureen Wilson in an
immigrant district of mostly Indian descent that Plant's interest in India and

Asia first began. Plant spoke to *Circus* magazine in 1976 about his girlfriend's family: "My old lady came from India, and her uncle was chief of the Calcutta mounted police during the '40s. He can speak about ten different dialects and he's a really great guy. In fact, one of the times that I worked – before the Led Zeppelin days – I had a job as a production control manager in a factory that he ran. I got the sack because I ordered enough steel to keep three factories going for about a year, but I managed to remain his friend …"

Plant quickly learned about Indian culture and customs. Most of all he loved the smell of hot curries and hounded local Indian immigrants for tales about their native country. He soon became well-versed in Indian music.

"I tripped over Asian music at school. The neighbours were playing it," he later told *Folk Roots Magazine*. "There was a lot of poetry and jazz going on and we listened to people like John Fahey. Ravi Shankar was there alongside Memphis Slim and the streets of West Bromwich were ringing out to the sounds of Hemant Kumar and all these Ghazal singers and, at the same time, Son House, Sleep John Estes and Willie Dixon were coming over. One ear was taking in the big Hindi pop songs of the day and the other one was taking in American blues guys singing about rats in my kitchen."

Through the next few years, Plant's love of music even filtered into Maureen Wilson's family. There was a young guitarist named Ernie Chataway who had jammed with Earth (prior to changing their name to Black Sabbath) on occasions at Henry's Blues House before he joined the first line-up of Judas Priest in 1969-1970: "I never did like him [Robert Plant,]" remembers Chataway during an interview with the author. "We never did get on but I did some recording with him. In fact, one of the first bands I got together was when I came to Worcester. It was [with] Ian Jennings … [and] Maureen's little brother, you know. I was trying to get a bit of R&B/B.B. King-type thing."

Plant's latest charges, the Birmingham-based Band Of Joy, was formed by Vernon Perara formally of the Stourbridge outfit The Stringbeats and a relative of Maureen Wilson's. The band was important to Plant in many ways despite having such a tumultuous and convoluted history.[11]

The Band Of Joy was directly inspired by the West Coast sound of the United States music scene, which Plant fully embraced. However, despite some minor success in the region, it soon became apparent that Plant would not last long in the first line-up. Ironically, some reports suggest he was allegedly considered to be a rather poor singer by certain people around the band, hence his departure in early 1967.

Frustrated but undeterred, Plant formed a second version of the Band Of Joy in 1967, unimaginatively called Robert Plant And The Band Of Joy, which lasted only a few months; this version used face paints in their stage act to attract the burgeoning hippy fans, as well as dressing in well-worn hippy attire. Their bizarre costumes, stage dances and Native American-inspired face paints made them look like character actors from Tolkien's Middle Earth. This version of the band consisted of: Mick Reeves, Vernon Perara, Peter Robinson and Chris Brown. However, part way through 1967, it became obvious that the second version of the Band Of Joy could no longer continue with so many internal arguments and so the line-up folded. In Alan Clayson's highly-recommended book on the genesis of Led Zeppelin, *The Origin Of The Species*, the author writes that Robert Plant and the Band Of Joy "created such a stir at the Rainbow Suite in Birmingham city centre that when Plant jumped into the crowd, frightened onlookers fled into the corridors beyond the auditorium."

Perhaps the third line-up of the band featuring Robert Plant – formed in West Bromwich in the second half of '67 – was more successful than the previous two versions because of one man – the formidable drummer John Bonham, who in July, 1966, had become the proud father of a baby boy named Jason.

Playing alongside vocalist Robert Plant and drummer John Bonham, the other members of the band included guitarist and vocalist Kevyn Gammond, organist Chris Brown and bassist/vocalist Paul Lockey. Previously of The Shakedown Sound, Gammond used the stage name 'Carlisle Egypt' during his tenure in the third line-up of the band.

Local blues-rock singer Al Atkins remembers the Band Of Joy quite clearly from gigging on the same circuit of pubs and clubs in the late 1960s: "I played on the same bill when I was in The Bitta Sweet at the Adelphi Ballroom. [Plant] only had a small Marshall P.A and a cheap mic, so he asked if he could borrow mine and I told him to 'Fuck off!' ... No, just kidding ... I let him borrow it."

The Band Of Joy even dared to venture down south to the capital to play the popular London clubs of the day. Kevyn Gammond remembers those road jaunts down to London as he told one writer in 1992 (*www.led-zeppelin.org*): "We played gigs at [places] like Middle Earth [and] the Speakeasy. And at that time, everybody was going down, like [Eric] Clapton, [Jimi] Hendrix. I'll always remember this guy who was running a place saying 'My God, this is the best band we've seen in the last three months!' ... They're saying we're the best band."

Alexis Korner, an influential blues musician, was in the audience at the Band Of Joy's gig at the Speakeasy and was reportedly impressed with Plant's obvious talents and enviable charisma.

Months went by and the latest version of the band played on bills that boasted such revered names as Terry Reid, Fairport Convention, Mick Farren's Social Deviants and Aynsely Dunbar's Retaliation – the blues drummer's own project. Evidently, not only did the Band Of Joy play gigs in their home territory and London, they also drove to the north of England where they occasionally had some misfired performances as Paul Lockey recalled when he was interviewed in the early 1990s (*www.led-zeppelin.org*): "On one of our tours, a one week tour up North [Yorkshire, Lancashire, Manchester;] mistakenly, they booked us at a working men's club ... where all the people play bingo and when a band comes [on] they want comedy or something ... so they thought we were a comedy band – Robert Plant and the Band Of Joy! It's a working men's club, it's dinnertime, you have a few pints and you watch a comedian or a ballad singer or a stripper [or] something like that. So what did we do? We didn't play any of our ... heavy blues but some simple rock tunes, hoping that these people had heard them before, and you could see that some of them enjoyed it but because it was [an audience of] older people – fifty, sixty or seventy – we didn't even finish ..."

Touring was laborious for them because they didn't have many roadies to help them set up their gear, although they did use Ross Crutchley, Steven Latham, who went under the nickname Big Bruce, and there was also a young lad named Ben Randle. Interestingly, Noddy Holder – who's real name is Neville John Holder – was a roadie for the Band Of Joy for a brief period of time before he joined The N' Betweens. Slade drummer Don Powell recalls: "Nod's dad was a window cleaner and had a van. Nod helped them out, driving for them, when we weren't working. Robert mentioned this from the stage when Zeppelin played Earls Court [in 1975.] He was talking about the past and when Noddy Holder was his roadie. We were in the audience that night."

For the most part, however, the band actually did their own driving and roadie work, to cut costs; besides, Holder would soon have his own career to worry about.

It was partly Bonham's talent as a powerhouse sticksman which kept the band afloat through those sweat-drenched nights playing heavy West Coast rock at various bars and clubs in and around Birmingham; Bonham was clearly the strongest musician in the band. Speaking in 1992 in an interview that can be found at *www.led-zeppelin.org*, Paul Lockey remembers Bonham thus: "I'm a guitar player, but during that time with Band Of Joy I learned to play the bass and to play it loud. You had to because Johnny Bonham was so loud, I stood next to him every night going 'Ahh!' Mindblowing..."

At this point in late 1967, Plant's taste in music undertook a major makeover; he was becoming less inspired by the blues and more interested in what was happening on the west coast of the United States, rather than in the Deep South. Recollecting his thoughts in 1992 (see *www.led-*

zeppelin.org) Kevyn Gammond said: "We all sort of loved this hard sort of West Coast stuff."

Temporarily disregarding the blues, Plant was listening to the Tennessee-born singer-songwriter-musician Arthur Lee and his LA psychedelic folk-rock band Love. Their 1967 debut album, *Forever Changes*, had a profound influence on Robert Plant as well as a generation of music lovers. Plant spoke to *Folk Roots Magazine* in 2000 about the West Coast music that has inspired him over the years: "Some of the songs we used to do with the Band Of Joy, they're songs that were cornerstones of a period of my life. I could never have written a song like Stephen Still's 'Bluebird'. When I first listened to Love's *Forever Changes*, I could never have come from that angle as a songwriter because my experiences are so different. But I've always been touched and moved by those songs. They've got such depth … I've always tried to get that Stephen Still's husky thing in my voice …"

Plant was also in awe of the sounds that fluttered out of San Francisco from bands like Jefferson Airplane and the Grateful Dead, as well as such Californian bands as Buffalo Springfield and The Byrds. He looked up to and admired artists like Stephen Stills, Joni Mitchell and Neil Young[12] and devoured as many imported records by those West Coast artists as possible. Bob Dylan was also an early influence and before him the legendary Woody Guthrie whom Dylan clearly imitated.

The Band Of Joy rapidly built up a reputation as a UK band that specialised in West Coast music and they were even runners-up in a regular poll by the 1960s magazine *Top Pops*. Plant spoke to the magazine at the time about his band's entry in the poll: "I have been confident that this group could do things," he enthused, "but being elected runners-up in the poll after such a short-time on the road is a sign of great things. It is really too much!"

It was the Band Of Joy's delicious but eclectic mix of blues, soul and psychedelic folk-rock that made them popular with the local Mods in both Birmingham and the more daunting confines of London. Speaking to one interviewer in 1992 (see *www.-led-zeppelin.org*) Paul Lockey said that Led Zeppelin's heavy contrast in music was "…just what the Band Of Joy was playing."

Even Robert Plant admits that the Band Of Joy was a definite precursor to Zeppelin, as he told *Record Magazine*'s J.D. Considine in 1983: "Maybe to me, [Led Zeppelin] was a progression from the Band Of Joy. I suppose Led Zeppelin became more like the Band Of Joy than the Yardbirds. Mainly because Bonzo and I were coming from the Band Of Joy … it was a natural extension of our American West Coast country-blues approach. That was where I was coming from." As quoted on *www.-led-zeppelin.org*, Kevyn Gammond said: "… a lot of the songs that came out of the Band Of Joy fitted right in to that first Zeppelin album."

Speaking to the now-defunct US rock magazine *Circus* in 1976, Plant recalled some of his earlier songwriting credits:"I wrote one song with the Band Of Joy called 'Memory Lane'. It was really quite funny, something about a chick on the back of a motorbike with a chrome horse between her legs. I suppose it was an early version of [Zeppelin's] 'The Wanton Song'."

Early demos composed by the Band Of Joy ultimately found their way into fans collections as very rare and expensive bootlegs. For the record, 'Memory Lane' and 'Adriatic Seaview' were original compositions while the rest were cover versions: 'Hey Joe' was a cover of a classic folk song which Jimi Hendrix made famous[13] and 'For What It's Worth' was a cover of the Buffalo Springfield tune. Those tracks were recorded at London's prestigious New Regent Sounds Studios. Intriguingly, 'Hey Joe' and 'For What It's Worth' cropped up on Robert Plant's praised duel-CD retrospective compilation *Sixty Six To Timbuktu*, released in 2003 on the Mercury Records label.

As quoted in a 1992 interview on the website *www.led-zeppelin.org*, Gammond remembered: "Denny Cordell, who produced all the Move records, picked up on the demos, and Robert said, 'Okay, I'm going to London with the demos, and Denny was really over the moon about them … and Robert was knocking on the door saying, 'Yeah, they love it!' But then somehow it got messed up, Robert said, 'Come on and let's go meet Denny' and he didn't come back. So we went down [to London] and he said: 'Great let's go in the studio.' And Denny said, 'There's a guitar,' he stuck it in my hand and said 'Write something!' At that age we really hadn't started writing, so he said, 'Okay, I'll give you a tenner or something and put you up at the Madison Hotel, go write a song and come back in the morning,' So we did this wild thing with like one bar, and went back the next day and, of course, that killed us … Paul [Lockey] picked us up coming back off the motorway about 10:30 that night, we had no money for the train fare, and he met us and we gave him the exciting news."

The band wasn't to be. Despite several demo recordings and three singles, any notions of making some decent cash out of the project were quickly quashed and, with morale low, the Band Of Joy called it a day.

After a tour of England, supporting the revered American singer-songwriter Tim Rose and alongside the famously robust English blues-rock singer Terry Reid, the third line-up of the Band Of Joy ceased activity in May, 1968. Speaking in 1992 (see *www.-led-zeppelin.org*) Gammond remembers that they "blew him [Tim Rose] off stage!"

Their exhilarating performances on that tour were one of the reasons why Bonham was offered work with Tim Rose; like a true journeyman, Plant was left wandering yet again …

★ ★ ★

It may have been the end of Robert Plant's tenure in the Band Of Joy but it wasn't exactly the end of the Band Of Joy *per se*, as that group has proven to be an integral part of his life outside of Led Zeppelin. So before we pick up on Plant's continuing journey in the late 1960s, it is interesting to note what happened after the third version folded.

After the demise of a pseudo country-rock band called Bronco (with guitarists Kevyn Gammond and Robbie Blunt, vocalist Jess Roden, bass player John Pasternak, drummer Pete Robinson and keyboardist Dan Fone) Gammond and Lockey re-formed the Band Of Joy in 1977.

This time around, the Band Of Joy consisted of Gammond and Lockey with bassist John Pasternak, keyboards player Michael Chetwood and drummer Francisco Nizza.[14] They released just two albums: the first, a self-titled release, in 1978 and the final record in 1983.

Paul Lockey spoke to an interviewer in 1992 (see *www.led-zeppelin.org*) about this late 1970s version of the Band Of Joy. "[It was] about ten years down the road [after splitting up in 1968.] Some guys from a band called Possessed [including ex-Band Of Joy member Mick Reeves[15]] had died in a car accident, including a good friend of Robert's, and so we all got together again and did some charity gigs to raise money for the families. So we turned up in various pubs and clubs in Kidderminster and Birmingham, and it was sort of organised chaos … that's when I met Kevyn after all those years, and we said yes, we'll get the band back together, Rob Plant and the Band Of Joy, and we'd make a record. That's what was happening, and in the end Robert never made it because of a tragedy in his family."[16]

Years later in an interview that can be found on the website *www.led-zeppelin.org*, Gammond gave some interesting details about the reaction the band received outside of the UK: "One nice thing about it was that we didn't try to sound like the Band Of Joy of old," he said. "We were totally, much more … fast, sort of up-tempo." The second album by this incarnation of the Band Of Joy was followed, two years later, by their eventual split.

★ ★ ★

In 1968, Robert Plant was left without a job after the demise of the third version of the Band Of Joy. One rumour claims that Plant was offered the vocalist job with Wolverhampton rockers The N' Betweens, who later changed their name to Slade. It's been alleged that certain members of the band detested Plant's flamboyant posing and showmanship so they opted for the talents of the down-to-earth Noddy Holder, a croaky but affable vocalist from Walsall, who was already a member of the band as guitarist.

Slade drummer Don Powell explains: "We all thought that Robert had such a unique voice and was a great frontman but our tour manager, Swinn said, 'You don't need anyone else, Nod can do the job.' Robert was never taken that seriously, although his voice really stood out!"

They therefore retained their set-up as a four-piece with Holder as lead vocalist and guitarist, Dave Hill on guitar, Don Powell on drums and Jimmy Lea on bass. In his 1999 autobiography *Who's Crazee Now*, Holder wrote: "The others didn't know [Robert Plant,] but I did. Personally, I didn't mind if we got another singer or not. I knew that I could front the band by myself, and I preferred being in a four-piece."

Plant's supportive and reliable girlfriend Maureen Wilson took pity on her artistically minded partner and supported him admirably. Plant even took a demoralising job laying tarmac on the busy roads of Birmingham for the construction company Wimpey; it was a job that barely made ends meet with only a few tuppances per hour; he justifiably felt his talents were being wasted on such poorly-paid and mind numbing vocations, so he quit to have a go at singing professionally, full-time.

He jammed with Alexis Korner for a while in Birmingham and London and they even made some recordings together with Steve Miller on piano in 1968 at a studio in London – 'Operator'[17] is one of them; it's often been said that Plant, Korner and Steve Miller intended on making an album together but it was cut short when Plant and Page hooked up for the New Yardbirds project (before it was renamed Led Zeppelin, but more on that in the next chapter). Steve Miller featured in Alexis Korner's outfit in which Plant was a co-vocalist and he even played the harmonica. The hard-blues rock band Free led by the Middlesbrough-born singer Paul Rodgers opened for them.

Korner – who was actually born in Paris, France – has often been dubbed 'the father of British blues' and his passion and knowledge reinstated Plant's interest in the genre after the Band Of Joy's days came to an end. Korner, who had previously seen Robert Plant with the Band Of Joy at that Speakeasy gig in London, could not fathom why such a unique singer – an alto[18] in technical terms – had not yet been discovered. Plant could sing falsettos that seemed unreachable to most British singers at the time.

Plant's next musical endeavour was the peculiarly named band Hobbstweedle – a name derived from J.R.R. Tolkien's *Lord Of The Rings* trilogy of books. In the late 1960s, just about every hippy, bohemian and eccentric artist had immersed themselves in Tolkien's mammoth set of books. Plant adored the ideas that Tolkien had created and was swept away by the immense landscapes, bizarre characters and the good-versus-evil style of story-telling (see Appendices). Hobbstweedle acted as a filler band until Plant could find something more serious. Right on cue, a more worthwhile band suited for Plant's talents and unrelenting energy was just around the corner …

* * *

In mid-1968, when Hobbstweedle were gigging around Birmingham, a guitarist named Jimmy Page was getting a line-up together for his band the New Yardbirds. Terry Reid – who had a soulful, bluesy voice similar to Paul Rodgers, Steve Winwood and Rod Stewart – was the singer that he had in mind.

Born James Patrick Page on January 9, 1944, in Middlesex, Jimmy had already compiled a notable list of credits by the time Plant was gigging with Hobbstweedle in '68. As well as being a member of The Yardbirds – first as a bassist and then second lead guitarist to Jeff Beck – between 1966 and 1968, he had also produced and/or played guitar on a wide array of studio tracks. He'd worked with The Kinks, The Who, the Rolling Stones, Marianne Faithfull and Them with Van Morrison as well as the forgotten pop group The Nashville Teens, 1960s teen idol Dave Berry and the American pop singer Brenda Lee. He'd also jammed on stage with fellow guitar wizards Jeff Beck and Eric Clapton as well as Alexis Korner's Blues Incorporated and the Cyril Davis All Stars.

Speaking about Jimmy Page's invitation for him to sing in the New Yardbirds, Terry Reid later told *The Guardian*: "I said, 'Yeah, I'd love to give it a shot. But I've just got to pop off for a minute to do this Stones tour and I don't want to be the one to tell Keith [Richards] I'm not going: you'll have to call him.'"

Fate conspired against Reid who went on to open for the Stones on their 1969 US tour instead of taking the New Yardbirds gig. In fact, it was Terry Reid himself who generously suggested to Jimmy Page that he should check out a singer in Birmingham named Robert Plant. The Band Of Joy had supported Terry Reid several months earlier and he was gob-smacked by Plant's voice. It has often been said that Chris Farlowe was another singer that Jimmy Page had in mind. Farlowe's 1960s R&B single 'Stormy Monday Blues' was issued under the pseudonym Little Joe Cock, which only fuelled the erroneous rumour that he was, in fact, black rather than a white English singer from Islington, north London. Like Steve Winwood and Paul Rodgers of Free, Chris Farlowe had one of the most distinctive and soulful voices of the late 1960s English rhythm and blues scene. Similarly, Plant had the right voice for the job but also had rock star good looks and flamboyant attire, with a long mane of hair, a slim torso and the appealing physique to make many sexually aroused teenage girls go wild. The stage moves and Elvis-inspired gyrations and hip movements also aided Plant in his quest for rock 'n' roll stardom.

As told in the Led Zeppelin biography *Hammer Of The Gods* and consequently every other book on Zeppelin, Jimmy Page, manager Peter Grant and Yardbirds bassist Chris Dreja made a trip up to smoggy Walsall to see Hobbstweedle in action in front of less than a hundred people at the run-down West Midlands College of Higher Education, an academic institution for students training to be teachers. In hindsight, Plant admitted to *The Independent* in 2005 that Hobbstweedle "weren't very good," on the night. "There was a lot of rubbish and flash, but not real content," he said.

At first, Page, Grant and Dreja were not sure what to make of Plant's voice or the stage act, which borrowed musical ideas from the Californian bands of the time and the striking visual imagery of the hippy movement. Hobbstweedle included songs by Buffalo Springfield and the San Francisco folk-rock psychedelic band Moby Grape in their set list. Very quickly, however, his stage aura won them over. Plant's vocal strength appeared to show few limitations as he screamed like a banshee before he slowed down for a tender verse. He pranced about the diminutive stage, showing he had charisma and sex appeal.

Why had this singer so far gone unnoticed?

In a feature by Mikal Gilmore for *Rolling Stone* in 2006, Jimmy Page revealed that he'd asked himself the same question: "I just could not understand why, when he told me he'd been singing for a few years already, he hadn't become a big name yet."

Plant and Page meet each other after the gig; Plant was asked what he thought about the idea of him singing in the New Yardbirds. As quoted in *Classic Rock* in 2003, Plant said: "I knew The Yardbirds had done a lot of work in America – which to me meant audiences who want to know what I might have to offer – so naturally I was very interested." Yet Page couldn't quite make out this enigmatic character and invited him down to his home near the capital for a chat to get to know each other some more.

Plant was initially a little hesitant, and took advice from his pal Alexis Korner, who encouraged the insecure singer to hook up with Page. And so Plant travelled more than a hundred miles south, down to London ...

At Page's boathouse on the River Thames in Pangbourne, Berkshire, the pair formed a quick rapport when they discovered they shared similar tastes in music such as Joan Baez's 'Babe I'm Gonna Leave You' and the Muddy Waters tune 'You Shook Me.' They spoke about music with light and shade, music that was not black and white but had different textures and layers. They spoke about making music that included acoustic guitars as well as electric riffs; music that took the listener to another psychological realm. Neither of them wanted to compose straight-forward pop or rock and roll records like those by The Shadows and their light-hearted ilk.

Despite some initial reluctance when they all met each other at that gig near Birmingham, on the boathouse in Pangbourne it quickly became apparent that Jimmy Page had found his singer.

Robert Plant returned home to the Midlands excited, nervous and a little overwhelmed. Shortly after, Peter Grant confirmed Plant's involvement in the New Yardbirds when he sent a telegram up to a pub called Three Men In A Boat in Walsall where Hobbstweedle were rehearsing. The telegram could not have come at a better time. Even so, the excitable Plant wasn't quite prepared for just how successful the New Yardbirds (later Led Zeppelin) would become once the keys were in the ignition and the band's engine was turned on ...

PLANTY
& THE LED ZEPPELIN SAGA
1969–1980

*"Zeppelin emerged from the embers of the Yardbirds, and had all
sorts of influences, such as blues and West Coast American music."*
Robert Plant speaking to *Circus* magazine in 1976

As mentioned in the introduction, this is not a book on Led Zeppelin
because such an endeavour would be a fool-hardy undertaking for a
number of reasons, one of them being the near-impossible challenge of
bettering such revered tomes as Stephen Davis' popular (and controversial)
book *Hammer Of The Gods* and Ritchie Yorke's detailed account of the
band in his weighty book *The Definitive Biography*. A special mention must
also go to ex-Led Zeppelin road manager Richard Cole whose book
(written with author Richard Turbo) on Zeppelin, *Stairway To Heaven: Led
Zeppelin Uncensored,* has caused as much notoriety as Davis's book, a
thrilling read for rock fans. The books by Led Zeppelin archivist Dave
Lewis are also highly-lauded.

There have, of course, been many other books on Zeppelin but those
three, primarily, offer a history of the band's entire life-span when others
have specifically focused on different aspects of Zeppelin's twelve-year
career; they also have the benefit of having an insider's view of the band.
While the formation of the band, the famous tales of sex with groupies,
drugs, fights, the occult and Aleister Crowley – and let's not forget a
famous story concerning red snappers – are incredibly exciting to read, this
book is solely about Robert Plant so inevitably many concessions in the
storytelling will have to be made. There are an abundance of 'Led Zep

issues' which are largely irrelevant to this particular text. Evidently, it is Robert Plant's role in Led Zeppelin which is the focal point of this single chapter and how this affected and pre-empted his post–Led Zep career.

*　*　*

It was in mid-1968 that Robert Plant agreed to join Jimmy Page in his band the New Yardbirds, managed by Peter Grant. Page and bassist Chris Dreja – both of them former members of The Yardbirds – had ideas for the name after the band folded. A disastrous gig at the Luton College of Technology on July 7, 1968 put a metaphorical nail in the band's weighty coffin. But neither Page nor Dreja were undaunted about forming under the unoriginal moniker of the New Yardbirds. They had a contracted tour of Scandinavia to fulfil to so they had to quickly form a new version of the band. Cue singer Robert Plant. However, Dreja had a change of heart and opted out of the bold project to follow a career in photography. Cue the next piece in the puzzle: John Paul Jones, born John Baldwin on January 3, 1946 in Sidcup, London.

By the late 1960s, the seasoned bassist was tired of constant session work and craved something new. In the studio, he had already worked with the Rolling Stones, Donovan, Herman's Hermits, Jeff Beck, Rod Stewart and Nico – a formidable list of credits by any standards. Speaking to rock writer and author Steven Rosen in 1977, which was later used as a fascinating feature in the September 2005 issue of *Classic Rock*, Jones said, "I'd been doing sessions for three or four years, on and off. I'd met Jimmy on sessions before." He continued: "I joined Led Zeppelin, I suppose, after my missus said to me: 'Will you stop moping around the house? Why don't you join a band or something?' And I said: 'There's no bands I want to join, what are you talking about?' And she said: 'Well, look, Jimmy Page is forming a group.' I think it was in *Disc* magazine … so I rang him … and I said: 'Well, if you want a bass player, give me a ring.'" After Dreja quit, Jimmy Page did exactly that.

There was one more crucial part of the outfit left to fill – the drum stool. As with the choice of singer, Page threw various ideas around before Robert Plant mentioned the name of his old pal John Bonham from his days in The Crawling King Snakes and the Band Of Joy. Bonham was still gigging with Tim Rose, earning the handsome sum of £40 a week, which may not seem much compared to the millions he would later enjoy in Zeppelin, but at that point it was a nice little bag of money. Plant persuaded Page and Grant to check out Bonham's thunderous drumming at a gig he played in London during his tenure in Tim Rose's band at the end of July, 1968. Considering the way Bonham pounded the drums and kept the rhythm tight and effective, there was no doubt in their minds that Bonham was the man for the job. There were times when Bonham hit the kit so hard his fingers actually bled. But he needed more than gentle persuasion if he was to give up his handsome, secure wage. It was down to Page and Grant to attract the energetic drummer to the prospect of joining a potentially lucrative band. Those who knew Grant were aware that he always got his own way; his stamina and persistence finally allured Bonham over to the new project after sending copious amounts of telegrams. Part of the reason for Bonham's change of mind was due to his friendship with Plant.

There was one other thing − a band name. Surely they couldn't or wouldn't want to carve out a career from the ashes of a previous band? It wasn't until they played their very first gig at the Gladsaxe Teen Club in Denmark on September 7, 1968 that they decided to adopt a new name altogether, so once their contracted tour of Scandinavia was done and dusted and they'd returned back home to England, they conducted some brainstorming sessions regarding a new moniker.[19]

★   ★   ★

It is commonly understood that the name Led Zeppelin derived from a joke told by The Who drummer Keith Moon at a recording session for the song 'Beck's Bolero' in May, 1966. In attendance at that session was Jimmy Page, Jeff Beck, Keith Moon and session musicians Nicky Hopkins and John Baldwin (he hadn't adopted the stage name of John Paul Jones at that point). After the success of that particular session, an idea was flung around about forming a super-group − Jimmy Page even approached both Steve Winwood of the Spencer Davis Group and Steve Marriott from the Small Faces about fronting the band but neither were free to take up the offer. Nothing came of the bold idea except a witticism from Keith Moon; to paraphrase, he said that a band like 'Beck's Bolero', with so many egos in the room, would probably go down like a lead balloon or even a lead Zeppelin. Page mentioned this little anecdote to Grant who was impressed, although he suggested they take the 'a' out of 'lead' so it would not confuse the Americans.

That tale has been disputed: some believe that the name actually came about because of a conversation Led Zep's road manager Richard Cole had with Keith Moon and John Entwistle of The Who at a New York disco. Moon and Entwistle were feeling disillusioned with The Who and Pete Townshend's domineering personality and actually thought about forming a band with Jimmy Page and Steve Winwood. Cue the line about a lead balloon again, this time allegedly from Entwistle. Cole reiterated the conversation back to Page when he returned to England and it was discussed with Peter Grant (often dubbed the 'fifth member' of the group).

The bulky-sized Grant was born on April 5, 1935 in London. Prior to the formation of Led Zeppelin, Grant had done a wide array of jobs, including working as a doorman at the famous 2i's Coffee Bar in central London, a bouncer, the entertainment manager of a hotel in Jersey and an actor. Most famously he played small roles in the acclaimed 1961 film *The Guns Of Navarone* and the 1963 film *Cleopatra* with Elizabeth Taylor in the starring role. He also starred as actor Richard Morley's double in several movies.

When the band first started rehearsing and gigging (still using the name the New Yardbirds), Plant appeared to take a back seat; he was slightly intimidated by Page and Jones who were both experienced London session musicians. As quoted in a retrospective piece in early 1987 for the defunct music paper *Sounds*, John Paul Jones said, "The first time, we all met in this little room to see if we could stand each other. Robert had heard I was a session man, and he was wondering what was going to turn up – some old bloke with a pipe?" Rehearsals were productive and new songs began to materialise.

From the word go, it was startlingly obvious that Plant took a step back to make room for the domineering talents of Jimmy Page. A hugely significant aspect at this time for all concerned was when Peter Grant and Jimmy Page flew to the States in November, 1968 to meet with record labels, hoping to secure a good deal for the band. Equipped with an arsenal of master recordings and the artwork for their first album, Grant secured one of the most famous deals in rock history. At that time the legendary Ahmet Ertegun was a senior executive at Atlantic Records, a hive of uniquely talented artists that included Ray Charles and Aretha Franklin, amongst a dazzling array of other revered musicians and singers. After some tense talks, Grant and Page walked away having signed a five-year contract which included a number of clauses and small print that essentially gave Led Zeppelin artistic freedom over the production and distribution of their music. Such a deal was literally unheard of at the time. They also walked away with a smile on their faces for one other reason; they secured an advance of legendary proportions – the grand sum of $200,000.

Plant had something to celebrate in 1968 when he married Maureen Wilson, his Anglo-Indian girlfriend, on November 9. She was several months pregnant with their first child, a baby girl, soon to be called Carmen Jane.

It would take some time before Robert Plant could offer contributions with confidence; at that time he was naïve about the record industry and took criticisms to heart. Nonetheless, his new band catapulted him on to an altogether different level.

★　★　★

What competition was Led Zeppelin about to face? Roger Daltrey was strutting his stuff on stage while singing recent hits like 1967's 'Pictures Of Lilly', 'I Can See For Miles' and 1968's 'Magic Bus.' Music had become faster, louder and far brawnier than the early days of The Beatles and Cliff Richard – Cream was a band that Led Zeppelin would follow. Their first album, 1966's *Fresh Cream*, proved that the super-group – in this case former John Mayall and The Bluesbreakers guitarist Eric Clapton, ex-Graham Bond Organization drummer Ginger Baker and veteran bassist Jack Bruce – could live up to the hype such weighty names would inevitably produce. Although their first album was a hit in the UK and gave them a reputation in the larger American market, it mostly consisted of old blues covers. It was their second album, the magnificent *Disraeli Gears*, which propelled them to enormous heights of success and reverence, especially in the States. They were famous for over-extended solos and onstage jam workouts which could last up to twenty remarkable minutes and more. Cream were made famous by songs such as 'Sunshine Of Your Love', 'I Feel Free', 'Strange Brew' and a stupendous live re-working of Robert Johnson's 'Crossroads'; but they said goodbye to the world's stages in November, 1968, after two gigs at London's Royal Albert Hall. It was an acrimonious spilt with divisions in the band caused by personality clashes and conflicting musical visions.

Other UK bands that enjoyed success during Plant's first days in Led Zeppelin included the Jeff Beck Group and the Small Faces – a Mod band whose singer Steve Marriott had the same vocal strength and stamina of Messr Robert Plant; in fact, Plant briefly flirted with a Mod image prior to his Band Of Joy days and modelled it on the legendary Marriott. At the time of Led Zeppelin's birth in 1968, a band called Free had gotten together in April; their singer Paul Rodgers has often been called the greatest white blues singer of all-time. The London-based Jimi Hendrix Experience enjoyed phenomenal success with their debut album in 1967 called *Are You Experienced?* which featured the classic song 'Foxy Lady.' Hendrix's wild style of playing immediately caught the attention of Clapton and Beck who quickly came to be in awe of the controversial American. Another Hendrix fan was Robert Plant.

Over in the States, the Southern blues-rock band Creedence Clearwater Revival led by the formidable John Fogerty had a tough time being taken seriously in 1968, primarily, because the main choice of music which most Americans steered towards was psychedelia. Also, Canned Heat released their second album, *Boogie With Canned Heat*, in the year Zeppelin formed.

Plant was soaking up as many influences as possible and although he loved the West Coast sounds, the latest blues-rock bands (particularly from the UK) offered something more dangerous and rebellious, which attracted his ever growing interests in all styles of music however eclectic, wild or controversial.

★ ★ ★

Led Zeppelin were ready to head over to the States by the end of 1968. It would be Robert Plant and John Bonham's first journey over the waters of the Atlantic. Plant was in awe of America on his first visit there; like an over-zealous child in a candy store not knowing which direction to head toward, Plant endeavoured to devour all the sights. In particular, he loved to chill-out at local bars and especially loved the female attention he received; he'd never seen such beauty before and what especially attracted Plant to American women was the sheer confidence they displayed when asking men out on dates. It was like a world away from rainy old England!

A few hundred white-promo vinyl copies of their debut album *Led Zeppelin*[20] had already been handed out to radio stations; as the band's main source of initial fame came from Page's association with The Yardbirds, the Led Zeppelin name was spreading like wild-fire.

The band's first set of American gigs was at the very end of the year and saw further dates in early '69; they even managed to play a gig at the Whiskey A Go-Go – a popular joint in Los Angeles. They were also booked to play the Fillmore East in New York and the Fillmore West in San Francisco, both of which were owned by the successful promoter, Bill Graham.

Zeppelin's first US gig saw them gain a support slot on the same bill as Vanilla Fudge and Iron Butterfly in Denver on Boxing Day, 1968. All three bands were signed to Atlantic Records. Mark Stein of Vanilla Fudge, a band that took Zeppelin under their wing in 1968/69, says, "I always thought Robert Plant was this incredible spirit! A great source of positive energy mixed with respect for his peers and, of course, an amazing singer. He was always easy to talk to and well, what can I say, to this day I've never lost any fondness for him, as famous as he became, whenever I ran into him over the years there was always that feeling that we were there in the beginning and always felt the respect he had for me again."

It was often the case on those initial US dates that Zeppelin would not even be included on the bill; they were an unknown band. Speaking to *Circus* in 1976, Plant said: "The reaction [for the first tour] was very good ... I remember the [poster] that read 'Vanilla Fudge, Taj Mahal plus Supporting Act!' I didn't care; I'd been playing for years and I'd never seen my name up there so it meant nothing to me. But the reception that we got was something else again, and that was especially surprising because in some of those towns the album had not yet reached the stores."

As referenced in the superlative *Led Zeppelin: The Concert File* by Dave Lewis and Simon Pallett, the band took some harsh criticisms from the local press. Colorado's *Rocky Mountain News* wrote: "Singer Robert Plant – a cut above average in style, but no special appeal in sound."

It was not unheard of that Peter Grant and road manager Richard Cole hid bad reviews or any negative criticisms from Plant because of his perceived naïvete and lack of confidence at that point. As mentioned, he took such criticisms to heart. Speaking to the author, Mark Stein of Vanilla Fudge has nothing but good memories of touring with Zeppelin. "The first time I heard of Led Zeppelin, I was at my manager's house with some of the guys and we were talking about the upcoming tour. Our agent was there as well and he played us the track 'You Shook Me' from the first Led Zeppelin album and when Plant's voice followed the downward slide of Page's guitar, it blew everybody's mind."

Mark Stein recalls that Led Zeppelin were a band who were more eager and zealous to play music than any other band he was aware of: "They were all so naïve and full of wonderment. We got to be good friends through it all," he says. "I started checking out their set thinking how much potential they had and I know this may sound a bit self-serving, but I think I told Robert to move more on stage and for Page to get bigger amps! Crazy isn't it?"

Despite Zeppelin's growing strength onstage – which some headlining bands would have been frightened of – Vanilla Fudge warmed to the young English band. Plant, in particular, was excited to be on the road with such a powerful and energetic group.

Stein: "Some other memories come back to me on that tour. Vanilla Fudge were the headliners in Salt Lake City, Utah. I watched [Zep's] show and was really blown away. They were so fucking powerful and dynamic and Page & Plant just wooed the audience into a frenzy, when they came off stage, after several encores, I looked at Cole and said: 'How do you follow that?' He said: 'Just go up and play.' Well, I've got to tell you that night we rocked the shit out of the house. Zep brought out the best in us, like one heavy-weight fighter doing it to another. What a night for rock fans!"

Zeppelin also supported Vanilla Fudge at Vancouver and despite what others have said, Stein did not sense any malcontent between Page and Plant or any of the other members: "To me, Page and Plant got on well; they, as well as Jonesy and Bonzo, were a collective force that no one would fuck with!"

Although some of the gigs that the band played on their first American road jaunt between December 1968 and February 1969 saw them opening for Vanilla Fudge on selected dates, they also opened for some other bands including, as mentioned, Iron Butterfly and also the MC5 on the East

Coast. Michael Davis of the famed Detroit garage rock band the MC5 recalls, "The only time I remember supporting Led Zeppelin was [at] a show in Boston at The Boston Gardens [in January]. We were the opener to a full house of 16,000 plus ..."

Plant in particular made an indelible impression on the MC5 bass player. Davis: "Plant was elementally different from the others. He was the 'one' – the golden boy, the shining star [and] the chosen [one] in the lead role. The supporting cast were well aware of their roles, and played them with discipline. The balance of stage persona was perfectly executed. They knew, really knew, their places. I particularly remember someone entering the dressing room and presenting Plant with the freshly released Rod Stewart album. Plant's reaction at the baiting was an exuberant exclamation of regard for Stewart's success, and a rather lavish approval of the package. Robert, the diplomat, the professional, came [out] front with a very positive response. It was also obvious that he was really into music and the music business – you just can't fake that.

So there he was, on stage, the torch bearer of the band, the golden-locked hero, sent to conquer the American lady folk with his English charm and good looks. Then he opened his mouth to sing, and to my shock, he sounded like a castrato ... just kidding, man! I wasn't used to hearing that high-pitched timbre in rock and roll – at least [not in] hard driving rock. I was used to gruff-voiced black guys or white guys trying to sound like down-home black guys. However, within a short time of their taking the stage, Led Zeppelin was in control of the audience and proceeded to [woo] the crowd at will. The band was that tight, and Plant just had the 'balls' even though his voice sounded like he did not!"

The US tour finished in mid-February; Frankie Banali, the drummer in the American heavy metal band Quiet Riot, was just a teenager when he witnessed the full force of Led Zeppelin on stage.

Frankie Banali: "I was fortunate enough to witness Led Zeppelin live on numerous occasions but ,without a doubt, the first time was for me a musical life altering experience. This performance was on February 15, 1969 at a club in Miami, Florida called Thee Image, which was a converted bowling alley. It was the most electrifying and amazing performance that I had ever witnessed. Led Zeppelin as a unit were at their most powerful ..."

Banali was especially impressed by Plant: "Robert Plant's vocals and charisma single-handedly defined [Led Zeppelin.] [He is] a vocal force to be reckoned with and his stage persona was the model for all those who came after him ... It really was inspiring to me even though I am a drummer rather than a singer. Robert Plant was able to effortlessly pour his heart out vocally on songs like 'I Can't Quit You' with such bravado and yet so honestly that it was endearing and frightening all at once ...

[He is] the image of, dare I say, a true 'Rock God' and I could not help but think to myself that [Led Zeppelin] is one lucky band to have someone like him ..."

In 1969, touring continued over in Europe after their debut US tour but work was being done off stage to prepare for the official release of their first album.

★ ★ ★

The band's first, eponymous album, was released in the United States on January 17, 1969. It was hardly a hit, reaching Number 99 on the *Billboard* charts. Back home in the UK where the band was taken less seriously, the album was delivered several weeks later than in America; it arrived in March at which time it had been flung into the US Top 10. It eventually reached the Top 10 in the UK in May, peaking at Number 6.

With constant touring (particularly in the States) to promote their initial opus, *Led Zeppelin* proved to be the most enduring albums of the year. As quoted in Ian Fortnam's astute retrospective feature in the June 2003 issue of *Classic Rock*, John Paul Jones was especially impressed with Plant's vocal prowess: "And when Robert roared in, the initial reaction from people was 'Where did you find him from?' His vocal approach was fantastic."

On the website *www.dailyvault.com*, one critic points out that much of the album "shows their willingness to go over the top, with Plant's outrageous, spastic singing leading the way."

Indeed, Plant really did give it his all; he had to prove that he could sing as robustly as Page could play the guitar. The most frustrating aspect of the band's first album, for Plant anyway, was the fact that his name was not able to appear on the songwriting credits because he was still under contract to CBS who had issued three singles by him in 1966 and 1967.

Filled with a few blues-folk covers which they had began playing under the New Yardbirds moniker, their debut album, which has since become known as simply *Led Zeppelin I*, opens with the robust 'Good Times Bad Times'; despite his youth, Plant's vocals are emotional, evocative and in control. His age betrays him because he sounds older, indeed, more mature than he actually was. 'Babe I'm Gonna Leave You' – an original Joan Baez song – is a tune that struck a chord with both Page and Plant when they first discussed forming a band in August, '68. Plant's vocals are vehement and heart-felt throughout the track. 'You Shook Me' – a cover of the Willie Dixon song – shows Plant on familiar ground, bringing that old American song up to date for the British blues boomers of the day. Plant can be heard playing harmonica and his vocals are magnificently energetic. Listen to Plant sing the chorus on 'Dazed And Confused' and one gets a complete understanding of his vocal prowess;

undoubtedly, it is a flawless centrepiece of a masterful first album. Despite not receiving any songwriting credits on this particular album, Plant's lyrical influence can be heard on 'You Time Is Gonna Come' with references to the Ray Charles number 'I Believe To My Soul.' Plant's passion for R&B had by no means been diminished by the time he spent taking inspiration from US West Coast music. Showing parallels to the Bert Jansch song 'Black Waterside', 'Black Mountain Side' is an accurate demonstration of Page's musical expertise rather than Plant's talent yet Plant is still in fine vocal shape. On 'Communication Breakdown' Plant definitely proves that he can wail and groan to a good rock song and not just an old blues tune or a folk ballad; unquestionably Plant had already begun proving his vocal versatility. 'I Can't Quit You Babe' is another Willie Dixon blues song and as such it is another perfect chance for Plant to show his affinity toward American blues music. The final song on the first album is the epic track 'How Many More Times' and again Plant's influence is felt in the lyrics with reference to Howlin' Wolf's 'How Many More Tears' and Albert King's 'The Hunter' – two of Plant's earliest blues idols. So despite the disappointment of not having any lyrical credit on Led Zep's debut opus, Plant's influence on those songs is nevertheless undeniable.

In the first half of '69, the band also found time to record some very successful and highly-lauded BBC sessions. The gigs were never-ending. The influential writer Nick Logan wrote in the *NME*: "It isn't hard to understand the substantial appeal of Led Zeppelin. Their live act is a blitzkrieg. There are few groups who could live with them."

They toured the UK in March visiting a series of small venues; West Midlands rock singer Al Atkins – who was fronting Judas Priest by this time – recalls seeing Zeppelin at a local gig: "We went to see them at Mothers Club in Erdington in Birmingham on March 22 in 1969, and they got paid £75 that night … I remember they were supported by Mick Abraham's band Blodwyn Pig … I said 'This is great! It's a crossover.' Cream was a loud, blues band … but this was heavier and louder. Having seen Rob sing in the past in various blues jams and also appearing alongside him in his group the Band Of Joy, I couldn't believe the transformation since teaming up with Jimmy Page. He had gone from being a fairly good blues singer into a rock icon overnight. The band totally blew me away … I loved it!"

Slade drummer Don Powell remembers that bassist Jim Lea's "brother Frank, saw them [Led Zeppelin] at The Lafayette Club in Wolverhampton [possibly in April, 1969] when they did a small club tour in England. We asked him what he thought of the singer, Robert Plant, and his reply was: 'I didn't think they had a singer, but there was a guy dancing around on stage!'"

Only a year before, Plant was a naïve and relatively young novice compared to the more experienced musical hands of Page and Jones, but with the heavy touring, Plant was quickly learning the admirable craft of leading, challenging and dominating an audience. In those early days, he did struggle to compete with the sheer, unrelenting volume of the band but in time he'd learn to work in unison with Page's riffs and Bonham and Jones' fast and taut rhythm section.

Zeppelin and their growing entourage went back to the States for the second time in April '69 before returning home to England in the summer. "For years, in Led Zeppelin, I went all around the world and never saw a thing," he explained to journalist Deborah Frost of *Spin* magazine in 1993.

At Peter Grant's insistence, the United States had become Led Zeppelin's stronghold; like a merry-go-round the band ventured back over the Atlantic yet again for a tour in July through to August.

In correspondence with the author, Vanilla Fudge's Mark Stein remembers, "There was the one time … [in] 1969, Vanilla Fudge was playing the Singer Bowl in Flushing, N.Y. Jeff Beck was on the bill and we were hanging out in the dressing room. Plant, Richard Cole, Bonzo [and us] were having a chat and … Plant spotted this music critic coming down the alleyway outside, which led to the dressing room, don't recall his name, but apparently he had written some harsh things about Zeppelin, there was a crate filled with pints of O.J. [and] Cole shouted: 'Let's get that fucker!' and they started stoning him with the O.J! I mean, really giving it to him as he ran back up into the alley where he was pelted with the things and ran for his life! Never to be seen again that evening, afterwards it was quite comical reflecting on that, especially now!"

Frankie Banali: "My [second] live Led Zeppelin experience was at a very popular, albeit very odd venue in Dania, Florida on August 23, 1969. Pirates' World, as it was called, was an amusement park, but the venue was nothing more than a stage set up in the unused parking lot of the facility! Though [it was] only six months from the first time I had seen the mighty Zeppelin, Robert Plant had already matured in both his vocal abilities and how he commanded the stage with his confident presence. Their set that evening was essentially the same as the first of the two shows I saw in Miami at Thee Image venue, but right from the very first wail in the opening riff of 'Train Kept A Rollin'" you could clearly hear that Robert Plant planned to take the vocals in this and each subsequent song to incredibly acrobatic heights. He never let go from that point on through what I remember to be a gymnastic vocal extravaganza. I could clearly see that Jimmy Page smiling, thought so too! The band was fantastic with Jimmy as the six-stringed master of ceremonies and the rhythm section of John Paul Jones and John Henry Bonham building a tsunami strength wall of sound. Truly a great memory."

* * *

The band's second album *Led Zeppelin II* was issued in the UK on October 22, 1969. On a commercial level, it was monster hit even if the critics were not totally overwhelmed by its intelligence and strength. However, things have certainly changed since 1969 with current critics and fans lauding the album loudly as one of Zep's heaviest. One fan writes on the e-zine *Treble* (*http://treblezine.com*) that as soon as you play the album, "Robert Plant comes wailing in, his voice another instrument, making himself much more than a vocalist."

Recorded at many different studios in the UK and US while the band were completing an incredibly hectic touring schedule, Plant's influence on the album is evident in the songwriting and he also offered many suggestions in terms of song arrangements. As quoted in a 2004 issue of *Classic Rock* in a feature on the album by the noted Led Zeppelin expert Dave Lewis, engineer Chris Huston remembered Plant at a session in Mystic Sound Studio in LA: "We did the tracks live, with Plant standing in the middle of the room with a hand-held microphone. You can hear that at the end of 'The Lemon Song', where Plant sings 'floor floor floor' – that echo was recorded in real time."

Led Zeppelin II begins with the fiery 'Whole Lotta Love' which is a perfect example of how Plant can sing in conjunction with Page's lead riffs. With lyrics inspired by Willie Dixon[21], Plant sounds utterly seductive as he groans and moans throughout the whole song. It's no wonder he became an object of desire for many young and lustful American girls during the 1970s; indeed, the second half of the song has one of Plant's most overtly sexual moments and as such it has been cheekily dubbed the 'orgasm section.' 'What Is And What Should Never Be' is a personal song for Plant and one which showed his talent strengthen as a credible songwriter. 'The Lemon Song' has picked up cult status over the years and, like 'Whole Lotta Love', also proved to be rather controversial. Plant would, throughout the next few years, often improvise these lyrics on stage. 'Thank You' is a slow dreamy ballad written by Plant as a love letter to his wife; it's a delicate ballad and his vocals are tender and dulcet. 'Heartbreaker' is a terrific 1970s rock song with an indelible groove; such a song as this invariably proved how much of an influence Plant has had on singers like Steven Tyler. 'Living Loving Maid (She's Just A Woman)' is a relatively obscure song despite its memorable chorus and fun rhythm.[22] 'Ramble On' is a superb track where Plant's interest in fantasy literature and in particular J.R.R. Tolkien is evoked in the song's lyrics. 'Moby Dick' is a track that sees Plant take a back seat while John Bonham takes the lead. 'Being It Home' is a nifty song inspired by Sonny Boy Williamson's 'Bring It On Home;' Williamson was an early inspiration on Plant when he was just a budding blues singer working his way through the busy Midlands blues circuit, so again Plant had plenty of input into this one.

Evidently, Plant had been given enough space for his talents to properly flourish. He offered his thoughts on the band's second long-form composition after its release; as reported in *Classic Rock* in 2004, he said: "On that album we were definitely deviating from the original Zeppelin intensity, but without losing quality. In fact, we gained a quality, because my voice was being used in different ways instead of confining it to a safe formula."

Speaking to *MP3.com* in December, 2006, Judas Priest singer and fellow 'Midlander' Rob Halford included *Led Zeppelin II* as one of his most inspirational albums. "Robert's voice is just phenomenal," he enthused. "He inspired me in a tremendous way as a singer."

After the release of *Led Zeppelin II* and a subsequent tour of the States, Plant flew home to the Midlands for a brief stay. On November 25, he found time to attend a showcase gig at a Walsall pub called The George which was organised by a young up-coming band called Judas Priest who had only formed in 1969. At that point, Judas Priest was fronted by Al Atkins and the gig was arranged for the attention of various record labels including the EMI offshoot Harvest, Decca and the independent label Immediate Records, owned by former Rolling Stones manager Andrew Loog Oldham.

One-time Judas Priest guitarist Ernie Chataway recalls with startling clarity: "I remember Planty there now. He'd got a purple velvet coat on and these big fur boots. He hasn't changed much has he?! And he'd got a load of people around him ... I didn't like him ... I never did like him; we never did get on ..."

With the growing commercial success of both *Led Zeppelin I* and *Led Zeppelin II* and due to their constant touring, the band found themselves financially comfortable in a relatively short space of time. It was around this time when Plant splashed out on a huge present for himself, his wife Maureen and their child: he bought a broken-down farm in Wolverly, close to his childhood home of Kidderminster. Although it needed some major reconstruction work, Plant was attracted by its rich history and could not resist buying it. It proved to be a comfortable base for him, seemingly light years away from the insanity of Led Zeppelin's success, especially in America. It was wise that the band never moved permanently to the States as so many of their contemporaries did. They probably would have imploded because of the constant temptation and the sheer insanity of the life of a British rock band let loose in a large country that loves excess; instead they would go onto enjoy America when need be; then they could go back home to the tranquillity of the English countryside and remember who they actually were.

* * *

With two album releases, it had been a hectic year for the band and they needed a break, but the gigs kept on coming, largely at Grant's insistence. At the same time that *Led Zeppelin II* was released, The Beatles unleashed their masterpiece *Abbey Road* in September in the UK and October in the US. By the start of 1970, *Led Zeppelin II* reigned supreme in the UK charts and the band began a full tour in January. It was perfect timing really; however, the final date of the UK tour (at Edinburgh's Usher Hall) on February 7 was rescheduled for the 17 after Plant was involved in a road accident on January 31 after driving home from a gig in Birmingham by the Californian psychedelic-rock band Spirit. He'd lost control of his expensive Jaguar and suffered facial injuries; he was sent to the nearby Kidderminster Hospital. Plant's relationship with his family was still uneasy after they struggled to understand his chosen path in life, so he gave the hospital staff Jimmy Page's contact details rather than his parents. Not long after the accident, Plant began building his broken relationship with his parents, especially with his father.

Plant's interest in blues and folk was influencing the rest of the band, allowing them to compromise on the choice of songs for the many tours they undertook. For example, when they played Europe in 1970 prior to the release of their third album, they threw various cover songs into the set list, not uncommon since they had been playing these from the moment they formed the band; but it was Plant's deep interest in Robert Johnson which undoubtedly led to them playing a version of 'Travelling River Side Blues' as well as 'Long Distance Call' by John Lee Hooker and even Neil Young's 'Down By The River' which proved he had not lost his interest in the Californian folk sound. A regular set-list would run as follows: 'We're Gonna Groove', 'I Can't Quit You', 'Dazed And Confused', 'Heartbreaker', 'White Summer', 'White Mountain Side', 'Since I've Been Loving You', 'Thank You', 'What Is And What Should Never Be', 'Moby Dick', 'How Many More Times'[23] and 'Whole Lotta Love'.

The sheer amount of energy the band portrayed on stage was unrelenting; not since Cream had any rock fan seen a band jam for such lengthy periods on stage. The fans were cooked up into a frenzy and Plant was swiftly dominating the stage. Cleverly, he worked both alongside Jimmy Page as well as competing against him to win the audience's affections.[24] "I was competing for attention in a four-piece band that was phenomenal, and I was trying to attack the blues from a kind of white English viewpoint as a singer ..." Plant enthused to *National Public Radio* in 2005. "I found myself overdoing it, but it worked. It was great, I was young ..."

Yet many of the negative criticisms the band received from the press were directed towards Plant and he did not take to kindly to some of these reviews. As referenced in the Dave Lewis and Simon Pallet's commendable *Led Zeppelin: The Concert File,* the *Montreal Star* had some pretty severe words to say about Plant after seeing the band live at The Forum on April 13, 1970: "Such miserable music would not be so offensive were it not for the fact that it is all so pretentious," wrote one journalist. "Robert Plant is without talent as a singer or performer. He waves his arms uselessly, he clutches the microphone predictably. He cannot dance and his moves are graceless and tasteless. He seems to think he is very sexy, but he has absolutely nothing interesting or original to offer."

After famously spending some time at an old cottage called Bron-Yr-Aur in Snowdonia, Wales in May, 1970 where they arranged some material for their third opus, Led Zep ventured back on the road in June, having also spent some time in various studios preparing songs. The European tour included a famous set at the Bath Festival.

They travelled back to the States in the late summer of 1970 and even headlined a gig at Madison Square Garden in New York. Despite being seen as something of a joke in their native country, over in America they could easily fill venues of 10,000 to 20,000 capacity; it was certainly not a bad feat by any band's standards, regardless of what the reluctant critics may have thought.

Vanilla Fudge's Mark Stein remembers seeing Zeppelin at a gig on the East Coast in August: "I went to see them [one] night along with the drummer in my new band Jimmy Galuzzi [who has since passed away]. We got backstage and there were a group of seats right behind the stage," he remembers, fondly. "Plant spotted me during Bonham's drum solo and came over and screamed: 'Are you writing?' I screamed back: 'Yes, I'm excited about my new band.' Vanilla Fudge had recently disbanded. Then he screamed to the crew: 'Tea, tea!' [Because] tea was good for the vocal cords after banshee [type] singing half the night. Lastly, Page came running over to me to say hello and as he extended his hand to me, there was a small space between the stage and our seats; he lost his footing and I grabbed him just as one foot had fallen through. He blurted out: 'You almost lost me!' Now to paint the picture, his guitar was flung over his back and the stage was maybe fifteen-foot high or so; Christ, if he fell it could have been a disaster! Crazy shit!"

Reviewing Led Zeppelin's gig at The Forum in Inglewood, California on September 4, David P. writes on his personal website *Led Zeppelin Live: The Reviews (http://users.adelphia.net)* that during the opener 'Immigrant Song' "Robert sounds as if he'll be in excellent voice for this concert."

Writing about the song 'That's The Way', David P. also recalls: "The comfortable interaction between Robert and the crowd is very evident here. It's like he's talking to his next door neighbours. The acoustic set starts off with one of my favourites and the band does not disappoint.

JPJ's [John Paul Jones] mandolin and Jimmy's guitar are in perfect harmony, though the song is played a touch too hurriedly. Robert sings fairly well throughout the song, but he misses during the chorus, not really (or wanting) to hit the notes. There's some great background vocals into the final strumming coda. A pretty rendition, though somewhat hurried."

David P. was also at the International Centre in Honolulu, Hawaii on September 6 and was especially impressed by Plant's performance during 'Dazed And Confused.' On his own website *Led Zeppelin Live: The Reviews* (*http://users.adelphia.net*) he writes, "the crowd loves every second. Screams of delight are heard throughout the intro. Robert's vocal entry intensifies the already heavy mood created by his band mates, but then the whole band erupts in the first musical chorus, creating a force of rock and roll power that makes the building tremble ... next up, Plant delivers another scream that overloads the channel prior to the second musical chorus, delivered as forcefully as the first, with the rhythm section solid and steady."

★ ★ ★

Led Zeppelin III proved to be their most versatile record yet. Released in October, 1970, the album was recorded at various studios in the UK and US; most famously they conducted recording sessions at a mobile studio owned by the Rolling Stones and more importantly they became acquainted with a dilapidated Victorian mansion in Hampshire called Headley Grange. Page spoke to Q magazine about the mansion: "It was very grey and damp. There was no heating. It had a boiler system that was like something that wouldn't have quite made it onto the Titanic."

Inevitably, the bold notion of recording at a spooky Victorian castle in England was Jimmy Page's idea. His deep interest in the occult and especially the Satanist Aleister Crowley had great bearings on the direction of the band's music and image. Yet the deep-rooted Celtic and folk themes of their third album unquestionably came from Robert Plant.

It was using a mobile studio at Headley Grange that Plant and Page would create some of their most inspired lyrics; indeed fans like to conjure images in their minds' eye of an enigmatic singer and lyricist and an eccentric guitarist and lyricist working by a coal-fuelled fire in a large Victorian living room that's seen better days with its peeling wallpaper, dusty furniture and damp rugs. But despite the aged décor, there was something oddly beautiful that could be found in the ugliness of the mansion. The boys would have a bottle of whiskey[25] and two half-empty glasses would sit on a nearby mahogany table as they wrote songs about Vikings, great mythological heroes and other fantastical characters.

Page told writer Mick Wall in October, 1990 for an interview in *Kerrang!*: "If I was writing something I was hearing Robert singing it, and you knew you were going forward all the time."[26]

Even though the sales of *Led Zeppelin III* would not be quite as high as its two predecessors, it nevertheless reached the top spot in both the UK and US charts. However, the album was criticised in many quarters of the music press who barked at Zeppelin for being arrogant and pretentious; they did not enjoy Zeppelin's use of acoustic pieces and folk music in the album alongside such rock numbers as 'Immigrant Song.' If anything, the album left many listeners feeling somewhat perplexed, although with the benefit of hindsight it now stands as one of their better and most inspired works.

Led Zeppelin III is an odd one; it opens with the outstanding rock tune 'Immigrant Song' and yet again, Plant's lyrics concern mythology, fantasy and powerful Viking characters that are prevalent in his earlier lyrics with Led Zeppelin. With the song 'Friends', Plant's liking for Crosby, Stills and Nash and Neil Young is evident in the lyrics and arrangement. The impact of playing in New York inspired Plant so much that he wrote the lyrics for the excellent 'Celebration Day.' 'Since I've Been Loving You' shows one of Plant's most inspired and moving vocal performances and it is partially inspired by a song called 'Never', composed by the late 1960s American band Moby Grape – one of Plant's favourite groups at the time. 'Out On The Tiles' is a lesser-known track but Plant's vocals are still resonant. Plant's growing interest in medieval Britain filters into 'Gallows Pole' but as for 'Tangerine', Plant had no lyrical input. 'That's The Way' is a wonderful song and Plant's delightful vocals reflect the harmony and remoteness of what it must have been like to write the song at the peaceful Bron-Yr-Aur cottage in Wales. 'Bron-Y-Aur Stomp' was originally written as 'Jennings Farm Blues;' the premise of the song is about Plant's dog Strider whose name is taken from a character in the popular *Lord Of The Rings* trilogy. 'Hats Off To (Roy) Harper' is a tribute to the eccentric English folk singer and was partially influenced by some of Plant's other idols – Bukka White, Robert Johnson, Sleepy John Estes and also Elvis Presley. The song gave Plant and Page the chance to jam on a gritty blues number and clearly they had an absolute blast doing so.

Led Zeppelin III has stood the test of time as one fan writes on the popular e-zine *Sputnikmusic* (*www.sputnikmusic.com*): "*Led Zeppelin III* offers a lot that you won't find anywhere else. Whether you're looking for epic blues, delicate acoustic songs, and even blue-grass anthems, the album will not fail to please you. And to all ego-centric reviewers, perhaps it is worth mentioning that even *Sgt. Pepper* garnered bad press? Ponder that a while."

With three albums under their belt, the battering ram style managerial strength of Peter Grant – who insisted that they continue such vast amounts of touring – obviously aided the band in many ways. By the time they hit the road (again) for a UK tour in March, 1971, rock music had changed significantly since Led Zeppelin had formed just three years previously …

* * *

Cream was nothing but a distant memory. Brian Jones – a founding member and rhythm guitarist of the Rolling Stones – had died in suspicious circumstances at the age of twenty seven; The Beatles had split up in April, 1970; the same year saw the deaths of two legends, Jimi Hendrix and Janis Joplin; and a band called Deep Purple were huge in the rock world, having built up a reputation as a challenging blues-rock band with their tremendous album *In Rock*, released in September of that same year.

Under the leadership of Syd Barrett, the arty progressive rock band Pink Floyd was enjoying modest degrees of success at the tail end of the 1960s with albums like *A Saucerful Of Secrets* and *Ummagumma*; they proved to be the antithesis of bands like Deep Purple, Led Zeppelin and another hard living blues-rock band, this time from Birmingham, called Black Sabbath. Sabbath are now recognised as the founding fathers of heavy metal, yet bands like Purple and Zeppelin undoubtedly (and unknowingly) lent more than a helping hand to the genesis of that style of music. Although in time all three bands would refuse to acknowledge themselves as a metal band – more rock or blues-rock than metal – many believe their heavy brand of guitars, bass and drums music created the glorious genre. Sabbath's first three albums – *Black Sabbath*, *Paranoid* and *Master Of Reality* – are masterpieces and in terms of strength and quality, they unquestionably offered strong competition to Zeppelin's first three albums.

* * *

Moving into 1971 and Zeppelin had around four to five months off the road; however, during what was – by today's standards – a very short break from the road, they had been working tirelessly at Headley Grange for their next opus. This workaholic attitude had a detrimental effect on the members, especially Plant, whose voice was understandably struggling to cope with their schedule of album/tour, album/tour, etc.

In the wake of *Led Zeppelin III*'s release, Grant and Atlantic wanted the band to continue to dominate American and European concert venues, so they were pressed for another speedy release before they hit the road again in March. This time the band played a series of gigs in the UK in smaller venues to re-establish a rapport with their audience who perhaps felt alienated in the bigger venues. They played various universities and small clubs, much to the dismay of some fans and critics who felt that such a successful live band should stick to playing 10,000-plus capacity venues. Also, some live dates had to be re-arranged in March, '71 so Plant could rest his vocal cords.

From 1971 and for the next few years thereafter, Zeppelin enjoyed the most hedonistic, decadent and successful period of their career. The sheer insanity of the Zeppelin circle was particularly felt on the live stage when the band regularly whipped the audiences into a visibly frenetic state. Bonham's drum solos sometimes lasted for an implausible twenty minutes and Page's riffs would exhilarate the crowd, making them even more wildly euphoric. Their sets grew from two-hours to two-and-a-half-hours to even three long hours of constant playing. Like Cream before them, Zeppelin simply got lost in the moment and felt powered by the audience, which meant they improvised and continued the set for even longer. Led Zeppelin were not just rock stars but *musicians*.

As Plant was the voice of the band, he would often have to calm the audience down, telling them to "Cool it," or "Move back, guys," or "You're goin' to have to take a minute to cool down." One riotous show in Milan, Italy at the famous Vigorelli Stadium in July, 1971 saw tear gas being let off by the Italian police who were out in full force. The police were dressed in full riot gear, with batons, protection shields and tear gas as they guarded and patrolled the 12,000 capacity venue. Undoubtedly it was one of the most frightening nights of their career and the band never returned to Italy. By now, Led Zep were justifiably fatigued and jaded with life on the road, so after the Milan gig they were keen to return home to their respective houses in England.

The iconic Jim Morrison of The Doors died in Paris in July, 1971 at the age of twenty seven. Like many musical bohemians, Morrison was plagued by personal demons which eventually got the better of him. If there was one rock star who could carry the baton after Morrison's path then it was Robert Plant: both of them were prototypical rock stars chronicled as legends in the annals of rock music. Morrison and Plant had several things in common in those early years: both men were adored by thousands of young women and became iconic figures to young men who wanted to imitate them. Morrison and Plant both had long hair, slim, well-toned figures and are known for using sexually provocative stage moves in front of excitable audiences. Both men were charismatic, overt yet mysterious and ambiguous, and most definitely controversial. When Morrison died, Plant quite easily became the most iconic (living) rock star in the world.

After a short sabbatical, the band, predictably, went back on the road; they returned to the States in August through to September for yet another tour. For band of such magnitude and offstage notoriety, it was not uncommon for them to receive death threats. After the debacle of the gig in Milan, the band became more concerned about their personal safety so Grant hired more security as they journeyed around America. The cliché 'better safe than sorry' certainly came into effect and there were times when Plant started to feel alienated from the real world. A necessary evil, but an evil nonetheless.

Proving that they were not spoilt, self-important rock stars, Led Zeppelin performed a charity gig on their first Japanese tour in September for victims of the American atomic bombings of Hiroshima and Nagasaki during World War II. Plant was especially emotionally affected by their trip to East Asia. They donated 7,000,000 yen from the charity gig at the Shiei Taikukan Municipal Gymnasium in Hiroshima to victims of the bombings; the town's Major then presented the band with peace medals at a special presentation.

As quoted in *Led Zeppelin: The Concert File* by Dave Lewis and Simon Pallet, Plant attended the presentation and reportedly said: "We were born after the atomic air raid. We are not in a position to blame anybody, as it just happened in the past history and it was a human being who did it. It is not our fault, but our 'past' should be blamed. We would like to express our sincere apologies about it. In this regard, we would like to help any victims who have been suffering from the bombing. Music can bring peace and joy to you. We, the musicians, will feel honourable if we can be of help to anybody."

After Japan, the band headed back home ...

★　★　★

The band's unnamed fourth album, *Led Zeppelin IV*, has been given many titles such as 'Zoso', 'Untitled', 'The Fourth Album' and 'Four Symbols'. Speaking to *Rolling Stone* in 2005, Plant said: "[It's] just 'The Fourth Album.' That's it." However, for the sake of clarity, the author will refer to the album by the more populist title, *Led Zeppelin IV* .

Again, this album was recorded at various studios including the Rolling Stones' mobile studio as well as facilities in London and LA. They also spent some time in the winter of 1970 back in Snowdonia at Bron-Yr-Aur; once again, the place proved a source of inspiration where they could peacefully prepare music and draw up ideas. As quoted in *Classic Rock* in 2001, Robert Plant had a particular affection towards Headley Grange: "Most of the mood for the fourth album was brought about in settings [that we] had not been used to. We were living in this falling down mansion in the country. The mood was incredible."

It was at Headley Grange that Plant wrote probably his most famous set of lyrics of his entire career; 'Stairway To Heaven' was conceived at the

Victorian mansion in Hampshire. As quoted in *Classic Rock,* Plant said: "The lyrics were a cynical thing about a woman getting everything she wanted without [giving] anything back."

The reason why the album was not given a title was because Jimmy Page especially wanted to make a stance against the confused response that greeted the ambiguous *Led Zeppelin III*; with a deep interest in the occult and esoteric, it was Page's idea to have the four symbols on the cover sleeve instead of a title. Each symbol was hand-picked individually by the four band members. Plant picked an Ancient Egyptian symbol which has connotations of honesty and fairness. Everything about the album was bold. As repeated in a *Classic Rock* retrospective feature by Mick Wall and Dave Lewis, Plant explained his opinion at the time of the album's release: "Now we've done *Led Zeppelin III*, the sky's the limit. It shows we can change, we can do things. It means there are endless possibilities. We are not stale, and this proves it."

Jumping straight into the UK charts at Number 1, *Led Zeppelin IV* was released on November 12, 1971. Again, Plant's influence on Zeppelin's forth album can be found in the songwriting and the album's overall texture. By now, Plant had become a dominant songwriting partner.

An undisputed masterpiece, *Led Zeppelin IV* begins with the fantastically exhilarating 'Black Dog' which showcases Plant's appetite for singing a good, bluesy rock tune. The tremendously powerful 'Rock And Roll' shows Plant keeping up to speed with Bonham's non-stop pounding of the drum kit. Plant duets with the late Sandy Denny of Fairport Convention on 'The Battle Of Evermore', which is another song that draws inspiration from the imaginative novels of J.R.R. Tolkien. 'Stairway To Heaven' is perhaps Zeppelin's trademark anthem and one of the most famous songs ever written, so there is little need to mention any more. The new age lyrics to 'Misty Mountain Hop' demonstrate Plant's influence on the lyrical content of the album. 'Four Sticks' has picked up a fan base over the years aided by Page & Plant's re-working of it on their *No Quarter* live album in 1994 and it is still played by Plant to this very day. 'Going To California' is purportedly a song about the singer-songwriter Joni Mitchell, whom Plant adored. The blues number, 'When The Levee Breaks', is a re-recording of the Kansas Joe McCoy and Memphis Minnie song of the same name; Plant was a big fan of the song and owned it on vinyl in his personal collection.

Led Zeppelin IV is perhaps their heaviest album and many commentators have declared it as a vital precursor to heavy metal, but Plant has always shot down those remarks: "The musicianship was such that people could go off on tangents and create passages that were compelling," he explained to *Record Magazine* in '83. "They were skull-crushing, in a way. But it wasn't through sheer, brute volume. It was the way it was played. It's a distinct difference."

Years later, he still refutes any claims that Zeppelin were heavy metal: "I don't think 'Stairway To Heaven' was very heavy metal," he said to journalist Chuck Klosterman of *Spin* magazine in 2002. However, some people disagree entirely. Despite Plant's vehement opinions, the self-proclaimed 'Metal God' himself, Rob Halford, told *MP3.com* in 2006: "To me they're [Led Zeppelin] a metal act to some extent..."

Also, Led Zeppelin biographer Stephen Davis wrote in *Rolling Stone* in 1976 that "Led Zeppelin's seventh album [*Presence*] confirms this quartet's status as heavy-metal champions of the known universe."[27]

They began a hectic tour of the UK in support of their fourth album during the cold winter months of 1971, playing such venues as the Free Trade Hall in Manchester, the Public Hall in Preston, the Wembley Empire Pool in London and, surprisingly, a couple of smaller shows at ballrooms in Bournemouth and Coventry, as well as various other venues in Britain. They continued touring throughout 1971 until their final gig on December 21 and, from there, Plant was able to spend a bit of time with his family on the farm.

★   ★   ★

Despite having not releasing any new material, 1972 proved to be one of the most important years in Robert Plant's life: in April, Maureen Plant gave birth to their second child, a boy named Karac. A simple name like Kevin or David would not have been appropriate for Plant, whose imagination was steeped in ancient British history, so he chose Karac which is a sturdy, age-old name based in Celtic mythology.

Another important aspect of 1972 was Plant's trips to the Indian city of Bombay. Plant had previously visited that country on a trip with Jimmy Page in October of the previous year; they also travelled to Thailand and Hong Kong when they were on something of a 'cultural high.'

It has been well-documented over the years that Plant has a love affair with India which goes back to when he first met his wife. However, his first visit was as a result of taking a different route to Australia and New Zealand for a very successful tour Down Under (they were refused entry into Singapore unless they cut their hair). Therefore, Led Zeppelin stopped, briefly, in Bombay whilst travelling with Air India and his love affair with that continent began.

On their return to England both Plant and Page (with road manager Richard Cole) decided to return to Bombay for a longer stay – two days was not enough. It would be sufficient to say that Plant was significantly moved by what he saw and experienced in the Indian city.

Bombay continues to be the most populated city in the whole of India; the sheer amount of people combined with the exceedingly high temperatures is overwhelming to any Westerner who travels there. Plant was intrigued by local cultures and delicacies and even took to drinking local Indian whiskey.

It was in March '72 when Plant and Page recorded 'Four Sticks' and 'Friends' with the revered Bombay Symphony Orchestra. "We should have stayed there and made the album," he explained to *Folk Roots Magazine* in 2000. "There were Indian instruments all over the place and it sounded fantastic. But we got the brandy out and got pissed and ... and the session fell apart!"

Although those two tracks have yet to see the light of day officially, there is a certain intrigue and aura around them; fans are keen to hear them on a band endorsed collection. Page and Plant also got the chance to jam at the only music club in Bombay. Ultimately working in Bombay had a profound and long lasting affect on Plant, one that continues to this day.

Perhaps most famously, The Beatles had spent time in India in 1968 where they studied transcendental meditation in the city of Rishikesh in Uttarakhand. They learned from the creator of transcendental meditation, Maharishi Mahesh Yogi; like Plant, it was George Harrison of The Beatles who was deeply inspired by their Indian visit more so than the other band members.

The amalgamation of traditional Eastern flavoured music with Western popular music was significant in more ways than one. More recently, the experience in Bombay had a great impact on the material used by Plant and Page for their 'reunion' in the 1990s.

The band returned to the States in May, '72 for another round of touring and excessive bouts of hedonistic fun, which hit uncharted levels of decadence.

The press often ignored them in favour of the Rolling Stones who also toured the States at the same time; nonetheless, the public adored them. The Stones enjoyed hanging out with famed artists and socialites while Led Zeppelin preferred their own entourage.

Plant was still something of an anomaly to the critics – some loathed him while others lauded his talents. The band was not exactly the critic's favourites although the staff at *Melody Maker* – then Britain's top music rag – were Led Zeppelin supporters.

As written in that weekly by noted Zep fan and respected critic Roy Hollingworth, Plant was nothing but exuberant about the success of the US tour. Speaking to Hollingworth, he said: "Something has really happened this time. Something has really clicked. It's fantastic, the spirit within the band is just fantastic." He explained further: "They'd never believe how good it is here back home. They'd just never believe what happened tonight [in New York]."

The US tour was such a success that on selective nights they even played *five* encores, although they did take a breather during the gigs to sit down for an acoustic set! It's certainly worth pointing out that the gigs they played in Southern California provided the material for 2003's magnificent live triple-CD collection, *How The West Was Won* and Plant's voice is especially resonant in that collection.

When Zeppelin played LA at the end of June, they stayed at the Continental Hyatt Hotel which can be found at 8401 Sunset Boulevard, West Hollywood. Zeppelin preferred staying there and it turned into a hive for many English rock bands of the day such as The Who and the Rolling Stones; it also helped that various rock clubs and pubs such as the Rainbow and the Whisky A Go-Go were closely located. Briefly jumping ahead to 1975, Robert Plant allegedly stood on a balcony at the Continental Hyatt and shouted: "I am the Golden God" during another tour. This is referenced in the Cameron Crowe film, *Almost Famous*.

As well as the tight touring schedule, their itinerary for '72 also included work on their fifth album, to be titled *Houses Of The Holy*. Alongside the trips to Bombay, another cultural highlight for Plant in 1972 was Zeppelin's second tour of Japan which felt somewhat predictable after having only visited the East Asian country the previous year; but Plant did find time to continue his love of soaking up local interests. By this point, midway into the year, his voice was showing considerable signs of fatigue and depletion. 1972 ended with a tour of Britain where Plant was really struggling to hit the higher notes of songs like 'Black Dog' and 'Whole Lotta Love'. Clearly being on the road so much proved to be a little too much for his voice; there were times when he wouldn't speak to anybody backstage because he did not want to exhaust his vocals before a big gig. He always had a cup of hot English tea before a gig to warm up his vocals.

During the rare but welcomed occasions when the band got the chance to return home, they never saw each other; not only did they need a break from touring and recording but also from each other. 1972 had been their busiest year thus far. Plant took those opportunities to continue the building work on his sheep farm although he did occasionally meet up with Bonham who also resided in his home county, the West Midlands.

★　★　★

1973 did not begin on a happy note for Robert Plant; he caught a bout of the 'flu after walking part of the way to a gig up in Sheffield, Yorkshire, with John Bonham, after the latter's car broke down – the illness subsequently affected his vocals. Plant was seen struggling throughout the gig at the Sheffield City Hall and the band had to drop 'Bron-Yr-Aur

Stomp' from the evening's set list. A couple of gigs in the north of England were cancelled and even when they hit the road again, on January 7, his vocals were still not powering on full thrust.

Zeppelin's fifth album, *Houses Of The Holy*, was released in March, 1973. Disliked by most critics at the time of its release, it has since proved to be one of their most enduring albums. Upon its release, *Billboard* declared: "The heavy beat boys of British rock have produced a standard package of intense rock material utilising their staunchest abilities to praise the beat and bury the melody."

Plant's lyrics are not as mystical or fantastical as his previous songs. The album opens with 'The Song Remains The Same', a staple of Plant's fondness for world music which has never waned over the passing years. It has been repeatedly mentioned that Robert Plant considers his vocals on 'The Rain Song' to be his most powerful performance while 'Over The Hills And Far Away' shows Plant giving a sensitive performance alongside Page's acoustic guitars. Plant gets funky on 'The Crunge' and he even mimics James Brown in the lyrics.[28] 'Dancing Days' is an obscure song that sees Plant singing merrily along while 'D-Yer Mak-er' is another funk-filled tune that Plant actually wanted to release as a single – the band did not concur. Plant enjoys himself on the last track 'No Quarter' and thus closes an imaginative and curious album.

With four albums under their belts, each member of the band, including Peter Grant, was making serious money – many millions of pounds in fact – so because of the punitive British tax system, it was shrewdly but hesitantly planned that the band should spend several months of each year outside of their native country; Plant was very reluctant to move, preferring the luxury and silence of his home in the West Midlands.

The band toured Europe before heading back over the Atlantic in May and with Danny Goldberg on board as the band's PR agent, Zeppelin started to gain some major coverage. Famously, they acquired a Boeing 720B called The Starship. In big, bold letters the name 'LED ZEPPELIN' was confidently printed on the side of the plane.

In America, Plant especially enjoyed shows in New Orleans because of its rich history of jazz and blues music. The *Houses Of The Holy* tour was unquestionably the most adventurous and wildest of their career and even Plant admitted they went a little too far into realms of hedonism and self-indulgence!

Writing in the *Buffalo Evening News*, one journalist said of the band's show at the Memorial Auditorium on July 16 that "Whatever isn't touched by the earthquake rumble of John Paul Jones' bass, John Bonham's gunshot cracks on the drums or Robert Plant's echoey heart of darkness voice is left quivering by the swooping electronic slices of guitarist Jimmy Page, especially his solo on the theremin."

However despite the overwhelming sound of the band, Plant received a bit of a bashing from this particular journalist: "Plant avoided some of the astringent high notes he puts on records, singing for instance a low harmony line for 'Over The Hills And Far Away.' And for all his gyrations, he was hardly as compelling as Mick Jagger or Rod Stewart."

Plant became ill during the tour of America which resulted in him feeling drained and exhausted during those July shows (hence perhaps some of the negative press he received) but he persevered and the US tour finished in front of a sold-out show at Madison Square Garden in New York on July 29.

Despite the busy schedule for the year, Plant managed to find time to buy a farm close to his home county; it brought karma to his hectic life. The constant touring had to draw to a lengthy close at some point, so the band took a break after the American jaunt and returned home. It is certainly plausible that one of the key factors that led to the subsequent 18-month break was the sheer strain that Plant was putting on his voice.

Lots of things happened during their late 1973/74 sabbatical: most importantly, they formed their own record label, Swan Song Records, after their five-year deal with Atlantic came to an end (although Atlantic would distribute Swan Song's music). For Plant, it was a chance to be at home in the English/Welsh countryside. Yet they did spend a significant amount of their so-called break recording material for their sixth opus. Finally in November, 1974 they began rehearsing in London for their forthcoming tour.

★ ★ ★

Physical Graffiti was released by Swan Song in February, 1975. A double album consisting of fifteen tracks that comprised of new material and previously unused songs, it was a massive success in the States, reaching the top spot; also, remarkably, it helped their previous five albums gain re-entry into the *Billboard* Top 200.

The *All Music Guide* says, "Most of these heavy rockers are isolated on the first album, with the second half of *Physical Graffiti* sounding a little like a scrap-heap of experiments, jams, acoustic workouts, and neo-covers. This may not be as consistent as the first platter, but its quirks are entirely welcome …"

Plant's influence on the album is felt on such tracks as 'Custard Pie' which sees him drifting back in time to one of his earliest blues idols Bukka White. 'Kashmir' is one of Zeppelin's most famous songs and was written by Plant while he was on holiday in South Morocco in '73, a country that he has repeatedly visited and turned to for inspiration. Interestingly, Plant picks up a guitar on 'Down By The Seaside' and attempts a Neil Young impersonation! Plant's clever lyrics form the basis for other songs on the album too: 'Ten Years Gone' is a love song, 'The Wanton Song' and 'Sick Again' are about women, although the latter specifically focused on 1973's out of control tour of America. Clearly Plant gave the song 'Black Country Woman' its name although it was initially intended to be called 'Never Ending Doubting Woman Blues'.

As for the touring side of things, they performed some small gigs in Europe before venturing to America in late January, 1975; they took The Starship along with them. Plant caught influenza and predictably it affected his voice, which many fans and critics noticed. It was a difficult time for him. Because of the bitter winter weather in parts of the States, some gigs were even cancelled such as the show at the Missouri Arena on January 25. Thankfully he did take time out to recover during a holiday in the Caribbean.

The North American gigs finished at the end of March.

Reviewing Plant's performance on March 4 at the Memorial Auditorium in Dallas, Texas, David P. writes on his website *Led Zeppelin Live: The Reviews (http://users.adelphia.net)* that during the opener 'Rock And Roll' "Robert Plant's voice could be a little more steady in this song (the whole concert for that matter)..." and during 'The Rain Song' "Robert's voice just wasn't as smooth."

Nevertheless, the gigs rolled on until mid-1975 when they finished with a series of concerts in May at Earl's Court – a huge 17,000 capacity venue in London. Those gigs were, in a way, a temporary goodbye and thank you to British fans. The band still had to spend time outside of the UK for tax reasons. Plant took a swipe at the British Prime Minister Harold Wilson and his Labour government during these shows, but he reserved most of his wrath for Denis Healey who, at that point, was the Chancellor Of The Exchequer. The British economy was in a bad way and the band, despite their wealth, felt a significant amount of financial strain. As quoted in a Led Zeppelin feature by Dave Lewis in a 2006 issue of *Record Collector*, Plant said to the crowd: "Somebody voted for someone and now everybody's on the run ... there'll be no artists in the country any more ... he [Denis Healey] must be dazed and confused."

As a break from the relentless touring, at the end of May, Robert and Maureen Plant took a holiday in Agadir in Morocco. Their trip to south-western Morocco inspired Plant to write the mammoth song 'Achilles Last Stand.' In a 2006 *Classic Rock* feature about the album *Presence,* Robert Plant said: "I definitely learned a lot from Morocco which I can relate to on songs."

Following on from that, August '75 was, in many respects, the most difficult period of Plant's entire life up to that point. While Plant, his wife Maureen and their children, Carmen and Karac, and Jimmy Page's daughter[29] were holidaying on the beautiful Greek island of Rhodes, a terrible accident happened.

The temporarily extended Plant family rented a car on August 4 and decided to go for a drive to check out the local area; Maureen drove with Planty in the passenger seat and the kids in the back. The car skidded and crashed into a tree. Plant broke his ankle and elbow while his family also suffered various major injuries. As it was such a remote part of the island, it wasn't until a local farmer picked them up on the back of his fruit truck that they received any medical attention. Plant was left temporarily paralysed and in a wheel chair. At a Greek hospital, Plant had trouble explaining to the staff that he was a famous rock singer. As quoted in *Record Collector*, Plant said: "I had to share a room with a drunken soldier who'd fallen over. He kept uttering my name and singing 'The Ocean' – it was bizarre."

The rest of the tour – which would have netted them many millions – was necessarily cancelled. Tickets had already sold out for a massive US stadium tour but Plant was told that he would not be able to walk for at least another six months. It was even erroneously rumoured in the press at the time that Plant thought the accident happened because of Jimmy Page's obsession with the black arts and, in particular, his famous fascination with Aleister Crowley; those rumours were fiercely denied as media jargon and remain deeply offensive.

Plant returned to England, briefly, before moving to Jersey in the Channel Islands, which also had more welcoming tax laws. The band began work on their seventh album, titled *Presence*. On account of the seriousness of his wife's injuries, Maureen and their children stayed in England while Plant moved around outside of the UK. It was especially emotionally difficult for him to be away from his family during such a fraught period. Away from Jersey, Plant also spent time in Malibu, which was at least a much warmer climate than anywhere on the British Islands. During this time, serious work had also begun on the band's first film, *The Song Remains The Same*.[30]

At the end of 1975, *Presence* was recorded in just three weeks at Musicland Studios in Munich, Germany while Plant was still in a wheelchair. The Rolling Stones wanted to use the same studio so Led Zeppelin were on an extremely tight schedule; Mick Jagger was actually surprised that they'd recorded the whole album by the time his band moved. It was in December when Plant built up some Dutch courage and began boldly taking his first steps, alone.

Presence was issued in March, 1976, and the reaction was bitterly divided. Many felt it was insubstantial and lacked imagination; it seemed mundane compared to their previous albums. Some fans and critics felt it was a rushed effort. Famed rock writer Stephen Davis, writing in *Rolling*

Stone, said that the album has "lengthy echoing moans gushing from Robert Plant and a general lyrical slant toward the cosmos."

Speaking to *Circus* in 1976, Plant said: "[*Presence*] was an album of circumstances; it was a cry from the depths, the only thing that we could do. I honestly didn't know what was going to happen and neither did anybody else."

Plant's influence is felt in the mammoth song 'Achilles Last Stand' which was written in Malibu while Plant was recovering from his accident; the song reflects his travels in Morocco and his love of Africa and Eastern countries.[31] Perhaps 'For Your Life' is Plant at his most uncomfortable as he thinks back to the excesses of his rock and roll lifestyle. Written about a hotel in New Orleans, 'Royal Orleans' is not an especially great song although the cheeky lyrics are interesting. 'Nobody's Fault But Mine' is a Blind Willie Johnson-inspired blues tune and you can almost feel Plant's excitement as he plays the harmonica. 'Candy Rock Store' is a little rock and roll number that harks back to the great music of Plant's idols like Elvis, Jerry Lee Lewis *et al.* 'Hots On For Nowhere' was written in Malibu and reflects some of the discontent Plant felt between himself and other members of the Led Zeppelin camp, namely, Jimmy Page and Peter Grant. In 'Tea For One' Plant expresses his isolation at being temporarily separated from his wife after the car accident; some commentators have said the song is a retrospective number about Plant having tea for one in a New York hotel when Zeppelin toured the US in the early 1970s; whatever the truth, the song reflects his isolation from the band.

Plant felt his muscles strengthen as a result of his departure from a wheelchair; he took his first brave moves in front of a live, paying audience several months later in May, '76. Along with Jimmy Page; they performed a two song encore with Bad Company – who were signed to Swan Song – at the Los Angeles Forum. As quoted in *Record Collector*, Plant said after the gig: "I want to get back on stage *so* much."

★ ★ ★

Evidently, spending time in a wheelchair gave Robert Plant some time to reflect on his life. Only a decade before, he was a struggling blues singer in the Midlands, making barely enough cash to get by. Now he was one of the richest rock stars in the world. He imitated his idols; great blues players like Muddy Waters and great rock and roll performers like Elvis. But now it felt weird because there were people out there mimicking him, copying his soaring vocals and even his sexually provocative stage moves (which made a lot of impersonators look plain daft). Speaking to *Record Magazine* in 1983, Plant said, "There are a lot of these English, second-generation whatever they're-called bands, the substance of which, and the sources from which they draw influences, are no longer Howlin' Wolf and Robert Johnson – they're me and Steve Marriott."

David Coverdale was surely one of them. Coverdale, who joined Deep Purple in 1974, was almost a spitting image of Plant and even sang like him too. Plant told Dave Dickinson of *Metal Hammer* in 1988: "I mean, when Coverdale's finished impersonating me, I can go out and be myself ... Coverdale is trite ... he could be Billy Ocean with a different drum beat."

Even now, one can see Plant's influence on Coverdale as he fronts the classic rock band Whitesnake. In *Led Zeppelin: The Concert Profile* by Dave Lewis and Simon Pallet, it is alleged that Coverdale saw Zeppelin live at the Owton Manor Youth Club in Hartlepool at the end of 1968 so perhaps it was there when Coverdale decided what his ambition in life was going to be? Such comparisons needn't be seen negative – Liam Gallagher famously aped Ian Brown; depending on your viewpoint, such 'impersonation' is actually just an influence.

Vocalist and bassist Geddy Lee of the great Canadian progressive rock band Rush was also inspired by Plant but as a singer rather than a performer. Zeppelin's influence can be heard in Rush's legendary 1976 album *2112*. Plant certainly influenced such 1970s rock stars as the legendary Steven Tyler of Aerosmith and Robin Zander from Cheap Trick.

Besides Roger Daltrey, perhaps the only rock star of the 1970s who came close to capturing a similar onstage presence, vibe, charm and wit as Robert Plant was Freddie Mercury; although when Queen began playing stadiums in the 1980s, Mercury undoubtedly showed that, for many, he was – and indeed still is, albeit posthumously – the greatest frontman ever, over fifteen years since his untimely death.

★ ★ ★

The band kicked off a tour of North America on February 1, 1977, after rehearsing in London. The set list opened with 'The Song Remains The Same' and finished with 'Rock And Roll'. The tour was a mammoth success which saw the band playing in front of fifty, sixty, seventy, even eighty-thousand crazed fans. During that tour, Plant's newly appointed personal assistant, Dennis Sheehan, was by his side twenty-four-seven if he needed anything sorting out.

The reviews for that tour were slightly more positive than usual. Yet the odd gig did not escape from scathing notices by reviewers reluctant to give them a break; the criticism was often aimed at Plant's vocals.

On the night of June 25 at The Forum, Plant sounded in a fiery mood – as quoted on the site *Led Zeppelin Live: The Reviews,* he bellowed to the audience: "Good evening! Good evening! ... Well, uh, it's Saturday night, yeah? [The crowd applauds loudly] I get a round of applause for knowing what day it is ... That's a pretty good start to a concert ... All right, tonight is the night – it's a celebrating night for the annual general meeting of all the LA Badgeholders. It's a very important night for badgeholding, badgeholding."

The band's concert at the Kingdome in Seattle on July 17, 1977 got a bashing in the press when it was claimed Plant's voice was in poor shape although the singer admitted he had gone temporarily deaf in one ear, no doubt as a result of the firecrackers various audience members were letting off during the acoustic part of the evening's set.

However one tragic event overshadowed even the most exhilarating performance. It was on July 23 and 24 when the band headlined the weekend-long Day On The Green festival at the California Alameda Country Coliseum in Oakland. Support came from the mighty Black Country heavy metal band Judas Priest and the American singer Rick Derringer.

"We had the opportunity to open up for Led Zeppelin towards the end of our very first American tour," Rob Halford said in 2007 on *The Hairball John Radio Show* in America. "We had just completed a very successful tour across the States and we got a call saying the Zeppelin was going to be doing two shows at the Oakland Coliseum, near San Francisco, and Robert Plant had asked if we were still in the States and if we would mind hanging out and opening up for them. Of course, we said yes..."

However, speaking to *Kerrang!* in the mid-1980s, Priest's observant main man Halford didn't sound so impressed with Zeppelin's actual show: "... I saw Led Zep at a Day On The Green show ... and you could tell they were bored shitless playing 'Stairway To Heaven' for the millionth time!"

After the California shows, Led Zeppelin and their entourage flew to New Orleans where a concert was arranged for June 30 with 80,000 tickets sold; the hype was considerable, claiming that their forthcoming show would be one of their most powerful and well-attended gigs ever.

However, on June 26, Plant received a phone call from home: as quoted in an article in a 2005 issue of *Classic Rock*, road manager Richard Cole told the respected journalist Steven Rosen: "The first phone call said his ... son [Karac] was sick. The second phone call ... unfortunately Karac had died in that time."

Karac was only five-years-old when he died; the cause of his premature and unexpected death was a virus that caused serious respiratory problems. Plant flew home to the Midlands and the rest of the 1977 tour was cancelled. In memory of his son, Plant wrote a song called 'All My Love' which featured on what would be the band's last album, *In Through The Out Door.*

Plant was left distraught; he no longer cared about Led Zeppelin, money, America, excess and all the other trappings that adorn a successful rock star's life. How could he? He'd just lost a son. Understandably, in the months after the chilling tragedy, he became reclusive and justifiably chose to stay out of the limelight for some time, instead staying at home to mourn the loss of his son.

★ ★ ★

The first half of 1978 was predictably a quiet period for Led Zeppelin's lead singer. Life away from the limelight suited Plant. But things soon changed. The business of the band began to return, slowly. Surprisingly, as the year progressed he worked with a Midlands punk band called Dansette Damage before he meet up with Led Zeppelin in May and November for rehearsals and recordings (in London and Stockholm, respectively) for their ninth opus.

Other appointments for the Led Zeppelin singer in '78 included a surprise appearance on TV in June; recorded in Birmingham, Plant was dressed in his beloved Wolverhampton Wanders football shirt when he made a cameo on the vintage children's programme *Tiswas*. The series, which use to air on Saturday mornings with *Who Wants To Be A Millionaire?* presenter Chris Tarrant, has now reached cult status in the UK and the press enjoyed mocking Plant for his decision to appear on the show.

Plant also spent a bit of time working/jamming with the blues-rock outfit Dr Feelgood in Ibiza and the Welsh singer Dave Edmunds in Birmingham: he'd also join Edmunds on stage in December, 1979 during an all-star charity gig at London's popular rock venue, Hammersmith Odeon.

Amongst all that activity, Plant even found time to work with another Midlands-based band called Melvin's Marauders, also known as The Turd Burglars. In September, he also attended Richard Cole's wedding in London with the rest of the band as well as Swan Song act Bad Company with ex-Free singer Paul Rodgers. Plant also paid a welcome visit to a charity auction at the Golden Lion pub in Fulham, West London. It was impossible to move on — ever, in a sense — from the death of Karac. One positive element had arisen in the months after that hideous event ... from a professional point of view, Robert found life outside of Led Zeppelin was proving to be rather wholesome and a lot less strenuous, particularly in light of the acute perspective that his son's death had just cast over his flamboyant working life.

★ ★ ★

Swan Song released *In Through The Out Door* on August 10, 1979, and like its predecessor, *Presence,* some of the major critics were left with a partially empty stomach. However, the influential US music rag *Billboard* gave the album a thumbs-up, saying, "the high powered quartet has not lost its grasp on contemporary rock trends. The seven tracks offered here bristle with Zep's patented heavy metal riffs yet the material is surprisingly diverse in content and delivery." However, there was still an undercurrent of feeling that the world of Led Zep was crumbling.

Consisting of only seven tracks, *In Through The Outdoor* shows Plant and the rest of band in a calmer mood than previously displayed on their other albums and, for the most part, it lacks the frenetic excitement they had shown in abundance on their first few albums.

Plant howls a great vocal riff during 'In The Evening' and, in competition, Page also gets a little self-assured too as he uses a violin bow reminiscent of earlier Zep songs. 'South Bound Suarez' is not an especially memorable track and Plant sounds a little worse for wear; it's almost as if he doesn't want to sing it despite it being a piano and guitar based Southern blues number. 'Fool In The Rain' is further proof of Plant's (and Page's) interests in other cultures, this time being South America. 'Fool In The Rain' was actually inspired by the theme tune for the 1978 World Cup that was held in Argentina. 'Hot Dog' could just well be a song about America and indeed it is; from Plant's perspective it was a chance to have a blast while singing an early Elvis rockabilly-style number. In 'Carouselambra', Plant is at a low ebb, he sounds buried amongst the rest of the band who dominate the proceedings which last a lengthy ten minutes; also, his lyrics are too ambiguous. As mentioned, 'All My Love' is a delicate song written by Plant in memory of his son Karac; it's a wonderful little track and Plant sounds particularly effective.[32] 'I'm Gonna Crawl' is yet another chance for Plant to go back to his adolescent influences and re-ignite his passion for Otis Rush, Wilson Pickett *et al.*

The band spent time in December, 1978 recording new material for a forthcoming album; much to the band's delight, Plant was somehow getting back into the swing of things after the death of his son and his dissatisfaction with the tumultuous music business.

★   ★   ★

By the time of Zeppelin's 'comeback', punk rock was the music of choice for many young music lovers in Britain and America and had been since it violently burst on the scene around 1976. Zeppelin were seen as relics from another era; rock dinosaurs who bared little – if any – relevance to modern day rock music. As quoted in a 1987 issue of *Sounds,* The Clash bassist Paul Simonon said, very famously, in 1979, "Led Zeppelin? I don't have to hear the music. All I have to do is look at one of their album covers and I feel like throwing up!"

Zeppelin's overblown stage performances, long-winded solos and, in particular, Plant's pampered looks were at odds with the punk ethos of social rebellion and their aims to make music with a political conscience. Producer Tim Palmer who worked with Robert Plant in the 1980s says, "The sort of kids who had grown up listening to Led Zeppelin, Pink Floyd and ELO were the sort of kids who use to do a lot of homework and I was definitely not in that crowd. We were all listening to The Clash, The Damned, the Pistols, you know, all the punk music …"

Some bands/artists such as Johnny Rotten of the Sex Pistols and The Clash loathed bands like Zeppelin, although NYC legends The Ramones and even guitarist Steve Jones of the Sex Pistols drew influences from Page's guitar style. Whereas Zeppelin bathed in the overt glamour of rock and everything that came with it (i.e. sex, drugs and millions of dollars) punk was a sub-culture of its own; an ideology and a movement that was emphatically anti-establishment and anti-authoritarian. Punk anthems like the Sex Pistols' 'Anarchy In The UK' and 'God Save The Queen' and The Clash's 'London's Calling' and 'Career Opportunities' focused on modern-day issues rather than fantasy and mythical legends. Even working-class singers like Billy Joel and Bruce Springsteen took a cue from punk bands and began their own political rants in their lyrics.

Zeppelin were the complete antithesis of this and someone as flamboyant as Plant became a target for punk bands to openly mock. As referenced in a Led Zeppelin retrospective in *Sounds*, Johnny Rotten declared his obvious hatred of Led Zeppelin and others like them: "I despise them. They live in their rich mansions, fucking completely out of touch with reality. They know nothing about reality, they're just drugged out arseholes."

It's probably worth pointing out that in 2007, Johnny Rotten aka John Lydon and Steve Jones both enjoy comfortable lives in LA. "Yeah, but now all the punks have become the mainstream pillars of reliable, acceptable, populist music," explained Plant to *Launch* in 1998. "Including John Lydon, the archetypal punk. It goes round and round and round. This is entertainment."

Despite the scathing assault that Robert Plant and Led Zeppelin received from the punk rockers and consequently their fans, it can easily be argued that Zeppelin bears more relevance to modern day rock music than any punk band from the mid-1970s. Such feelings were clearly not held at the time.

While punk bands for the most part loathed the likes of Robert Plant and Led Zeppelin, there were, however, a significant amount of rock bands out there that loved Zeppelin's heavy blues style of rock and also drew influences from fellow Brit rockers Black Sabbath and Deep Purple. Heavy Metal was in full force in Britain and from the late 1970s to the early 1980s, Britain produced too many metal bands to name here but a small selection included Iron Maiden, Saxon, Motörhead[33] and Diamond Head.

Judas Priest, a Midlands metal band who released their debut album in 1974, also claimed Led Zeppelin as important influences. Rob Halford, the powerful lead singer of Priest, was one of few singers who could match – and even better – Plant's falsetto and screeches. Popular music was like a boxing ring with heavy metal on one side and punk on the other but Zeppelin ran their own show and didn't fit in anywhere.

★ ★ ★

The year 1979 began on a high note as Maureen Plant gave birth to Logan Romero Plant on January 21; given the tragic loss of Karac, news of the new arrival was especially poignant.

Professionally, Plant spent more time doing bits and pieces such as making an appearance at a Bad Company gig in Birmingham in March, plus further appearances at gigs by Melvin's Marauders and Little Acre in the Midlands. A press announcement was made in May, 1979 that the band would play some live dates in July with rehearsals being held the previous month. On June 9, Plant gave his first interview in two years on the Radio One broadcast *Rock On*.

Although the band would play a live date in Denmark on July 23 it would, however, be their enormously anticipated return to the UK that gained them the most press. They played two nights at Knebworth on August 4 and 11. Most major critics were not bowled over by the Knebworth gigs and the fans complained at the length of time in between both shows even though the gigs themselves appeared to impress the majority of the Zeppelin fan base.

Paul Morley of the *New Musical Express* declared: "I didn't expect or demand anything from them. I don't need them. I don't care whether they go away for another bunch of years. But over 140,000 people can't be wrong. And neither can I."

Conversely, writing a feature on Robert Plant for *Metal Hammer* in 1988, Dave Dickson, recalled that "the three hours that Zeppelin held the stage were amongst the most magical of my life ..."

Writing in a retrospective piece on Led Zeppelin in *Metal Hammer* in 1989, Chris Welch – a Zeppelin devotee and friend of the band – was less eager than Dickson: "It was the first and last chance many people would have seeing Zeppelin and although they played well, there wasn't quite the old magic."

Plant later admitted that the Knebworth shows could have been better despite what was for the most part a thumbs up from the fans and some (but not all) quarters of the normally harsh British press. Plant informed Chris Welch in 1988 that, "The decision to do Knebworth after two warm-up gigs in Denmark was a bad move ... I felt like I was cheating myself because I wasn't as relaxed as I could have been, and I'd played to that many people loads of times. There was so much expectation there and the least we could have done was to have been confident ..."

Aside from some random press interviews, the rest of the year was pretty uneventful. 1979 was over and things had slowed down. The Starship had long since grounded, Plant was less confident, Page was having his own personal troubles, Jonesy doubted his future in the band and Bonzo was drinking heavily. Consequently, the sense of fun and excitement that they had from 1971 to around '75 had diminished. Plant seemed happier being at home with his family at their sheep farm.

★   ★   ★

As 1980 began, ideas were thrown around the band's inner circle about a possible tour and even heading over to America for some selective live dates. Plant was not too keen about making any trips over the Atlantic and the idea was to ease him into a touring schedule by playing small venues closer to home. He did finally agree to tour the States after much persuasion from Peter Grant but he only wanted to stay there for the maximum of one month. Plant was also displeased with certain people in the Zeppelin camp, and there were tensions with road manager Richard Cole. Plant didn't care for the excessiveness and camaraderie in the camp that had given previous tours major press headlines; he even began to think about moving on altogether, to do his own thing.

The rehearsals began in April and the tour dates had been confirmed; they kicked off their 1980 tour – dubbed *Over Europe* – in June at Dortmund's Westfalenhall in Germany. Reviewing the band's show at Mannheim in Germany on Thursday, July 3, David P. writes on his website *Led Zeppelin Live: The Reviews* that "Certainly Plant's voice has fully recovered from the dark years between 1973-75; he's actually a pleasure to listen to as he vocalises this very muscular tune."

Plant was well aware that Zeppelin were used as the butt of jokes by punk bands and as a nice piece of irony he would often make cheeky references about dinosaurs (as in Led Zeppelin/rock dinosaurs) to the paying crowds.

The gigs continued and the band seemed to have undergone a transformation with a renewed sense of friendliness between each other and themselves and their fans. Despite the odd muted show and a lack of rapport with certain audiences, Plant in particular seemed to be enjoying himself and was singing well on most nights. He was enthusiastic as he sang songs like the opening number 'Train Kept A Rollin" and the old favourites like 'Black Dog' and 'Rock And Roll.' They finished each set with 'Whole Lotta Love' and as usual, on some nights it was extended.

However, little did they know that on Monday, July 7, 1980, their gig at the Eissporthalle in Berlin would be their last ever concert as a four-piece band.

★ ★ ★

On September 25, 1980, John Bonham was found dead at Jimmy Page's new mansion in Windsor; he died from an overdose of alcohol which caused him to asphyxiate on his own vomit.

On September 24, Bonham had been downing double and even quadruple vodkas all day; his binge drinking began at a local pub, swiftly continued at Bray Studios where the band spent the day rehearsing and carried on well into the evening when the band retreated to Jimmy Page's mansion after drawing an early close to a series of unproductive rehearsals.

The band were preparing for their up-coming North American tour that was due to commence in October, having last toured the continent in 1977. Tony Harnell, a Led Zeppelin fan and former singer of the Norwegian melodic rock band TNT, says, "I was supposed to see them in New York the year Bonham died. Bummer."

Reportedly, at 13:45, Robert Plant's roadie Benji Le Fevre found Bonham dead. Previously, one of Page's assistant's had checked in on Bonham at 8am and he was sleeping fine. Bonham was only thirty two years old.

The band went their separate ways with Plant going back to the Midlands to visit and pay his respects to Bonham's wife, Pat, and his children, Jason and Zoe. Bonham's funeral was held on October 7, 1980. Yet again frivolous, erroneous and deeply offensive rumours of Page's involvement in black magic in relation to Bonham's death found their way into the press.

Would the band be able to continue with another drummer?

What happens next?

On December 4, 1980, a brief statement was issued to the press on behalf of the band: "We wish it to be known that the loss of our dear friend and the deep respect we have for his family, together with the deep sense of harmony felt by ourselves and our manager have led us to decide that we could not continue as we were."

Plant confessed to *Sounds* in 1982: "No one could ever have taken over John's job. Never, ever! … You couldn't have found anybody with the same kind of ingredient to make the band really take off like John did."

83

After Bonham's death the remaining members of Led Zeppelin went their separate ways … it was all over.

★ ★ ★

There are still a few important aspects of Led Zeppelin that need to be mentioned briefly before the great beast can be put to rest, so we can sink our teeth into Robert Plant's solo career.

Coda was released in 1982; comprising of unreleased session material it was a counter-attack to the sheer amount of bootlegs that had been illegally released over the years. It's an unspectacular album that was overshadowed by Zeppelin's previous compositions. On the other hand, some reviewers were rather impressed with the album. Kurt Loder wrote in *Rolling Stone*: "*Coda* is a resounding farewell from the greatest heavy-metal band that ever strutted the boards."

Despite vowing never to return to Led Zeppelin, Robert Plant has taken part in several 'reunions' since the band announced their decision in December, 1980 not to continue without John Bonham.

Plant was adamant that he would never sing 'Stairway To Heaven' ever again but he went back on his word in 1985 when himself, Jimmy Page and John Paul Jones (along with drummers Phil Collins and Tony Thompson and bassist Paul Martinez from Plant's solo band) performed a short set at the mammoth *Live Aid* concert at the JFK stadium in Philadelphia on July 13, 1985. The set-list was 'Rock And Roll', 'Whole Lotta Love' and 'Stairway To Heaven.' Yet despite the euphoria that greeted the band from the massive crowd, their performance was lacklustre, Plant included.

Curiously, Plant, Page, Jones and drummer Tony Thompson made some tentative plans for a Zeppelin reunion in 1986 and actually began rehearsals but, alas, Thompson was involved in a serious vehicle accident and those plans were quickly scrapped.

Four other so-called 'reunions' followed: the first took part at Atlantic Record's 40th anniversary on Saturday May 14, 1988. Held at Madison Square Garden in New York, the band (with Jason Bonham on drums) played 'Kashmir', 'Heartbreaker', 'Whole Lotta Love', 'Misty Mountain Hop' and 'Stairway To Heaven.' Again it was considered to be a poor performance as Jimmy Page told Mick Wall in 2001 for *Classic Rock*: "Well … that was awful, because we'd actually rehearsed it. [Plant] was involved in his own solo tour, which always seems to happen whenever there's something to do with Zeppelin coming up. He's always got his own agenda going on …"

On the day, Plant must have been nervous? He hadn't played under the Led Zeppelin banner since the underwhelming Live Aid performance (he

84

was not keen about singing 'Stairway To Heaven' but he went ahead with it, despite his reluctance). Page also did not have his best gig ever. The audience loved it but the band was less enamoured.

The second reunion happened at the 21st birthday part of Plant's daughter Carmen in November, 1989. The third reunion of the remaining Zeppelin members took place on April 28, 1990 at Jason Bonham's after-wedding party at the Heath Hotel in the West Midlands. Plant-Page-Jones-Bonham played in front of a small audience of fewer than 200 hundred people; the set-list was 'Bring It On Home', 'Rock And Roll', 'Sick Again', 'Custard Pie' and 'It'll Be Me' by Jerry Lee Lewis. The band's unofficial fifth member, manager Peter Grant, attended the wedding reception.

Finally, on January 15, 1995, Jason Bonham joined his late father's former band to perform a high-profile set at the Rock And Roll Hall Of Fame in the States. Rumours of more Led Zeppelin reunions with various drummers[34] swiftly followed but for the most part Plant vigorously denied ever wanting to go back to his old band.

Fast-forward to mid-2007 and the *Birmingham Mail* printed a full-page article called 'Led Zeppelin To Go Back On Road.' The article stated that plans were already underway for a Led Zep reunion with (possibly) Jason Bonham on drums; the premise of this reunion would be for a memorial concert for Atlantic Records founder and former head Ahmet Ertegun who died in 2006. A world tour by the reunited Led Zeppelin would net them a reputed £300 million. In the article it is quoted by an unknown source that "… this is the closet they have ever come to a reunion tour."

In September 2007, the popular metal news online resource *Blabbermouth* reported major concert promoters such as Harvey Goldsmith have warned fans not to accept fraudulent tickets for four concerts in the English capital. *Blabbermouth* stated: "Despite no official confirmation from the band, hotel and ticket packages are being sold for upwards of £269 for gigs at London's O2 Arena."

It would be an expensive luxury but one which would be the highlight of a fan's life, especially a fan not old enough to have witnessed the band during their legendary heyday. After all, this is a band who since 1980 has won major awards such as the Q 'Merit Award', a 'Lifetime Achievement' Award in Mumbai, an 'Ivor Novello Lifetime Achievement' Award, the Grammy 'Lifetime Achievement' Award and The American Music Awards 'International Artist' accolade. Yet they hadn't played live for years.

Despite all the hyped-up talk of a Led Zeppelin reunion, it has always been Robert Plant who is the least enthusiastic about such a prospect; the thought of singing 'Stairway To Heaven' yet again turns his stomach into knots. But people can change their minds …

On Wednesday, September 12, 2007 it was announced that the remaining members of Led Zeppelin – with John Bonham's son Jason, would indeed reform for a one-off gig at the O2 Arena, a 22,000 capacity venue, in London in memory of Atlantic's Ahmet Ertegun. In a press statement reported on the metal news-site *Blabbermouth*, Plant said: "During the Zeppelin years, Ahmet Ertegun was a major foundation of solidarity and accord. For us, he was Atlantic Records and remained a close friend and conspirator – this performance stands alone as our tribute to the work and the life of our long-standing friend."

Not surprisingly, the announcement circled the globe's press at the speed of one of Page's fastest Zep riffs; it seemed that the story featured in every British tabloid, broad-sheet and popular culture magazine. Even the bloated British gossip magazine *OK!* featured a brief article about the band's reunion!

PR heavyweight Harvey Goldsmith was in charge of organising the special event to be held on Monday, November 26, 2007 (changed to December 10, after Jimmy Page broke his finger), which at the time of writing was also set to include Pete Townshend, Bill Wyman & The Rhythm Kings, Foreigner and Scots singer Paolo Nutini. Tickets were limited to two people and only made available through *www.ahmettribute.com* and, like Wimbledon tickets, were only for sale via public ballot at a hefty cost of £125. It was reported in the press that prior to the September 17 deadline, approximately 89.9 million people tried to register for tickets in a 12-hour period and with just 22,000 available tickets on *www.ahmettribute.com,* the site went into meltdown, unable to cope with the shocking demand. Necessarily, the deadline was extended to September 19; a few days later it was reported on *Blabbermouth* that almost 20 million people had successfully registered for tickets. Apparently, an approximate total of 852 tickets had been reserved for corporate use only costing a minimum of £1000. Nearly thirty years on from Bonham's death, Zeppelin fever had hit an all-time, record-breaking high.

Profits from the concert were set to go to the Ahmet Ertegun Education Fund, which provides scholarships to universities in America, Britain and Turkey, Ertegun's native country. Things had certainly changed since Plant spoke to *Mojo* magazine earlier in the year: "I'd like to talk to him [Page] but I never do. Lives change." However, he was correct when he said in the same interview, "The unfortunate thing is that whenever John, Jimmy and myself meet up, the points of reference are always about the past. If there wasn't any previous triumph, then we probably wouldn't be in touch."

Considering the amount of interest in this reunion, the notion of a full-scale global tour that would net ludicrous amounts of money around the world was inevitably mooted, but with Zeppelin, money is not a major issue; it is certainly a case of artistic merit and whether or not the three of them could work closely together for months at a time after more than twenty five years apart. At the time of writing, the song most definitely remains the same. It was reported in the British newspaper *Daily Express* that a Led Zeppelin tour would never happen. "There'll be one show and that'll be it ..." said Plant. "We need to do one last great show because we've done some shows [before] and they've been crap."

Alongside the several live appearances since 1980, there have been many acclaimed Led Zeppelin releases from the early 1990s onwards that have kept the band consistently in the limelight and their accountants in a jovial mood. Yet those releases have often laid a very large and dark shadow over some of Plant's solo material. There has also been plenty of bootleg/unofficial material released over the years, much to Jimmy Page's frustration.

1990s *Remasters* CD is a very effective compilation comprising of Zep's best music. Several box sets were released during the 1990s, which forced music critics to re-evaluate their opinion on Zeppelin's music. 1994's *The Complete Recordings* is an exhaustive box set featuring every one of the studio albums. In 1995 Robert Plant recorded a version of 'Down By The Seaside' with Tori Amos for the Led Zeppelin tribute album *Encomium*, released via Atlantic Records.

Perhaps more importantly, the band released their terrific *BBC Sessions* in 1997 to high acclaim; one fan writes on the well-known e-zine *2 Walls* (*http://www.2walls.com*) "It's loud, hot rock, served up fresh during the band's first creative peak."

In 2000, *The Song Remains The Same* was released on DVD for the first time; despite its many flaws it has since become a cult film. The tremendous three-disc live extravaganza *How The West Was Won* was issued in 2003 and reached the Number 1 spot on the *Billboard* Top 200 in America. Reviewing the album on the website *Audio Video Revolution* (*http://www.avrev.com*) one critic wrote: "Recent performances from Robert Plant highlight his reduced vocal range, but in 1972 he could go balls to the wall and 'Immigrant Song' is a perfect example of places Plant could reach vocally that others could not."

Just as significant as *How The West Was Won* was a DVD simply called *Led Zeppelin*, also released in 2003: a double disc set, it features gigs recorded at the Royal Albert Hall in 1970, Madison Square Garden in '73, Earls Court in '75 and finally Knebworth in '79. *Led Zeppelin* peaked at Number 1 on the music DVD charts in the US and UK and received top marks in literally every review it received. The *Led Zeppelin* DVD is a great introduction to the band and shows Robert Plant in his prime both as a singer and performer.

It has been reported that sales of Led Zeppelin albums had exceeded 300 million by the time of their 2007 reunion. Also, November 2007 saw the release of a 'Best Of' two CD compilation called *Mothership* that conveniently coincided with the reunion concert in London. The eagerly awaited set was made available in various deluxe editions as well as a basic two CD package but many of those songs were already available in other collections. Released simultaneously, a special edition DVD of *The Song Remains The Same*, produced by Kevin Shirley, was issued with 5.1. Dolby Digital surround sound and forty minutes of scrumptious extra features. A revised special CD soundtrack was also issued to coincide with the film's re-release. As reported on *Blabbermouth,* Jimmy Page stated: "We have revisited *The Song Remains The Same* and can now offer the complete set as played at Madison Square Garden. This differs substantially from the original soundtrack released in 1976 ... When it comes to *The Song Remains The Same*, the expansion of the DVD and soundtrack are as good as it gets on the Led Zeppelin wish list."

Evidently, Led Zeppelin has really never gone away and as a consequence of that Plant has always been sure to distance himself from Zeppelin's history, speaking about himself during that period in the third person. "I'd love to be in the same room as that guy [Robert Plant] from Led Zeppelin, to listen to him doing an interview fifteen years ago," he enthused to *Music Express Magazine* in 1983. "I do know that the work we did was occasionally very good."

But let's not forget that Robert Plant has also made some very good music as a solo artist ...

PLANTATIONS:
BUILDING A SOLO CAREER
1981–1983

"In those days, Led Zeppelin was legendary. It was still alive. I thought,
maybe I should just quit now [because] nothing could be like that.
But on the other hand the great challenge was, what's it going to be like?"
Robert Plant speaking to *National Public Radio*

In 1980, Robert Plant was left in a tricky situation. Imagine: is it plausible that he could/should carve out a solo career for himself? Or should he simply disappear into obscurity, adding more hype and intrigue to the Led Zeppelin mythology? Should he become elusive or should he stay in rock's limelight?

Other legendary singers have tried building a solo career outside of successful bands and, for the most part, failed. Plant was lucky. Freddie Mercury had a go and was greeted with little acclaim; Mick Jagger has tried it and gotten nowhere; and unfortunately, everything has worked out well for Sting. However, unlike Mercury and Jagger who used their solo albums as creative outlets, Plant was going to battle with a non-living entity; by forming a solo career he was going to compete with his past, a near-pointless exercise for even the most talented artist. How could he better Led Zeppelin? But Plant was clever and we shall see why …

★   ★   ★

Aside from jamming with an R&B covers band called The Honeydrippers – which we shall get to in the next chapter – in early 1981, Plant's first

89

serious musical endeavour was getting his debut album lifted off the ground. He was keen to burst the Led Zeppelin bubble that had held him tightly: "I've had to go from fourteen years of insulation," he confessed to *Record Magazine* in '83, "away from everybody, pick my own way through everything, and come up with a record that some people actually enjoy."

Plant took a holiday in Morocco with his wife and devoured local music, which would influence the direction of his debut solo album. Then, after teaming up with seasoned blues guitarist Robbie Blunt in The Honeydrippers, the pair formed some ideas and made a demo in the second half of 1981 with the intention of making an album together.

Blunt was instrumental in helping Plant get his career moving in the right direction. From Worcestershire, he'd been in various Midlands rock bands such as the Steve Gibbons Band, Chicken Shack, Savoy Brown and Bronco which featured Plant's ex-band mates from the Band Of Joy. He contributed to Silverhead's 1973 album *16 And Savaged*. Evidently Blunt had a good reputation in the Midlands area.

As a partnership, Plant and Blunt were pleased enough with their first song – 'Fat Lip' – that they began recording an album in August and September, 1981, after rehearsing for three weeks at Plant's home. Travelling to south Wales, Plant chose the famous Rockfield Studios in Monmouth as their recording zone while staying at the studio's rehearsal area, Old Mill House. Black Sabbath had previously recorded there and Queen used it to create 'Bohemian Rhapsody'.

As producer and all round main man, Plant brought a set of reputable musicians with him for the ride: Phil Collins – who was still in Genesis at the time as well as a solo artist in his own right – played drums on half a dozen songs, while the late, famed drummer Cozy Powell contributed his drumming talents to two songs, namely, 'Slow Dancer' and 'Like I've Never Been Gone'. Session musicians Paul Martinez and Jezz Woodruffe were also recruited on bass and keyboards respectively. Martinez had previously been in Paice, Ashton and Lord while Woodruffe had worked with Sabbath. Also, Raphael Ravenscroft was hired to play saxophone on 'Pledge Pin'. Obviously Plant was the key songwriter on his debut album – eventually titled *Pictures At Eleven* – but major contributions also came from Robbie Blunt and Jess Woodruffe.

Out of all the musicians, Phil Collins was a real coup for the ex-Led Zeppelin singer. When asked about the origins of their collaboration, Plant informed music journalist and author Barney Hoskyns in 2003: "It came about because we were both on the same label. He had some dealings with Atlantic's Phil Carson and had said to him that if I was doing anything he would love to hold out."

Plant explained his respect for Collins to Geoff Barton at *Sounds* in 1982: "He was a great surprise. I love his drumming, his use of dynamics on things like 'In The Air Tonight.' His phrasing on the kit is great; he works around the beat rather than on top of it. With Phil we did six tracks in three days, which was phenomenal, really … before he arrived we were all going: 'Fucking hell, what if he's a bit of an arsehole?' We'd never met him before he came up to do the session, you see."

Speaking to *Classic Rock* in 2007, guitarist Robbie Blunt let loose a little anecdote about Phil Collins: "One of my favourite memories was watching Phil throw up in the bedroom next to mine after he'd been on a night out with us. That was amusing."

As well as Collins, the late, great drummer Cozy Powell fixed a memorable impression on his fellow musicians as Jezz Woodruffe told *Classic Rock* in 2007: "What a smashing bloke he was … he'd always wanted to work with Robert. Always. And now here [in Rockfield] he was doing his spectacular, powerful drumming, and smiling from ear to ear."[35]

Pictures At Eleven took around two months to record. Speaking about the completed album, Plant spoke to *Record Magazine* in 1983: "It's a departure. On this album there's been a movement toward the creation of more space and light within the whole thing. There is still a lot of intensity, but the delivery is different."

It would be sufficient to say *Pictures At Eleven* was a hit when it was issued in the UK on June 28, 1982. The album was released through Zeppelin's own label Swan Song even though the company was going through its final days of existence.

The album peaked at Number 5 on the US *Billboard* Top 200 Albums chart and in his native Britain, *Pictures At Eleven* made it to a respectable Number 2 slot in the Top 40. Reviewers were generous with their choice of words and Plant was praised in his confident attempts to walk away from Zeppelin. With all that in mind, Plant was justifiably in a good mood. The album spawned a radio-friendly single 'Burning Down One Side' (with the B-side 'Moonlight in Samosa') in September. Although not a big hit, it proved that unlike Zeppelin, Plant was eager to embrace the media and press. He also made a promo video for it. Radio broadcasters in the States were keen on the album and gave it generous time slots, choosing to play the US radio promos 'Burning Down One Side', 'Pledge Pin', 'Slow Dancer' and 'Worse Than Detroit.' A US-only single of 'Pledge Pin' (with the B-side 'Fat Lip') was unleashed but with little success in the charts.

Most of the critics seem pleased with Plant's first solo album and a tad surprised too. Geoff Barton wrote in his lengthy review of the album in *Sounds*: "Got to admit, I didn't have particularly high hopes for this album. I imagined it was going to be a crumbling collection of hackneyed Honeydrippin' R&B tunes, over the hills and far away from Zep-style glories of yore. I reckoned there was no way *Pictures At Eleven* was going to deserve anything less than a pitiless pasting."

Like many rock critics, Barton's initial thoughts were squashed when he heard the entire album. He continued: "… it's gratifying to find Plant back with a bang, and with a record that may be 'solo' by name but it is really 'Zep' by nature. Yes, it's that good, to these ears the best thing our silver-throated screamer's been associated with since the mighty muscular *Physical Graffiti* … *Pictures At Eleven* sounds so vital and alive, it's something of an eye-opener. It has such class, it makes you realise how the quality's slipped, how you've become accustomed to praising the mundane and slinging superlatives in the direction of the utterly average"

Kurt Loder wrote in *Rolling Stone*: "If Robert Plant were young and hungry instead of nearly 34 and famous, this album might have been a real barn-burner. As it is, even though there's nothing new going on in these grooves, the sheer formal thrill of hearing someone who knows exactly what he's doing makes *Pictures At Eleven* something of an event almost in spite of its modest ambitions … But when the good stuff on an album cuts all the other cock-rock competition in sight, only a curmudgeon would complain."

With all the justified acclaim that greeted *Pictures At Eleven* upon its release, Plant was actually taken aback: "I was honestly expecting to get an absolute hammering from everybody," he told *Sounds*. "I don't really know why, because I'm really proud of what I've done."

However, not every critic lavished praise on *Pictures At Eleven*. One journalist wrote in the *Detroit News*: "Former Led Zeppelin lead singer arrives in America with a confining and unimaginative solo LP *Pictures At Eleven* … Commercially it's working. *Pictures At Eleven* may be the hottest album in the country particularly in the rock-religious Midwest and East. Much of that early spurge is due to standing respect for Led Zeppelin. I always thought Plant's voice capable of more subtle shakings than the primal whine which became his trademark."

Pictures At Eleven opens with the evocative 'Burning Down One Side' which features some delicate guitar work by Robbie Blunt. 'Moonlight In Samosa' is a tender ballad reflecting Plant's desire to shift away from the heavy rock associated with Led Zeppelin; his voice is especially resonant. 'Pledge Pin' is an infectious, moderately-paced pop song although for some hardcore fans it may be too close for comfort to a cheesy Phil Collins song. 'Slow Dancer' is a much better track with some Mark Knopfler Dire Straits-era guitar work from Robbie Blunt; it's a curious song with different layers of musical styles and sporadic moments of latterday Zeppelin. 'Worse Than Detroit' is perhaps the song that has the most apparent Zeppelin influences with deep grooves and a heavy bounce; again Blunt shines and it's almost as if it's his album rather than Plant's. 'Fat

Lip' is another slow one on an album that is more akin to commercial pop than serious hard rock of the previous decade (not necessarily a bad thing). 'Like I've Never Been Gone' is a slow effort but one of the album's more emotional songs; Plant sounds especially laid-back. The final song, 'Mystery Title', is a fast-paced and fantastically enjoyable song; it's a good way to finish the album and again the Dire Straits sounds are apparent.

Overall, it's an imaginative and richly diverse album with moments of Zeppelin inspirations – clearly Plant could never really get away from his past. In the scheme of things, it's not a rock album *per se* as Plant delves into different styles of music. Sadly, there are none of his famous wails and groans circa 1970.

The album was reissued and remastered in 2007 by Rhino Entertainment; it features two bonus tracks, namely, the previously unused 'Far Post' and a live version of 'Like I've Never Been Gone' which was recorded in Texas in 1983.

The reissue was reviewed on the revered e-zine *Vintage Rock* (*www.vintagerock.com*) in 2007 and predictably given a small round of applause: "*Pictures At Eleven* … incorporates elements of the bombastic slam for which the golden voice earned his stripes; however, the tone and sheen resonates with a forward-thinking ebb and flow."

Rock Is Life (*www.rock-is-life.com*) also had praise for the reissue: "*Pictures At Eleven* is definitely a musical portrait of an artist in transition from one stage of his career to another, but even that doesn't hold Plant back … The album has lots of musical ideas and notions to reel in the listener with nifty guitar work, pounding rhythm section work and, of course, the magic of Plant's vocals. The best thing is that this was only the beginning. He gets not only better as the albums progress, but also more important as a musical artist."

Also, writing in *Classic Rock* in 2007, Mick Wall shrewdly declared: "Co-written, sung and produced by Plant at a time when Jimmy Page was still hiding away reclusively, licking his wounds, it was the first encouraging glimpse Zeppelin fans would have of what the post-Zep future might actually look and sound like."

One interesting development in 1982 was that Plant was not averse to making regular television appearances, whereas Led Zeppelin shied away from appearing on the box. He even underwent something of an image change; he trimmed his hair and dressed smartly: "I just went to some shitty shops. Fucking hell!" he told Q magazine in 2005. "I was the stylist, the worst stylist Wolverhampton has ever seen. I had purple satin jodhpurs."

To drum up support for his debut solo album, he gave many interviews throughout June in the States and on July 21 for his first live performance he sang 'Worse Than Detroit' at the Prince's Trust concert at the popular

Dominion Theatre in London's West End. He was joined by The Who's Pete Townshend, Phil Collins, Robbie Blunt, Midge Ure of Ultravox who played guitar and keyboards and Mick Karn of Japan who played bass.

Ure: "George Martin who was producing an Ultravox album at the time ... and asked me to perform my current single 'No Regrets' at the show. Pete Townshend was in charge of the show and [also] asked me to play after hearing the solo on the record ... During Robert's part he desperately wanted some 'vibey' movement from the band but Mick Karn and I just stood like showmen dummies, still trying to be cool! ... it was very Zep-like with riffs and time signature changes."

Plant also joined in on the obligatory all star climatic version of 'I Want To Take You Higher' which featured all those artists who took part in the charity event.

In September, Plant performed 'Burning Down One Side' on the classic music show *Whistle Test* hosted by Bob Harris.

The biggest and most serious question fans aimed at Robert Plant's new solo venture was: when will he tour? Even though Plant's debut album was a significant success on both sides of the Atlantic he wanted enough solo material to justify a full set list and tour, instead of relying on old Zep tunes.

★ ★ ★

In October, 1982, Plant began steadily rehearsing for a second solo opus. Again, Plant chose the quiet surroundings of Rockfield. But this time, rather than acting as solo producer, he hired Pat Moran who engineered Plant's first album and Benji LeFeure who also worked on *Pictures At Eleven* as a mixing assistant and had worked for Led Zeppelin for several years. There were a few changes in Plant's band this time around too: he hired ex-Jethro Tull drummer Barriemore Barlow for some percussion work. Also joining Plant for his second ride were backing singers John David and Ray Martinez as well as Robbie Blunt, Paul Martinez, Jezz Woodruffe and his famous pal Phil Collins. Recording was completed in May, 1983.

Prior to the release of his second solo studio venture, Plant got his new band together – which included Roger Taylor, the brilliant drummer in Queen – to record a set on the cult TV music show *The Tube* at Tyne Tees studio in Newcastle. Joining him for this performance were guitarists Robbie Blunt and Bob Mayo (previously of AOR giants Foreigner) keyboard player Jezz Woodruffe and bassist Paul Martinez. Plant was not happy with the performance and it was not screened.

By this point Swan Song – Led Zeppelin's own label – had shut its doors; with the help of Peter Grant, Plant got a distribution deal with Atlantic and formed his own solo company Es Paranza. Grant was having personal problems of his own and, in effect, *Pictures Of Eleven*'s distribution through Swan Song was Plant's last connection with Led Zeppelin. The release of Plant's second album through his newly developed label proved that he could go the distance alone.

The Principle Of Moments was released in the UK on July 11, 1983. It reached Number 7 in the UK Top 40 and jumped into the Top 20 in *Billboard*'s Top 200 albums.

The Top 20 UK hit success of the single 'Big Log' (released on July 4) helped sales of the album significantly. It was rapidly becoming clear to fans and critics alike that Plant was a different man with a different attitude from his days in Led Zeppelin. His former band refused to make music videos but for 'Big Log', Plant had a change of heart and shot a trendy clip in the States. Suitably equipped, he could now appear on music shows like the extremely influential *Top Of The Pops*. Also, *MTV* had first aired in America on August 1, 1981, so Plant could clearly see the potential of music videos and television appearances; decent mainstream media exposure would massively boost sales of his albums and singles and with that in mind he could stick his middle finger up to those cynical hacks who said he would never have success in his own right. Indeed Plant performed 'Big Log' on *Top Of The Pops* on July 28. He also appeared on the now deceased UK TV show *Pop Quiz*.

A second individual release, 'In The Mood', was also let loose as a single in the winter of 1983 and reached a respectable Number 39 in the States but made little impact in the UK. But it was 'Big Log' that ended up as the song everybody spoke about in reference to Plant's career post-Led Zeppelin; it remains one of his most endurable and well-known singles.

Again, most of the critics took a liking to the new album and picked up on some of Plant's Zeppelin-esque moments. David Fricke wrote in *Rolling Stone*: "... much of *The Principle Of Moments* finds the singer trying to get around that dilemma by toying with weird hard-rock alternatives and singing in a restrained, though powerful, manner ... It is also his declaration of independence from the past – not a denial of it."

The Principle Of Moments opens with the superlative track 'Other Arms'; Plant's voice drips charisma and charm. 'In The Mood' is a wonderfully contrived song although the chorus gets a little monotonous. 'Messin' With The Mekon' is a mid-paced tune with a funky rhythm yet it lacks the spark and wit of some of the other songs on this album. 'Wreckless Love' follows Plant's fascination with Indian music; Plant's dulcet voice is wrapped in an exotic melody. 'Thru' With The Two Step' has a melody that's dealt with care and precision but the song is still a tad annoying and not very entertaining.

'Horizontal Departure' speeds things up and Plant sounds like he is having a great deal of fun; Blunt's precise guitar solo in the centre of the song is actually rather soothing but too short. 'Stranger Here ... Than Over There' is a peculiar song with lots of sounds thrown into the musical melting pot and even though it doesn't make exhilarating listening, it is an intriguing song. The album ends with the hit song 'Big Log;' it's an emotional song with a poetic guitar work courtesy of the indispensable Robbie Blunt while the backing vocals of John David and Ray Martinez are delicately smooth.

The Principle Of Moments is a good – albeit short – pop album with some genuine moments of inspiration and some fine melodies, but it suffers from too many mid-paced songs and not enough of the sweaty excitement that made his 'previous career' so illustrious. Having said that, this was exactly what he wanted, to move in a different direction.

In 2007, Rhino Entertainment released *The Principle Of Moments* in remastered and expanded form with four bonus tracks: live versions of 'In The Mood', 'Thru' With The Two Step' and a live cover of the Bob Marley tune 'Lively Up Yourself' – all of them recorded in Texas in 1983. The unreleased studio track 'Turnaround' was also added; it was recorded during the initial album sessions at Rockfield in 1983. *The Principle Of Moments* reissue was reviewed on a wide array of popular websites and magazines, giving mass exposure to Plant's back catalogue: *All Music Guide* (*www.artistdirect.com*) said, "Robert Plant's follow-up to *Pictures At Eleven* places much of his debut's style and vocal meandering into a new and more exciting bunch of songs ... Plant's voice is so compelling in any state, the convolution of his writing tends to take a back seat to his singing in most of his solo work, which is definitely the case in most of the songs here."

Connolly & Company (*www.connollyco.com*): "Once again, Robert Plant doesn't stray too far from the sound of Led Zeppelin's *In Through The Out Door*. And why should he? *The Principle Of Moments* is an excellent album, no apology necessary ... He could get by simply by singing, as Bryan Ferry and Roger Daltrey have done, but Plant instead continues to grow on his own, fertilised (if you will) by the creative chemistry cultivated in an actual band."

To the delight of thousands of fans, Robert Plant announced in the middle of 1983 that he would hit the road for the first time as a solo artist in his own right; he finally felt confident enough that he could entertain an audience for a couple of hours without relying on Led Zeppelin songs.

Rehearsals began at Shepperton studios in early August. Plant and his band would tour the States from August through to October and swiftly follow that road venture with a tour of Britain.

In the US, his live band consisted of: drummer Phil Collins, guitarists Robbie Blunt and Bob Mayo, bassist Paul Martinez and keyboardist Jezz Woodruffe. Jezz spoke to *Classic Rock* in 2007 and said that the tour "just got better and better. And I loved that old plane we toured on … rumbling across America in this 1960s prop plane."

Their first stop in the US was at the Rosemont Horizon in Chicago on August 1. Before playing on stage to a sold-out crowd at the large indoor venue, the Philadelphia Spectrum, Phil Collins told music journalist J.D. Considine (*www.led-zeppelin.org*): "You'd think with 20,000 people every night that there would have to be some people screaming for 'Stairway To Heaven' or 'Kashmir' but we haven't heard it."

Aside from Plant's solo numbers, they played some vintage rock and roll tunes, inevitably inspired by The Honeydrippers project; they flew through 'Little Sister', 'Treat Her Right' and 'The Young Ones.' They finished tour proceedings in Vancouver on October 1. Plant had the show at the Summit Arena in Houston on September 20 recorded for future use.[36]

In a 1983 issue of *Kerrang!*, the respected rock scribe Malcolm Dome wrote in the news section of the magazine: "On November 22 at the Glasgow Apollo, Robert Plant will step out on stage for his first major British live performance since the Knebworth concert four years ago. And over the following month, he will play a total of 17 more shows."

It was about time: Plant finally hit the UK for a tour in the winter of '83. Phil Collins had immediate duties in Genesis and was replaced by the revered sticksman Ritchie Haywood, previously of Little Feat. There was one little issue though, Plant vehemently refused to play any Zeppelin songs. Yet there was still a Led Zeppelin connection: Plant and his band played segments of lyrics from 'Since I've Been Loving You' and 'Trampled Underfoot' and merged them into his own songs. Also, John Paul Jones joined Plant on stage at the Bristol Colston Hall during the encore for a version of 'Little Sister'. At the famous Hammersmith Odeon in London, Jimmy Page joined Plant on stage, again during the encore, for a version of 'Treat Her Right.'

Plant spoke to writer J.D. Considine in 1983 (*www.led-zeppelin.org*): "The band is enjoying playing together, they're getting conscientious rather than carrying on in darkness, wondering whether I was trying to press them into being clones of Led Zeppelin, which is not what I'm trying to do … as far as my performance … I want it to be very clean and structured."

The tour was a huge triumph with extra dates being added in major UK cities like London, Birmingham, Manchester and Newcastle. However, the venues he played were not the biggest Britain had to offer at the time as he explained modestly to *Sounds*: "I can't play places like Birmingham NEC … I don't think I've got the audience that would fill the NEC anyway."

The UK road jaunt finished at the Birmingham Odeon on December 24; Plant was joined by Jason Bonham for the climatic encore. Winding the tour up in the Midlands on Christmas Eve gave Plant enough time to drive home and relax over the festive period. Plant also found out that in the annual *Sounds* reader's poll for 1983, he was voted sixth 'Sex Object Male'. His arch nemesis David Coverdale landed the top spot!

He had lots to celebrate yet the year had not gone so well in his private life. One cloud over the ex-Led Zeppelin vocalist was his divorce from Maureen – albeit an entirely amicable one for the sake of their two children. Plant confessed to Q magazine in 2005 that, "We had reached a point in 1983, not long after Bonzo left us, where we had exhausted the terms that we began when we were 17. We've probably got better terms now than we had at any time before, because we know where we're at. We're mates, we've got great kids and we have a good time together."

Plant continued his road jaunts into early '84; he toured Australia in February where he was joined by Elton John in Sydney for a version of 'Treat Her Right'. He played selected dates in parts of East Asia, finishing up in Tokyo on February 24. Things just got better: 1984 brought big bouts of excitement, nostalgia and an opportunity to indulge in his passion for 1950s rock and roll …

THE HONEYDRIPPERS:
PLANT, PAGE, BECK & OTHERS
1984

"I have to surprise myself, I have to try and push myself
into an area where I'm a little unsure, take myself out of character
and surprise myself."
– Robert Plant speaking in an interview with MSN Music in 2007

As mentioned in the previous chapter, The Honeydrippers was Robert Plant's first taste of a musical endeavour after Led Zeppelin. In early 1981, inspired by 1950s R&B and rockabilly, Plant surreptitiously joined a Midlands covers band called The Honeydrippers. After some thought, Plant appeared to be the most eager of ex-Led Zeppelin band members to move forward with his career and The Honeydrippers proved to be the most immediate opportunity.

The band featured a set of respected Midlands musicians: guitarists Robbie Blunt and Andy Sylvester, drummer Kevin J. O'Neil, bassist Jim Wickman with Ricky Cool playing the harp and Keith Evans playing the saxophone. Plant did not announce this to the press as the band played in pubs and clubs across the Midlands and around the North. They played Albert King, Otis Rush and Gene Vincent songs as well as old blues tunes like 'I Got My Mojo Workin'' and 'Stormy Monday'. Also, the set included two Zeppelin tracks, albeit covers themselves: 'Bring It On Home' by Sonny Boy Williamson and 'How Many More Years?' by Howlin' Wolf.[37]

The Honeydrippers never made it to London for the scheduled debut gig at the tiny Dingwalls club. However, Plant rather prudently kept the name alive and never shut the door on the project despite going ahead with his first studio album shortly after. Thus, in 1984, The Honeydrippers were reborn with a different line-up.

★   ★   ★

Reportedly Plant had recorded some demos on a four-track tape during his time in The Honeydrippers in '81 and during his first US tour as a solo artist in late 1983 he recorded a cover version of 'Philadelphia Baby' by Charlie Rich at Sun Studios in Memphis; the song was, rather oddly, used as part of the soundtrack to the movie *Porky's Revenge*. These sporadic acts of nostalgia got Plant's brain ticking: what if I do a whole album of my favourite 1950s rhythm and blues numbers? Atlantic Records boss Ahmet Ertegun was keen to get such a project lifted off the ground and persuaded Plant to go ahead with it.

In March, 1984, Robert Plant and a group of respected session musicians got together under The Honeydrippers moniker to record a mini-album at Atlantic Studio A in New York, with a spot of recording also done in London. What was special about this project was that it teamed Robert Plant up with Jimmy Page for the first time on record post-Led Zeppelin while Page's old Yardbirds buddy Jeff Beck was asked to participate too.

As quoted in the excellent unauthorised Jeff Beck biography, *Crazy Fingers* by Annette Carson, Beck said: "I went along there with my guitar in hand, plugged in, and I think we did the whole lot in one afternoon. Nobody knew what was going on, and that's what was so good. We didn't have any more studio time booked, so we just rattled them off. I think we did two takes of each song, no overdubs – it was just one, two, three, four, off we go!"

As well as Robert Plant, Jimmy Page and Jeff Beck, The Honeydrippers consisted of such esteemed session players as rhythm guitarist Nile Rodgers, pianist Paul Shaffer, bassist Wayne Pedziwatr, drummer David Weckl and arranger Dave Matthews. David Weckl recalls the haste of the project: "I was working a lot with Nile Rodgers in that period, and I suppose I was the first drummer available on a Sunday morning! It was a last minute call for the session!"

The mini-album was produced by 'Nugutre and the Fabulous Brill Brothers': 'Nugutre' was Ahmet Ertegun while the 'Brill Brothers' were Phil Carson and Robert Plant. Their name was a nostalgic homage to the Brill Building on 1619 Broadway in New York – the hub of 1950s and 1960s R&B music where many classic songs were written.

Weckl: "Ahmet was kind of just hanging … and played more of a spectator role from what I remember. He was just loving the moment, and enjoying all the stories Robert would tell us on the small breaks we would take."

What happened during the recording sessions in NYC?

Weckl: "It was, of course, a bit intimidating but exciting and sort of freaky at the same time! I mean, all that talent, all that history in the room, and me – the 'just-turned-twenty-four-year-old-kid' – in there trying to hang! I believe it was sort of a group effort, and we just played the tunes! I thought the 'group' that gathered that Sunday morning hit it off really well, gelled nice. 'Rockin' At Midnight' was live, either a first or second take, I do believe. No fixes or overdubs, and I think that is what they were after … it wasn't stressful at all. In fact, it was very relaxed, and I remember we had a ball! We were all in the big open room together, and Robert was in the airway between the studio and the control room, looking at us through the small window pane in the door as we played, and he sang. We just kind of ran all the songs down once and hit the record button. Maybe two takes of each song. I don't think we were there more than four, five hours or so, if that …"

As a young drummer, Weckl was justifiably in awe of the ex-Led Zeppelin front man: "Just shuffling away on 'Rockin' At Midnight' and seeing Robert, with all that hair, through that small glass window. It was a gas … the band was grooving, and that voice was coming through the cans – definitely one of those moments in one's career you never forget."

For the completed mini-album or EP, Plant chose the better recordings; he mixed together songs recorded at the London and New York sessions. Page played solos on 'I Get A Thrill' and 'Sea Of Love' at the London session after Plant made his trip to NYC.

Page told Chris Welch at *Kerrang!* in the mid-1980s: "I overdubbed guitar solos on a couple of tracks. Then I heard Beck's performance on 'Rockin' At Midnight' and thought, 'Bloody hell, that's good.' It's a beautiful solo. I was happy with my 'Sea Of Love' solo, but I didn't get the other one together. I felt what I did was really laboured."

The completed, released EP featured 'I Get A Thrill' originally written by Rudy Toombs and sung by Hank Ballard and The Midnighters, 'Sea Of Love' originally written by George Khoury and Philip Baptiste and sung by Phil Phillips, the Ray Charles penned song 'I Got A Woman', 'Young Boy Blues' originally written by Doc Pomus and Phil Spector and sung by Ben E. King and, finally, 'Rockin' At Midnight' which was originally written and sung by Roy Brown.

Weckl: "Well, I know it was our group on the 'Rockin' At Midnight' version that they chose, but [I don't think] it was us on 'Sea Of Love' … It was nice to hear them on the radio as much as I did though. Just wish we could have done more!"

★ ★ ★

The Honeydrippers: Volume One was released in the UK on November 12, 1984 by Es Paranza. The press reviews were certainly enthusiastic. One reviewer wrote in *Sounds*: "I didn't expect a croony, pre-bubblegum, woo-dropping pack of good natured rock 'n' roll oldie cream cheeses, y'know? ... This is Robert Plant with his heart on his sleeve. The big log ain't such a bad old stick!"

To promote the EP – which would go on to sell a respectable 100,000 copies in America – Plant and The Honeydrippers (with Brian Setzer from The Stray Cats on guitar and Paul Shaffer on piano) appeared on the popular US comedy show *Saturday Night Live*, hosted by Eddie Murphy, on December 15; they played 'Rockin' At Midnight' and 'Santa Claus Is Back In Town'. Unfortunately, the EP failed to ignite any interest in the UK, reaching a poor Number 56 in the charts. As well as America, the EP took off in Japan where 'Sea Of Love' was used as a theme to a Hitachi VCR commercial.

The EP conceived a huge Top 5 US single in 'Sea Of Love', released on February 2, 1985. 'Rockin' At Midnight' was planned to be the lead single, but it ended up as the B-side for the former song, much to Plant's obvious frustration. 'Sea Of Love' unexpectedly turned Plant into a crooner, something he was not exactly at ease with (although his mum gave it the thumbs up) and as such a follow-up never materialised.

The Honeydrippers: Volume One is a cool slab of modern-day 1950s R&B nostalgia. It begins with the enjoyable bop of 'I Get A Thrill'; Plant really sounds like he is in his element. He sings the slow ballad 'Sea Of Love' with a great deal of affection before the rockabilly of 'I Got A Woman' kicks into action. 'Young Boy Blues' certainly doesn't leave the listener feeling the melancholy blues; it's a charming little song with wonderfully melodic backing vocals. 'Rockin' At Midnight' is undoubtedly the highlight of the song; it's a slick production with a fluent rhythm and the excitement only heightens as it reaches the final crescendo.

The album was reissued and expanded in 2007 by Rhino Entertainment with some minor press coverage.[38] *The New Rolling Stone Album Guide* was less keen than others, as referenced on the magazine's website: "Excessive orchestrations distract from Plant's restrained interpretations, while the guest hotshots (Jimmy Page, Jeff Beck, Nile Rodgers) are under-utilised."

The Trades (*www.the-trades.com*): "The difference between this version and the original that closes the mini-album is negligible. Plant's vocals are more echo-y, and it clocks in nearly a couple of minutes shorter, eschewing the rousing concluding improvisational jam ... The only knock on this project is that in about eighteen minutes, it's done. The additional track is not essential, but it's still a nice inclusion."

All Music Guide: "… an unabashedly retro-rock project that hauled out five golden oldies from the pre-Beatles era and served them up authentically, or at least as authentic nostalgia. There is a certain sense of pastiche here … It may not be much more than a lark, but it's truly fun, even if it might have been slightly more fun making it than it is listening to it."

With a solid EP under his belt and a string of live appearances (albeit with different line-ups), Plant had a change of heart about a new release by The Honeydrippers, thinking it could be a good thing. "I had an idea of doing 'Stay Alive' by the Clovers, which is on the flip of 'Love Potion No. 9'," Plant informed *Billboard* in 2007, "and then [Ertegun] could tell me some more stories about Bobby Darin. That's what would have made it worthwhile."

But in October, 2006, the former head of Atlantic Records, Ahmet Ertegun, fell backstage at a Rolling Stones concert in New York. He died in hospital in December 2006; his sad death put an abrupt end to any tentative plans for a new release by The Honeydrippers. It was reported on the website *Rock Radio (www.therockradio.com)* that Plant told the press: "We'd been in touch. I knew he was thrilled with the idea of it – [it was] something that we were both looking forward to."

Many fans would love to see a return of The Honeydrippers on record; in early 2007, one journalist wrote in Malta's *The Times* that, "Robert Plant could do us and himself a good favour if he goes back to rhythm and blues, as he did so well with The Honeydrippers two decades ago."

Putting studio talk aside, The Honeydrippers have reformed under various guises over the years and with alternating line-ups, mostly for charity events so it is worth noting here that during Plant's 1985 *Shaken 'n' Stirred* tour he incorporated a mini-set of The Honeydrippers material into his usual solo affair.[39] Influenced by 1950s America, a Cadillac was the stage's centerpiece; joining Plant on stage was the touring line-up of The Honeydrippers namely, guitarist Robbie Blunt, bassist Paul Martinez, keyboard player Jezz Woodruffe and drummer Ritchie Hayward. Joining them for the special act was the backing band The Uptown Horns (also known as The King Bees) and backing vocalists The Queen Bees.

There have been other performances by The Honeydrippers since the band's only release. On January 18, 1985, The Honeydrippers – billed as 'The Skinnydippers' – played an eighty-minute benefit gig in Monmouth. The gig has been in wide circulation as a bootleg for years. In March, 1986, Robert Plant teamed up with local rhythm and blues band The Big Town Playboys which featured former Honeydrippers band mates Ricky Cool and Andy Sylvester; the line-up was completed with Michael Sanchez, John Spinetto and Ian Jennings. They played the Birmingham Heart Beat benefit show as well as a couple of low-key university appearances. They performed classic rock and roll songs such as 'Rockin' At Midnight'.

On December 16, 1986, The Honeydrippers played a set at the Civic Centre in Stourport in memory of the late Midlands musician John Pasternak who had played in the Band Of Joy. Jimmy Page and Robbie Blunt made special appearances to play old 1950s R&B songs and some blues numbers. They even finished the night with Zeppelin's 'Rock And Roll'.

A new version of the band performed a seventy-minute benefit gig in front of 600 elated fans at Kidderminster Town Hall on December 23, 2006. The night was billed as 'Robert Plant & The Return Of The Honeydrippers' and was organised in aid of his Kidderminster neighbour Jackie Jennings who was suffering from a brain tumour; the money contributed to a target of £100,000 which she needed to have a life-saving operation in Boston. A campaign was launched to raise £25,000 from the public with the remaining cash coming from government sources. It was reported in the West Midlands newspaper the *Express & Star* that a close friend of the family said: "Robert knows Jackie from living in the area and as soon as he heard about her he wanted to get involved. We are so grateful to Robert because he will give us a good chance of reaching the sum in time."

Other bands appeared on the bill but surprisingly The Honeydrippers did not headline, although it was evident that the hundreds of excitable fans were there primarily to see Robert Plant strut his stuff. Keyboardist Mark Stanway says: "The tickets sold out in hours, which was amazing considering that they were not officially advertised and people from literally all over the world booked tickets and came to the show. It brought it home to me just how popular Robert Plant is."

The line-up on the night featured guitarists Robbie Blunt and Andy Sylvester, bassist Wayne Terry, Mark Stanway on keyboards and Steve Atkins on drums and two backing vocalists.

Mark Stanway: "Robert asked me if I would play keyboards on the song 'Big Log' ... In order to perform this particular track keyboards are essential. So I had my keyboards taken to [a] rehearsal at Robert's house and we ran through 'Big Log' and it sounded great. Just for the fun of it, I just busked along for the rest of the rehearsal and both Robert and Robbie were instantly convinced that I should play keyboards on everything. Originally, along with Mo Birch, there was another backing vocalist called Nadine Edwards but her West End show commitments did not allow her to do all of the rehearsals required, so Mo bought in another Wolverhampton girl called Nadia Pearson, who is actually my son's partner."

The evening's set list ran: 'Mess Of Blues', 'Little Sister', 'She Little Sheila', 'It's Gonna Work Out Fine', 'Black Magic Woman', 'Keep On

Loving Me', 'Big Log', 'Can't Be Satisfied', 'Rattlesnake Shake', 'Big Hunk Of Love', 'Daddy Rolling Stone', 'What I'd Say' and 'Silent Night/Santa Claus'.

Mark Stanway: "Robert obviously had the final say [on the set list] and indeed the initial suggestions as he ... front[ed] the band and sang the songs but the whole affair was most democratic and Robert is always open to suggestions."

In January, 2007, it was announced that Robert Plant was going to reform The Honeydrippers for the second time in just a few short months to celebrate the 60th birthday of his long-term sound engineer and friend Roy Williams – again profits went to aid cancer research.

Mark Stanway: "The amount of interest these gigs made was truly amazing and obviously the charity concerned raised a considerable amount of money. Robert does an amazing amount of work for charity mostly non-publicised and he is a genuinely benevolent person, one of the most generous I have ever met in fact."

The second gig, also featuring local R&B band The Big Town Playboys and an unlikely impromptu three-song performance by Jeff Beck with drummer Jimmy Copley and bass player Ian Jennings, was held at the 1000-capacity club, JB's in Dudley on February 14. The night was dubbed 'An Evening Of Rhythm And Blues'. Mark Stanway recalls the excitement on the night: "I have never seen so many people in JB's ever ... let alone the amount of fans outside that couldn't get in but were there just for a glimpse of the man. He could have done a month of consecutive shows!"

For Plant, it was another chance to delve into the music of his youth whilst also commemorating a worthy charity and the birthday of his good friend. Mark Stanway remembers how the rehearsals went: "They were ... constructive and enjoyable when the whole band was actually all there together, but with Robert's busy schedule – writing and recording with his band [The] Strange Sensation and jetting backwards and forwards from the States to put finishing touches to an album he had recently recorded with Alison Krauss coupled with a few of the other members who had daytime commitments – [rehearsals] were 'spasmodic' to say the least! We did, however, enjoy some wonderful food and wine after most rehearsals ... which was all very nice."

Local journalist John Odgen wrote in the West Midlands newspaper, the *Express & Star*: "There followed a leisurely lesson in soul, rock and blues. The climax, a belting version of 'Daddy Rolling Stone', had the crowd roaring for an encore."

Indeed Mark Stanway, keyboard player in the classic Birmingham melodic rock band Magnum, remembers how easy it was to work with Plant on the two shows in Kidderminster and Dudley: "It was fantastic to work with Robert; he is a true professional and has a most focused attitude. I personally found him very easy to work with and we shared a lot of side-splittingly funny Midlands/Black Country humour together. He can be as sarcastic as me, so a lot of fun was enjoyed along the way."

RAMBLE ON:
FURTHER SOLO ENDEAVOURS
1985–1993

"Freedom is something that I wouldn't have considered with Zeppelin, because I was quite happy. By that I'm finding my own foot, I can see that my approach and my whole ideology have changed tremendously."
Robert Plant speaking to *Record Magazine* in 1983

In the mid-1980s when punk rock had long since waned, yet heavy metal was still enjoying tremendous success, Robert Plant was in the early stages of what would be a very successful solo career; indeed, he was making music vastly different from any of his rock star peers from the decadent 1960s and 1970s; and he was enjoying a surprising amount of success too.

Critics bashed Rod Stewart's solo albums with surprising gusto; the former singer of The Faces and The Jeff Beck Group had little success in the charts too. David Bowie had been washing himself with the dance sounds of the decade and provided his fans with uncomfortable songs like 'Let's Dance' and a cover of 'Dancing In The Street'; the latter, a laughable duet with Mick Jagger, was issued in 1985. Eric Clapton had left the blues behind and went for a more polished and commercial sound by working with Phil Collins as producer. Tina Turner had achieved a major comeback instigated by a cover of Al Green's 'Let's Stay Together' but her solo work lacked the gritty R&B vibe of the Ike and Tina years. Elton John and his writing partner Bernie Taupin had (temporarily) fallen from public favour; having enjoyed enormous critical and commercial success in the 1970s, it seemed that their creative spark had faded and in the 1980s they churned out mostly uninteresting pop songs. The Rolling Stones had not made a good album since 1978's *Some Girls* and the only highlight of 1981's *Tattoo You* was the opening track 'Start Me Up'.

While all that was happening, Plant was observing events in the American and British pop charts and mostly he detested what he heard. In one corner, the likes of the 'New Wave Of British Heavy Metal' heroes Def Leppard did little for the former lead singer of Led Zeppelin. A genre known as Hair Metal invaded the US charts and achieved success in Britain helped by music magazines like *Kerrang!* and *Sounds*. Those bands were largely nothing more than glamorised pop poseurs who enjoyed moderately heavy riffing in their music. Bands such as Bon Jovi and Mötley Crüe – albeit highly entertaining and fun to listen to – appeared to know more about the latest in hair styling products than the origins of rock and roll or even heavy metal. Most of the hair metal bands lived in southern California and hung out on Sunset Boulevard: Dokken, Quiet Riot, Poison, Ratt and Warrant, amongst plenty of others. Besides, it was not the first time that a rock star had been criticised for having too much hair and extravagant preening and pouting ...

In the other corner, there were the New Romantics; mostly based in Britain, those bands hit the charts in the early 1980s and partially managed to spread their music over to the States. Instead of guitars, they mainly used synthesisers and wore brightly coloured fashionable high street clothes rather than denim jeans and white shirts. As is the case in any movement, there was a myriad of New Romantic bands; the most popular being Duran Duran, Spandau Ballet, Soft Cell, Ultravox, Adam & The Ants, Culture Club and The Human League.

Yet Robert Plant was on his own, doing his own thing ...

1985 was a busy year for Jimmy Page, Plant's erstwhile cohort, as he launched The Firm, his new band with Paul Rodgers, the former singer of Free and Bad Company. It was also another busy year for Robert Plant with the release of his latest album.

It was during the second half of 1984 when recording of *Shaken 'n' Stirred*[40] commenced at Marcus Studios in London. He spent just a few short weeks in the city before transferring to Rockfield Studios in Monmouth where the band spent a couple of months in the wilderness of south Wales. Robbie Blunt, Paul Martinez and Jezz Woodruffe were there as was Plant's live drummer, the American Ritchie Hayward, who also added his considerable talents to the album. A recent inclusion was singer Toni Halliday, previously a backing singer for the Eurythmics and later of the band Curve.

The album was produced by Robert Plant and Benji LeFeure and co-produced by Tim Palmer. The latter studio expert remembers: "Robert wasn't particularly tight but one thing that was funny was that when I first got the phone call when it was first happening, my manager called so that the deal could be done and for the first time ever he had to do the actual recording deal with the artist. He actually had to do the deal with Robert himself; he likes to take care of all the contracts so my manager had to negotiate with Robert about how much I would get paid and stuff like that."

Exactly how did Palmer get involved with the project?

"From a technical point of view, I'd started in a studio when I was 18 and because of the 1980s most of the music that came through our studio was electronic. I'd engineered records for people like Dead Or Alive, I'd worked with John Fox and done some mixing for Cutting Crew. I didn't have a lot of experience recording rock bands at all, so when Robert called me up one day and said, 'I'm making a new album and I'd like you to think about coming along and engineering it' and asked me about things that I'd done, I wasn't that quick to point out that I hadn't actually recorded that many drum kits at this point. I knew basically what to do but I hadn't actually recorded many real drum sets on albums; it mainly being drum machines …

Robert really wanted to find somebody who, in his opinion, was more familiar with contemporary modern keyboard sounds, etc., and he thought I'd be able to help in that department. Truth is, I wasn't really happy doing pop and the type of music I'd been doing so I was happy to exchange and go over and learn a bit more about rock, which is what I always wanted to do. I didn't want to be a pop producer; I wanted to be a rock producer. So it was an interesting one because I was really not prepared!"

As a self-proclaimed rock 'novice', Palmer was in an unusual environment and had to learn the ropes quickly. "It's amazing that I ended up working with Robert Plant. I was 22 so I was pretty young and very inexperienced really," he recalls. "And to be honest, I was really not that familiar with most of the Led Zeppelin catalogue. I'd heard the obvious songs on the radio: 'Stairway To Heaven', 'Whole Lotta Love' and all those sort of things [but] I really wasn't very well prepared with the history of Robert Plant and Led Zeppelin at all … They [Plant and LeFeure] were trying something new and they were hoping I could bring something to the table that they hadn't seen before and I hoped that I did."

At the London studio, Palmer remembers that Robert Plant was very patient with him. "We had a full band set-up and for me it was very daunting, something quite new in a way, having so many musicians playing at the same time," he explains. "We were setting up the drums, having a lot of microphones to deal with and all the fold-backs for each individual member and we were working on a Harrison Board and I'd never worked on a Harrison Board before and I really was having trouble working the whole thing out and at one point Robert was getting annoyed and luckily for me he thought it was the studio going wrong so he started complaining to the studio manager at Marcus and the studio manager said the guy you've got in there doesn't know what he's doing, which was sort of true! But luckily for me, Robert and I were getting on well and I stayed on and we started working on the drum sound and it was coming together by this point. Robert started making references to Led Zeppelin songs and I had to say I really don't know those songs. He didn't care and he said, 'Okay, fair enough, what songs do you know?' I said, 'I know 'Whole Lotta Love'.' I said I haven't got any Led Zeppelin albums. And the following day he came into the studio and plopped down a pile of albums and said: 'Check my old band out, see if you like 'em.' So that was the way I was introduced to the music of Led Zeppelin. We did actually have points of reference that we could share. Robert was very aware of The Damned so we talked about the drum sound on 'New Rose'. Anyway, it was an interesting way to start my relationship on the project."

Palmer explains that Ritchie Hayward's drums played a fundamental role in the overall sound of the finished album. "We worked really hard on the drum sound … now I do know that the majority of the sound comes from the drummer and having Ritchie Hayward playing the drums already gave us a great start. It was a great sounding room, a great sounding kit and in the end we got a great sounding drum sound. It took a while but it was worth the effort. To this day it's still one of my favourites. I love the sound of the drums on 'Little By Little.'"

Despite the passing of over twenty years, Palmer has a little anecdote about one particular recording session in London: "When we were recording at Marcus Studios, we had the full band set-up and we were doing the backing tracks, I had my first experience of what we imagined the Led Zeppelin recording experience to be like. We used to go over to the pub and have a few beers and we came across some Robert Plant fans hanging out [there]. There was one particular girl that wanted to come back over and have a listen [at what we'd recorded] so she came over to the studio and had a listen and [when] we politely asked her to leave … she didn't wanna go so I remember I set up a headphone mix on her flight case and she danced as we cut the backing tracks from the band and it was pretty funny to watch. To top it off she took her clothes off, which was quite nice to look at through the glass instead of the members of the band!"

Serious work began at Rockfield where Plant and his band had recorded their first two albums. "We stayed there, they have accommodation provided; it was a house on top of a hill, it was separate from the studio, it was quite a hairy drive down," remembers Palmer. "Some of the band were living in Monmouth at the time and I think Robert was living there and I know Paul was living there and I think Robbie was not too far as well. So most of the band were close at hand."

In terms of the songwriting, Plant took a less restrained approach, as Palmer remembers, "As far as lyrics on *Shaken 'n' Stirred*, I know for a fact that we had all sorts of working titles for the songs. I found out the real titles of the songs about a week before it was in the shops. I guess the lyrics were also 'work in progress'. I know Robert had ideas and he would always sing a guide track but I think the lyrics were being written as we went along."

If anything, *Shaken 'n' Stirred* is an album that shows Plant wanting to move away from his rock star persona and into a new 1980s-sounding direction; he perhaps wanted to be somebody akin to Peter Gabriel? With his first two albums – both interesting and imaginative in different ways – Plant didn't appear to fit alongside most of his peers but with his third album, *Shaken 'n' Stirred*, he perhaps hastily embraced the electronic age of synthesisers and the glamour of MTV pop. Okay, he was pushing the boundaries of music and attempting to try new sounds but in this author's opinion, he got it wrong.

"Robert's a fun person to work with," says Palmer. "He can push you, push your buttons but he knows exactly what he wants. He has a very clear vision of how he would like the record to sound. He antagonises people to bring out the best in them. He'll wind you up and look for that extra mile that he can drag out of you. It seems to work!"

Palmer recalls another anecdote from the Rockfield sessions: "We'd take our dinner break and go to the pub most evenings then head back to the studio. One evening, the drinking session went on a lot longer than usual," he says. "I'd had more than a few too many; I just really couldn't keep up to be honest. The band found it all very funny and because of this they insisted I attempt to play a guitar solo on one of the tracks; I think it was 'Pink And Black'. So we headed back to the studio and I really wasn't in good shape at all and they put a Les Paul on me and somewhere in the vaults there is my attempted guitar solo and it was not good! We had a good laugh about it in the morning.

"I went outside to get a breath of fresh air and started to walk up this country road and head back to the house for the night and I saw in the distance the headlights of a car racing up the hill. Right at the last minute they slowed down, I just collapsed right on the bonnet of the car and I completed the rest of the journey up to our little cottage basically unconscious; definitely one too many that evening."

Robert Plant has lots of stories to tell; surely he must have mentioned the Led Zeppelin years?

Palmer: "I don't remember Robert sitting around talking about Led Zeppelin that much. He talked about Wolverhampton Wanderers a lot. And we discussed the merits of a good curry. We talked about the music that we were working on. Obviously you get a few stories here and there but

I think I probably got more Led Zeppelin stories from Benji. We were having fun in our own little world so we didn't need to be too much looking over our shoulders."

Shaken 'n' Stirred was the album that broke Plant's first solo band; he was determined to create a masterpiece, something that would define him and his new image despite a conflict of interest with some of his musicians.

Palmer: "It was a very old school way of making a record. All the band had strong ideas about what they wanted to achieve with their own parts and the music was constantly developing. A lot of time had been spent in rehearsals so everyone had a strong idea of where the music was gonna end up. It was about choosing the right sounds and getting the right performances. At the time, we were very [much] into making a special sounding record so we did spend a long time on getting everything to sound just so … I don't remember it being very stressful; I was only 22 and it was just very exciting for me. We had a lot of really good fun times making that record."

Plant decided that he wanted the album to use a relatively new instrument much to the annoyance of his blues-based guitarist. Palmer: "I don't remember too many arguments going on. I remember Robbie Blunt was using a brand new guitar synthesiser and that was quite frustrating for him at times to get the sounds that we were looking for out of this box. It was very new and quite fiddly; it wasn't consistent. Robert's always pushing people to take it to the next level so he can try and wind you up but it's all coming from a good place."

In hindsight, such an instrument was typical of the 1980s – even heavy metal legends Judas Priest caught onto the appeal of synthesiser guitars and recorded their entire 1986 album, *Turbo*, using them. ZZ Top also used them on their mega-selling 1983 album *Eliminator*. Both albums have since become cult classics.

Yet despite what Palmer says, reports have suggested that the three month recording sessions were fraught with difficulties and tension, primarily between Plant and Blunt, who had different opinions on how the album should sound. Blunt disliked a lot of the 1980s-sounding material that Plant championed. No wonder it was the last album to feature the Blunt/Martinez/Woodruffe/Hayward line-up.

Blunt had made an equally indelible impression on the young producer/engineer as Robert Plant had. "Robbie Blunt's quite an amazing guitar player," Palmer enthuses. "I have great memories of watching him play. He's very precise, there's nothing going on that record that isn't meant to be. At this particular point, he wasn't using too much in the way of pedals. The sounds that we got were either from adjusting the amps or the guitars themselves [as well as] changing guitars; it was a very natural sort of approach. I thought the parts that Robbie played were musically very interesting. He's not one to just play the obvious notes; he'll look for something a little more special than that and the music really benefited from that."

By the end of the recording and mixing sessions, Palmer's role had changed significantly. "I was not asked to come along and produce it, I was asked to engineer," he explains. "I contributed quite a lot to the sessions and Robert gave me a co-production credit in the end, which was great but really I was brought in at the beginning as an engineer."

Shaken 'n' Stirred was released in the UK on May 20, 1985, by Es Paranza and it was a massive disappointment. It seems that Plant's bold notions of creating a contemporary pop masterpiece had worked against him. "With things like *Shaken 'n' Stirred*, people scratched their heads," he confessed to Barney Hoskyns.

The album reached a poor Number 19 in the UK charts, dropping out after just a month while in the States it also achieved little success, climbing to Number 20 before quickly disappearing from view. In the UK, the album spawned two singles: 'Pink And Black' and 'Little By Little'. None of them set the singles charts alight. In the US, 'Little By Little' reached a respectable Number 36 but was followed by the flop single 'Too Loud'.

Tim Palmer: "To be honest, the album, it twists and it turns. It doesn't stick to the rules of usual rock or pop arrangements and even melodically Robert takes a few chances, which is a refreshing thing for somebody to be doing. He never just takes the easy way out. I was very proud of the way the record sounded. I think we did a great job there. Looking back on it, it was a very brave record to make. There weren't obvious singles; Robert wasn't driven to have a hit single. He was making some music that he felt proud of and he didn't really care if it sounded like Led Zeppelin and he didn't really care if it sounded like anything else; he just wanted to feel proud of what he did. I'm glad that we did that. It was definitely in a time when artists were allowed to be able to do that; that's definitely not the case now. It didn't bother me that it didn't sell as well as maybe the record [label] hoped because for me personally it was a great experience to work with one of the most legendary vocalists of all-time and I had a bloody good time doing it."

Reviews of the album were bitterly divided with many critics claiming Plant had literally lost the plot and should have stuck with the musical patterns portrayed on his first two solo albums. Many music writers noticed how much Plant had let himself be influenced by the pop artists of the era. It is certainly arguable that Plant was not at all concerned about that fact that he had taken a less organic approach to his new music; nevertheless, it certainly had an affect on the opinions of his fans and critics.

Parke Puterbaugh wrote in *Rolling Stone*: "For starters, it sounds like he's been listening to the last couple of records by The Police and Talking Heads, and some of the new stuff coming over from Africa ... he's banking on the present, reinventing himself as a chameleon with a sharp ear for new sound."

Shaken 'n' Stirred commences with 'Hip To Hoo'; the dance beats and backing vocals of the opening song emphatically put Robert Plant into the 1980s music scene. Plant cheekily quotes Led Zeppelin on the peculiar song 'Kallalou Kallalou' but unfortunately for him it makes the listener yearn for a good Zeppelin rock song.[41] Plant attempts to rap on 'Too Loud' and as such it leaves a sour taste. 'Trouble Your Money' is a slow, plodding tune with Plant's usual desire to add varying layers and textures. 'Pink And Black' is a funk-filled song and one of the album's rare highlights; Blunt makes a short and unlikely guitar appearance. 'Little By Little' is certainly the centre-piece of the album and a highlight of his first three solo albums. 'Doo Doo A Do Do' is a frustrating song despite the humorous title; it sounds confused and convoluted. 'Easily Lead' is a fast-paced song with some slight flourishes of guitar by Blunt and a deep, steady bass line. Finally, the moody 'Sixies And Sevens' is one of just a few reasonably good songs on this album.

Shaken 'n' Stirred is certainly not one of Plant's more digestible solo albums. He draws liberally from the pop stars of the 1980s – surely not the former lead singer of Led Zeppelin, what happened to the influence of Robert Johnson or Love? This album is deeply fixed in the 1980s and as such it sounds a little dated and makes for uncomfortable listening. It is a disjointed album.

The 2007 remastered and expanded version released by Rhino Entertainment also received little acclaim.[42] The *Blogcritics* online magazine (*www.blogcritics.org*) declared: "In the 1980s, it was all about electronics, and *Shaken 'n' Stirred* was no exception ... That's how this CD sounds, sugar-coated ... The synthesised guitar and keyboards rehash over the same chords as they did the track before. With the exception of his voice, the music sounds the same."

Vintage Rock (*www.vintagerock.com*): "*Shaken 'n' Stirred* and its single 'Little By Little' piled on the pop fragrances and alienated various sectors of the flock ..."

Inevitably, with the release of a new studio album, Plant ventured out on the road with his band for a bombastic arena tour; beginning in Vancouver on June 13, they toured North America for several weeks, finishing at New York's famed Madison Square Garden on August 5.

Tim Palmer: "I went out to [America to] record one of the shows on the tour and I had no idea just how big the tour was. I really didn't understand the phenomenon of Led Zeppelin in America. It was a rock and roll dream for me, to be honest, riding in the limos with the police escorts and getting up to all sorts of trouble with the band [plus] I got to ride on the tour bus. I'd be dumped in various small towns when we'd go out and no-one would tell me how to get home and they'd see if I managed to survive; it was always like seeing if I could make it back in one piece and it was just great – I had the best time ever."

After the States, Plant and his band continued their road jaunt, travelling to the UK for just two dates: the Birmingham NEC on September 8 and Wembley Arena on September 10. With that, the tour was over. In many ways 1985 was the end of an era for Robert Plant ...

★ ★ ★

Due to well-documented differences of opinion between Robert Plant and Robbie Blunt on *Shaken 'n' Stirred* and the negative response and poor sales that greeted the album, Plant became disillusioned with the music business and decided to take a break after making four albums in as many years; he disbanded his solo band and effectively started his solo group from scratch.

Regarding his split with Blunt, Plant told *Kerrang!*'s Chris Welch in 1988: "Maybe all the work we did in a short space of time drew a lot of energy out of people and their creative powers just weren't as hot as they were at the beginning. So it had to stop."

As previously mentioned, Plant worked briefly with remaining members of Led Zeppelin and he also staged gigs with The Honeydrippers but other than that, very little occurred between the second half of 1985 and the beginning of 1987. He spent time living in his new flat in London and thinking up ideas. As quoted in *Metal Hammer* in 1988, Plant said: "No, I didn't disappear. I was wandering around bleak streets, talking and starting to write."

Plant appeared onstage with Fairport Convention at the Cropredy Festival in Oxfordshire on August 9, 1986. Bassist Dave Pegg told *Get Ready To Rock* (*www.getreadytorock.com*) in 2006: "One of the greatest joys for me at Cropredy [has] been backing people like Robert Plant and doing Led Zeppelin material ..." Besides that Plant spent much of the year outside of the limelight.

Importantly Plant began tentative work on his fourth solo album during the autumn of '86. He had made demos with producer/songwriter Bruce Woolley who had previously worked with The Buggles and Grace Jones. But what mainly instigated Plant's decision to go back in the studio to make a complete album was some material he wrote with Robert Crash at the behest of Dave Stewart of The Eurythmics.[43] Crash had co-produced The Eurythmics' second album – the breakthrough hit *Sweet Dreams (Are*

Made of This). Speaking to Dave Dickson of *Metal Hammer* in 1988, Plant explained: "We both had a comprehension of garage punk stuff … we had common ground on which to start the great adventure."

Plant was psyched by what he'd created with Crash and was even more excited about the prospect of a new album when, sometime in November '86, Virgin Music handed him an interesting demo by an outfit called The Rest Is History.

Plant was keen to meet with the creators of the demo, producers Dave Barrett, Phil Johnstone and drummer Chris Blackwell, who were then working as session musicians. Blackwell had just finished a tour with Bucks Fizz and Phil Johnstone was valiantly producing largely disposable records for relatively obscure acts.

Johnstone spoke to *Raw* in 1990 about when he first got the job working with Plant: "At the time I met Robert, I was actually working on a song about him, because some girl told the Vermorels [Fred and Judy] that she had this fantasy about Robert coming down and screwing her. 'He's like a huge golden lion conquering me.' So it was quite weird when I met the Golden Lion himself."

The demo contained a song called 'Heaven Knows' which was engineered by Mike Gregovic; it had actually been made a year before Plant even heard it himself. Blackwell writes on his website (*www.chrisblackwell.co.uk*): "I came home one day to find a message on the answer phone from somebody claiming to be Robert Plant asking if I wanted to join his band! He had heard me drumming because Virgin [Phil Johnstone's publisher] had sent him tracks as possible singles, and I had been drumming on them. [I] called him back thinking it was a wind up. Turned out it wasn't. [I] nervously went along to rehearsal. First thing Robert said to me was, 'Would you like a cup of tea?' and I was immediately at home! [He] needed a guitarist and bass player, so I suggested Doug Boyle and Phil Scragg. Phil Johnstone was already on keyboards, and there was the band!"

Before Boyle was given the opportunity to work with Plant, he was working at the complaints department of a London-based holiday company and only found time to gig in his spare time at pubs and clubs. Plant explained to *Metal Hammer* in 1988: "Phil Scragg and Doug Boyle … came as a twin set. I don't think either of them had any stadium or arena or rock experience to speak of, and quite politely didn't have anything to do with rock or even want to."

They formed a professional relationship and began to compile new material with the prospect of brand new studio album at some point in the near future. Plant later confessed to *Kerrang!* scribe Neil Jeffries the details of the close-knit relationship he would quickly form with his new band. "Without *them* I don't exist," Plant explained. "Without me *they* don't exist

– but they can do something else. They have to sit back and go, 'Fucking hell! Here he goes again.' They've really got a good patience factor!"

* * *

Elsewhere, one of the most important things Plant did in mid-1987 was to sign up with Bill Curbishley's London management company, Trinifold. Curbishley has quite a reputation in the business as a dedicated manager, passionate about music as both an art form and as a business industry. Famously, he is known as the manager of The Who but he also manages heavy metal legends Judas Priest. Plant told Chris Welch at *Kerrang!* in 1988: "He's hasn't just dealt with tiny tots! He's dealt with people who have been around, had knocks and bangs, lost and won."

* * *

By mid-1987, Plant had fully formed his new band and was happy with the demos and pre-arranged material and lyrics. The album included two songs written by Robert Crash and Robert Plant as well as important lyrical input from Dave Barrett, Phil Johnstone and Doug Boyle. *Now And Zen* was produced by Robert Plant, Tim Palmer and Phil Johnstone and engineered by Rob Bozas and Martin Russell.

Recording of Plant's fourth studio album – to be titled *Now And Zen*[44] – commenced in September after rehearsing at London Docklands. The session musicians were: Phil Johnstone (keyboards) Dave Barrett (keyboards) Doug Boyle (guitars) Phil Scragg (bass) and Chris Blackwell (drums and percussion).

Doug Boyle spoke to *Raw* in 1990 about the band's relationship with each other and Plant: "It's kind of democratic," he explained, "but the onus is on somebody different all the time. It all depends on who's feeling particularly dominant that day. We all struggle and fight to get out particular ideas and approaches through ..."

It was certainly refreshing for Plant to have young, feisty musicians on board who ultimately helped to revitalise his career. "I don't know if it's a revitalisation process," Plant explained to *Music Express Magazine* in 1990, "but it is certainly a mutual stimulation."

Tim Palmer: "I went down to rehearsal and everything was beginning to take shape; it was a very different process to the *Shaken 'n' Stirred* sessions [because] it was a lot more contemporary in the way that we put it together. There was a lot more sequencing and a lot more keyboard parts really; by this point, I think Robert had been affected by Depeche Mode and the whole 1980s sound. At some level, I like the fact that Robert's voice was being surrounded by these new textures [but] on some levels

I was a bit worried by how much people would enjoy hearing Robert Plant surrounded by keyboards [and] synthesisers, not that Led Zeppelin didn't use them but Robert Plant with guitars behind him was something that everyone knows and loves and we were really going a long, long way from that and I was concerned about that.

I would sometimes argue and fight for more guitars behind the vocals rather than the keyboards, but that's not really the right way to approach it with Robert because he doesn't want to be held back and have to do things the way it was done before; he likes to do new things and go in new directions so it was a little bit of a battle but I think we found a good compromise."

In 2007, Palmer can still remember the recording sessions in some detail: "The album once again was started at Marcus studios and the overdubs and mixes were done at a studio called Swanyard up in Highgate," he explains. "We spent quite a long time in Marcus laying down the drum machines and then we started putting down real drums on different tracks [and] putting the sequence parts down so we got the basic shape. We ate a lot of curries; I remember each day we would go out for a curry and we would get that lovely pick-me-up in the afternoon when the spice had kicked in."

Having spent the years in between *Shaken 'n' Stirred* and *Now And Zen* working with bands like Texas and The Mission, Palmer was much more confident working with an understandably domineering and extremely talented artist like Plant.

Palmer: "Robert was his usual self, prodding and poking, trying to bring out the best in us all by pushing us further, sometimes to good effect, [some] times to bad effect. Some of the newer members of the band, I think [for example] Doug struggled with [Robert's] constant harassing him to play more and in different styles and to learn about some of the roots of some of the solos that he was doing but in the end it worked out for the best; Doug played some amazing stuff on that album."

Having such a young band backing Plant inevitably affected the working atmosphere in the studio, as Palmer recalls: "There was a lot of joking and laughing around and everyone seemed like they were in a good spirits. There was no tension, it felt very relaxed. It wasn't an easy album to produce, it took a while. The songs were quite complex in some ways, there were a lot of parts to get right and a lot of experimenting with sounds and trying different approaches but also I remember Robert was giving up smoking at the time so there was a period there in the middle where he wasn't the happiest bunny to work with."

Now And Zen included some valid contributions from outside musicians including backing vocalist Marie Pierre. Palmer: "We had a lot of musicians coming in to deal with … [on] backing vocals the late Kirsty McColl came and sang some amazing stuff. She did all the big block vocals on 'Heaven Knows', which we stacked up and multi-tracked, it was based on the idea from the demo that Phil [Johnstone] and Dave [Barrett] had done and we basically got Kirsty to do all these voice parts and they sounded fantastic; she made all that 'Heaven Knows' chant in the chorus and we had another backing vocalist, Toni Halliday come and sang on the backing vocals as well, we had somebody playing the jazz double bass on 'White Clean And Neat' ... it took a long time."

Plant and his musicians and producers did a lot of playing around with sound effects and samples: "On 'Tall Cool One', the samples of the Led Zeppelin songs was based on an idea that was on Phil and Dave's demo," remembers Palmer. "We just took it to the next level of the record. I remember putting all the samples into an AMS Sampler with Phil and just playing them in, changing the pitch and it came out sounding really fun and people really like the sense of humour of hearing Robert with the old Led Zeppelin samples behind him."

Plant spoke to *Metal Hammer* in 1988 about that song: "The first samples in the end of the last verse, that's 'Whole Lotta Love' right down in the background. Then you get bits of 'Custard Pie' and 'The Wanton Song' ... it actually made me laugh because there's that little tease at the beginning that makes you stop and go 'Wait a minute, wasn't that... ?' And then further on there's a segment more. And then of course at the end it all comes out."

'Tall Cool One' included contributions from one Jimmy Page; he plays guitar, taking inspiration from the song 'The Train Kept-A-Rollin'' by Johnny Burnette Palmer: "I don't remember whose idea it was to bring Jimmy ... It was something we always wanted to do. I imagine it was Robert's idea – the idea was given its blessing by him, that's for sure. The day that Jimmy came down to the studio, it was funny, I always remember that ... in studios you get an assistant if you're lucky [and] the day that Jimmy was about to arrive, suddenly I noticed that I had two assistants and I also noticed that the techs were in there fixing compressors and checking bits of equipment, just hoping to get a glimpse of Jimmy Page and Robert Plant together, so I knew it was going to be a pretty special day and it was amazing. The way that Jimmy played was a bit like a cartoon caricature of himself: when he puts the guitar on and the cigarette and has the beer and pulls the faces, he didn't let me down at all.

Basically, I wasn't going to start telling Jimmy Page what to play; we just gave him some open tracks, turned it up and said: 'Do what you feel's right.' In the end, once the parts had been chosen and we put them into the songs, I really feel they took away from some of the programmed sound ... the way that Jimmy bends the strings gave it the human touch that was needed to take it out of that pre-programmed sound – on the tracks that he played on, it really brought them to life."

Jimmy Page told Mick Wall in an interview for *Kerrang!* in 1988 that he didn't know Plant was going to sample some Zeppelin riffs on 'Tall Cool One'. Page: "Oh, it was his idea. When I did it, I didn't hear any of that stuff. I think he put it on right at the end … it was a surprise … it was an eye-opener."

Speaking to *Metal Hammer* in 1988, Plant said: "But to get him to come and play on the single and playing him 'Tall Cool One' when it was finished … it was really funny because he looked at me as if to say: 'What do you mean by this?' Ha!"

Ultimately it was Plant's album and he had full command although there was one little mistake which was beyond Plant's control, as Palmer explains: "The album was all mixed to half-inch tape and we were very meticulous when we were recording … there was nothing on that record that wasn't supposed to be there. When the CD came out and on the back it should have read 'AAD – Analogue Analogue Digital' which would have been correct but it was written on the back of the CD that it was a digital recording which as quite a nice compliment really because it wasn't digital in any way."

Palmer's final say on the album is mixed: "Looking back on it, to be honest, I still feel it was a little bit too 1980s but I think we made good progress in other directions. I think the songwriting was stronger [than *Shaken 'n' Stirred*] and I think we had hooks and choruses for the first time and I think we made a much more accessible album without making too many compromises."

Promotion for Plant's fourth album and his new band began as early as December 1987 when he played two very low-key gigs. On December 17 they played Leas Cliff Hall in Folkestone; what made this gig especially interesting was that his new band was billed as the Band Of Joy and for the first time in his solo career he played Zep songs live on stage. For those fans fortunate to be there, they heard Plant and his new band play 'Misty Mountain Hop' amongst a small set of other Zep tunes.

Also, on the December 30, again billed as the Band Of Joy, Plant played a local show at Stourbridge Town Hall, which included a performance of the classic Zep songs 'Rock And Roll' and 'The Lemon Song'. Other numbers played on the night included 'Tall Cool One', 'Ship Of Fools', 'Little By Little', 'Heaven Knows' and a welcome cover of The Doors classic 'Break On through (To The Other Side)'. Oddly enough, Duran Duran guitarist Andy Taylor made a surprise guest appearance.

Chris Welch enthusiastically reviewed the gig for *Kerrang!* and wrote: "The show was a fantastic success … a happy, smiling Plant rocked out with a great young band … If Robert was feeling any touch of nervousness, he didn't betray it. He positively glowed with confidence and satisfaction, and a big smile showed how much he was enjoying himself."

Now And Zen was preceded by the release of the album's first single, 'Heaven Knows', which was unleashed on January 18, 1988. The accompanying music video was filmed in Morocco: "The fear of videos has gone out of the window now," he explained to *Kerrang!* in '88, "and I decided to make something deep and meaningless, like most of the music around. I thought it was time to go to some far-away place and do a Bounty [chocolate] advert!"

The single reached Number 33 in the UK charts and entered Number 1 on America's *Mainstream Rock Charts* and achieved considerable radio play. To build up support for his first solo release in two years he played a number of important albeit small gigs at various universities in January and on February 3 he played a set at London's famous Marquee Club. This was Plant's first time on the Marquee's stage since the early rumblings of Led Zeppelin. Right up until the album's release, Plant was busy with interviews, press conferences and low-key gigs. He was in a good mood, with not a single grey cloud over his head.

★　★　★

Now And Zen was issued by Es Paranza on February 29, 1988 in Britain. It was a sure-fire hit; it reached Number 10 in the UK Top 40 and Number 6 in America's *Billboard's* Top 200 albums. *Now And Zen* was also a hit in such far-away countries as New Zealand where it enjoyed a healthy position at Number 7. In the UK the album spawned further singles: 'Tall Cool One', which seemed to take on a life of its own in the UK and US markets through incredible amounts of airplay, was released in April and entered the Top 30 proceeded by 'Ship Of Fools' in September.

Tim Palmer: "The album did a lot better than *Shaken 'n' Stirred* because it was a lot more accessible. The songs were simpler to understand [and] melodically they didn't go off on any strange tangents. There were stronger hooks and stronger choruses but also it didn't do any harm that ... Jimmy played guitar solos with Robert [after Led Zeppelin] which got a lot of people excited about the record and there was the track 'Tall Cool One' which generated a lot of interest. We had a very strong ballad in 'Ship Of Fools' with fantastic guitar work and a very strong melody. It sort of had a bit of everything, the album, which at that point you really needed to have."

Fans may have bemoaned his 'rehashing' of some old Led Zeppelin songs and a sound which was perhaps too pristine, but on the whole the dedicated Robert Plant fan base was positively pleased. What about the reaction from the music critics? Reviews could not have been more positive.

The New York Times declared enthusiastically: "A vocal tour de force. At its very best, *Now And Zen* suggests Mr. Plant and his young collaborators, are capable of making music as visionary as the best of Led Zeppelin. Plant seems to have reached a point where he can accept the past, but he continues to move forward."

Kurt Loder wrote in *Rolling Stone*: "This record is some kind of stylistic event: a seamless pop fusion of hard guitar rock, gorgeous computerisation and sharp, startling song craft … It is exhilarating to discover such lyrical substance in music already so technically arresting."

Howard Johnson wrote in *Kerrang!*: "*Now And Zen* has to be Plant's most satisfying album since *Pictures At Eleven* … The tunes are insidious, working their way into your brain with relentless restraint … *Now And Zen* is by no means a failure, it is a highly palatable reconciliation of old and new, a set of tunes which stand in their own right."

Dante Bonutto wrote in *Metal Hammer*: "It's the production that truly makes it shine, a heady and sophisticated cocktail with plenty to reward the attentive, can-encased ear … This is comfortable rock that dips a toe into the mainstream, yet could never be accused of being wet. Plant now seems comfortable with glories past and is all set to move ahead."

Now And Zen opens with 'Heaven Knows' which is a beautifully constructed and emotional soft rock song with some nifty guitar work. 'Dance On My Own' has some wonderful backing vocals and a haunting melody and stands tall as one of the album's best songs. Despite a typically 1980s intro, 'Tall Cool One' – which takes its title from a 1959 Wailers instrumental – builds itself up to be a strong number; it's especially memorable for those Led Zeppelin references and samples. 'The Way I Fell' is an extraordinary pop ballad with different layers of synthetic sounds and some refreshing guitar work. 'Helen Of Troy' is a top-notch electronic pop tune and the riff invites a rock audience into the equation. 'Billy's Revenge' is a brilliantly enjoyable 1950s bopper and unlike a majority of its sibling it is led by guitars and bass rather than keyboards and drums. 'Ship Of Fools' is a powerful and evocative ballad and remains one of Plant's more memorable solo songs. 'Why' is slightly monotonous but again the varying textures and tones lift it up from being an ordinary pop song. 'White, Clean And Neat' is Plant's tribute to his past when rock and roll first came onto the scene in the 1950s. Finally, 'Walking Towards Paradise' is a sharp and crisp way to end the album.

Now And Zen is an excellent album, which still doesn't sound too dated largely because the guitar work and melodies are fantastically contrived and original. It maybe the case that on previous albums Plant tried as hard as possible to cut off his connections to Led Zeppelin, but on *Now And Zen* he fully embraces them which is one good reason why this album works so well. Again, as evident on previous albums, he disregards the blues and his famous white boy wails and attempts varying styles of music in one eclectic melting pot. This album works magnificently despite some occasional moments of mundane Dire Straits-type riffing. The sound of the album is clearly influenced by the electronics of such European pop bands as Kraftwerk and even Roxy Music. The lyrics have been carefully constructed and Plant's voice sounds alert and vehement.

The album was reissued and expanded in 2007 by Rhino Entertainment and the reviews from the music press were mostly positive.[45] *All Music Guide* (*www.allmusic.com*) said: "Plant, who often uses mysterious (and mystical) lyrics, writes some of his most direct songs, and the way in which the lyrics complement the melodic arrangements are partially responsible for the commercial success of *Now And Zen*."

Dubbed *Non Stop Go* and supported by the acclaimed progressive rock band It Bites, Plant kicked off his UK tour on March 16, 1988 and finished on April 17 at London's Hammersmith Odeon, where he was joined by Jimmy Page for the encore. Plant and his band played such venues as Newport Centre, Newcastle City Hall, Edinburgh Playhouse, Oxford Apollo, Liverpool Royal Court and the Manchester Apollo.

The were some changes to the touring line-up of Plant's band as producer Tim Palmer explains: "Phil Scragg played bass on the album [but] after the album was complete, Robert was actually looking for a new bass player and I had a friend in a band called Violent Blue that I'd produced called Charlie Jones and he'd only ever really played in small shows and small venues but he was a great bass player. I suggested to him that he come down and meet Robert so he came straight down and stayed in my apartment and went to meet Robert the next day at the studio. The two of them really hit it off and, because he's a great bass player, he got the gig. It's a fantastic story because he literally went from playing in small venues around Bath and the next show he's playing he's in front of a huge stadium in America."

Charlie Jones spoke to *Raw* in 1990: "Well, I knew [Plant] had a history. But you can't let that history dictate how you feel otherwise you're going to be moon-eyed all the time … I didn't know what to expect – I'd heard his solo album *Shaken 'n' Stirred* when I was in Violent Blue and I realised that here's somebody who was striving for something different. So that's what I was in awe of … I was gobsmacked when I met him."

The US leg of the tour began in May and finished in November.

Plant spoke to *Kerrang!* in 1990 about his renewed success: "*Now And Zen* cracked it. Opened the whole thing wide open. I was getting audiences in America that didn't know what band I was in before …"

Throughout the American tour, Plant was supported by several artists including Cheap Trick, Stevie Ray Vaughan, The Mission, The Georgia Satellites and Joan Jett, previously of The Runaways.[46]

Despite having to cancel a gig in Dallas because Plant suffered heat exhaustion, it was a long, exciting and very successful road jaunt which included an appearance by Robbie Blunt and Brian Setzer at the popular LA Forum on June 14.

It was the first time some members of Plant's band had visited the States so it was obviously an eye-opener especially being on the road with the guy who used to front Led Zeppelin. Chris Blackwell told *Raw* in 1990: "When we first got to America, [Plant] was talking about what it was like out there and how wild everything was, and he organised a backstage room full of girls picked out of the audience with passes on, and led us in there and then ran away leaving us among thirty or forty young American girls who desperately wanted to get back to the hotel! Most of the time I think he delights in putting us into situations and seeing how we get out of them, and that was one occasion. We got out of it quite well actually."

The music press praised the tour. One *Kerrang!* scribe reviewed Plant's show at New York's famed Madison Square Gardens thus: "On this evening, Plant proved all doubters (including myself) wrong … Plant's voice was absolutely flawless … Plant exhibited a unique talent for taking his definitive voice for the full acoustic ride … It was totally refreshing to see Plant do his show in his own special way, adding further to his hard rock mystique."

Instigated by his sampling of certain Led Zeppelin songs on *Now And Zen*, Plant also embraced Zeppelin songs on tour: he played, amongst others, 'Misty Mountain Hop', 'Rock And Roll' and 'Communication Breakdown'. Fans were especially keen to hear Plant sing the songs that essentially made him an international rock icon; in the States, Plant enjoyed repeatedly sold-out shows hence the length of the tour.

An important event took place during the US road trip as Tim Palmer recalls: "I remember halfway through the tour, I got a phone call from Charlie [Jones] saying how great everything's going and he said to me, 'I have something to tell you,' and I said, 'What is it Charlie?' and he said, 'I've fallen in love with Robert's daughter.' I wondered if this was a very smart move and I said, 'Does Robert know?' and Charlie said, 'Robert knows, I've told him.' Soon after he proposed to Carmen and they got married so Robert went from being his boss to being his father-in-law and still is. In fact, Charlie made Robert a granddad!"

The US tour brought an end to Plant's hectic diary for the year and he took a well-earned break in December 1988 was the most exhilarating and rewarding year Plant had enjoyed since the release of his first solo album back in 1982.

★ ★ ★

"In my lust and desire to be different, I think I now need to take stock and latch on for a couple of years to one thing that I really like," he enthused to *Kerrang!*. So, in January 1989, Plant began swift work on his next studio album. Amongst other minor things, a collection of Plant's music videos was issued on VHS in February. Speaking about the collection, which was titled *Mumbo Jumbo,* he told *Kerrang!* in 1990: "It's hilarious. The song is what counts, but if you're gonna do something around the song, it's got to be a little tongue-in-cheek. Like 'In The Mood', there are so many silly things. The guy is galloping towards his true love and she's looking out the window. Then something happens, you go back, and he's still galloping towards her but [he's] further away."

His fifth release – titled *Manic Nirvana* – was recorded at Olympic Studios in London after Plant had spent time writing songs at his farm in Monmouth. The album was produced by Robert Plant, Phil Johnstone and Mark 'Spike' Stent, mixed by Bill Price and engineered by Stent, Michael Butterworth and Jeremy Wheatley.

The line-up of the band went unchanged since the *Shaken 'n' Stirred* sessions: drummer Chris Blackwell, guitarist Doug Boyle, keyboard player Phil Johnstone and bassist Charlie Jones. "I haven't a lot of faith in myself," he confessed to one *Kerrang!* scribe in 1990. "I have to work with other people and to be exposed to other ideas to get the best out of myself ... With younger musicians there's more of a hunger and less bullshit."

The sessions included contributions from several backing singers, with Plant wanting to continue making more melodic music; those singers were Rob Stride, Lalia Cohen, Micky Groome, Carolyn Harding, Jerry Wayne and Siddi Makain Mushkin.

Plant was especially pleased with Jones; he told *Metal Hammer* in 1990: "With our guys there's some great moments. Charlie Jones for example, comes up with some great riffs. There was a track called 'One Love' which nearly made it to the album, for which he came up with an inspired rhythm with a kind of Bo Diddley feel crossed with Muddy Waters and almost sounded like The Cure."

The recording of *Manic Nirvana* was finished in the autumn of 1989. Plant expressed his thoughts on the album to Sylvie Simmons at *Raw* magazine in 1990: "This record says, 'Take it or leave it, I don't really care,' ... I think there's quite a bit of humour in this outing – like 'Tie Dye On The Highway' for one."

In November, he took part in an impromptu jam session with remaining members of Led Zeppelin at the 21st birthday party of his daughter, Carmen, in Birmingham. He also made a welcome appearance at a gig in Kidderminster by the local outfit Day Of Awareness; the set list included numbers by Bob Dylan, ZZ Top and even Bryan Adams.

★ ★ ★

Manic Nirvana was released by Es Paranza on March 19, 1990 in the UK and was greeted with warm reviews but sluggish sales; it peaked at Number 15 in the UK Top 40 and Number 16 in the US *Billboard* Top 200 Albums. The first single off the album was 'Hurting Kind (Got My Eyes On You)' which was issued on March 26 and reached Number 46 in the US charts and Number 45 in the UK.[47]

Malcolm Dome wrote in *Raw*: "The power and substance that have screamed from all of Plant's works is very much in evidence ... he is in control of his own destiny and can make modern rock music that elaborates the senses. A fine tome."

Kerrang! called the record the thirteenth best album of 1990 and in his review, Jon Hotten wrote: "Percy sings every number like he's on the verge of orgasm ... With *Manic Nirvana*, Planty's cooking ... [he's] back and he's bastard-well good." In a four star review, *Rolling Stone* declared: "..This new sound is even more exciting than the old ... [it] may well be the singer's most important work to date." Q magazine also gave *Manic Nirvana* four stars and called it the eighth best album of 1990.

Plant expressed his own opinion of the album to *Music Express Magazine* in 1990: "Well, I feel *Manic Nirvana* has flair, because I don't really care. It's pop music, and it has a whole lot of heart and soul. It doesn't need a revival of anything else."

Manic Nirvana opens with the excellent guitar based soft rocker 'Hurting Kind (I've Got My Eyes On You)' before the fiery and melodic 'Big Love' kicks into action. 'S S S & Q' is led by a terrific hard rock riff and also features a pretty good guitar solo, while 'I Cried' is a fairly ineffective acoustic ballad at best; it slows things down too early after such an energetic start. 'She Said' opens with a Zeppelin-esque vintage rock riff and 'Nirvana' is an equally refreshing rock song albeit more polished than any of Zeppelin's early, grittier work. 'Tie Dye On The Highway' is a peculiar song with an electronic-based rhythm and a rock steady riff; very similar to the songs on *Now And Zen*. 'Your Ma Said You Cried In Your Sleep Last Night' is a cover song (originally sung by Kenny Dino) that brought Plant slap-bang up-to-date with modern sound technology but it's one of the weaker songs on the album; it feels more like a cut-and-paste effort especially with yet more references to Led Zeppelin. 'Anniversary' is a brooding, sluggish but interesting song. 'Liars Dance' is a wonderfully controlled acoustic folk-blues number. Finally, 'Watching You' is a hitting, drum beating opus with all sorts of Moroccan beats and effects.

Manic Nirvana is a much better album than it has sometimes been given credit for; indeed it does rely on some Zeppelin-type melodies and riffs but it is an album that represents a period of Plant's career when he was embracing his past after spending much of the 1980s trying to distance himself from it. There are some great melodies on the album and more than a couple of decent songs. "This is the best thing I've come across in along time," he told *Kerrang!* in 1990. "It's much more hard-hitting and positive."

Manic Nirvana was reissued and expanded in 2007 by Rhino Entertainment[48] and even years after its original release, the press greeted the reissue with only minor enthusiasm; some critics felt that there should have been something more wholesome inside.

The Daily Vault (*www.dailyvault.com*): "This is a weak effort that nearly reduces Plant to a bad Zeppelin clone, though he does hold out some promise towards the end. But *Manic Nirvana* proves that the good ol' days of Led Zeppelin were, at the time of this release, ten years behind Plant, and it might have been a good idea to let those days finally go after exorcising them on *Now And Zen*."

The *Manic Nirvana* tour, which spread its exhausted wings from 1990 to 1991, saw a solo Plant visit mainland Europe for the first time; previously he had only toured the UK and Ireland. The tour commenced on May 1, 1990 at The Hague; he visited such cities as Dusseldorf, Milan, Barcelona, Stockholm, Copenhagen and Oslo. Again, Plant embraced the Led Zeppelin legacy and included some well-known songs in his performance. A typical set list ran as follows: 'Watching You', 'Nobody's Fault But Mine', 'Billy's Revenge', 'Tie Dye On The Highway', 'In The Mood', 'No Quarter', 'Liar's Dance', 'Going To California', 'Heaven Knows', 'Nirvana', 'Immigrant Song', 'Hurting Kind (I've Got My Eyes On You)' 'Ship Of Fools', 'Misty Mountain Hop' and 'Tall Call One'.

Somewhere amongst the craziness of the tour, Plant found time to spend two hours with guitarist Mick Green recording 'Let's Have A Party' for the charity tribute album to Elvis Presley, *The Last Temptation Of Elvis,* organised by Roy Carr of the *NME*.

With Canadian singer Alannah Myles as support, the *Manic Nirvana* tour arrived in the UK on May 31 with the first stop being the City Hall in Newcastle. From there, he played Sheffield, London and Birmingham. Writing in *Raw*, Malcolm Dome reviewed one of the Hammersmith Odeon shows and enthused, "as a modern rock show, this was magnificent. Plant has become adept at creating a mood of euphoric, seductive escarpments within which he showcases sympathetic songs."[49]

On June 22 in London, Plant accepted the Silver Clef award for their 'Outstanding Contribution' to British music. Plant has often said he is very humbled and even embarrassed when it comes to collecting awards because something like the Silver Clef means one has been in the business for a long time, possibly too long. Perhaps he shouldn't be so modest …

He played a set at the Knebworth Silver Clef Festival on June 30 and Mr. Jimmy Page was invited to participate in the three song encore;

inevitably, more (unfounded) rumours of a Led Zeppelin reunion dominated the press.

Plant's US tour was divided into two parts with the first leg starting on July 5 when they played in Albany, New York. Alannah Myles supported Plant for the first leg followed by The Black Crowes and Faith No More for the second leg.

They ventured all around the States, playing New Jersey, Connecticut, Maryland, Ohio, Pennsylvania, Florida, Texas, Arizona and more. The US set list differed slightly from the UK one. In Texas, Plant played: 'Watching You', 'Nobody's Fault', 'Billy's Revenge', 'Tie Dye On The Highway', 'In The Mood', 'Little By Little', 'Heaven Knows', 'Liar's Dance', 'Going To California', 'Nirvana', 'Immigrant Song', 'Hurting Kind (I've Got My Eyes On You)' 'Ship Of Fools', 'Wearing And Tearing', 'Tall Cool One' and 'Living Loving Maid (She's Just A Woman)'.

The US tour finished in Oklahoma on November 26 and if that wasn't enough, Plant even returned to the UK to play some shows in December: he visited Newcastle, Manchester, Wolverhampton and Newport. But he had to reschedule some intended shows at the Town & Country Club in London because he contracted laryngitis – those shows were moved to early January 1991.[50]

Neil Jeffries reviewed one of the London gigs in *Kerrang!*: "[With] a band of extra-terrestrial talent and a final night crowd who know when to laugh as well as when to cheer … you get one of the truest, warmest, *bestest* Percy gigs I've ever seen … tonight's show was pure magic."

Yet another album was in the shops and another tour was completed and Plant looked back on yet another tumultuous decade. He told *Metal Hammer* in 1990: "I've been through a lot in ten years. I've learned a lot. I've really grown up. Up until then I'd been living in the world of *Spinal Tap* in Zep."

★ ★ ★

Since Robert Plant released his first single in 1966, he had seen bands come and go including, of course, Led Zeppelin. He'd witnessed the rise and decline of fickle music trends and he'd been laughed at by a generation of punks. He saw himself imitated by younger rock stars and influence a plateau of wannabe rock gods. In summary, he was by this point a bona fide rock legend and had nothing left to prove.

At the beginning of the 1990s, he was at the height of his creative powers, even if his pure sales figures were not especially magnificent and his tickets sales in the UK were not exactly record-breaking.[51]

Alternative rock and grunge music was the music of choice for many rock fans in the early 1990s. Seattle-based bands like Nirvana and Alice In

A 19-year-old Robert visits the office of Charge d'Affaires of the Republic
of China to offer the services of the Band of Joy, November 15, 1967.
Part of the letter he is carrying reads:
"We are prepared to play for a period of time, free of charge,
as we feel very strongly about a united world."
Photo courtesy of PA/PA Archive/PA Photos

Led Zeppelin in the beginning, 1969: Page, Jones, Plant & Bonham.
Photo courtesy of ADC/Rex Features

The powerful force of Led Zeppelin on stage: the Royal Albert Hall, 1970.
Photo courtesy of Ray Stevenson/Rex Features

Robert Plant & Jimmy Page onboard The Starship, January, 1975.
Photo courtesy of Neal Preston/Retna Ltd

Led Zeppelin performing live in the mid–1970s.
Photo courtesy of Neal Preston/Retna UK

With fellow Honeydrippers, Page and Beck at The Old Racon.
Photo courtesy of Richard Young/Rex Features

Making history: Live Aid, Philadelphia, 1985.
Photo courtesy of Sipa Press/Rex Features

Freddie Mercury Tribute Concert, Wembley Stadium, London, April 1992.
Photo courtesy of Andre Csillag/Rex Features

A rekindled romance: Page & Plant live in the mid-1990s.
Photo courtesy of Ross Halfin/Retna UK

Phil Collins, Ahmet Ertegun, Robert Plant & Eric Clapton at a dinner
hosted by The Music Industry Trust in October 2002. Ertegun received
an award as one of the most important producers of all-time.
Photo courtesy of Richard Young/Rex Features

A life-long passion – his Wolverhampton Wanderers memorabilia.
Photo courtesy of Chris Taylor/Haymarket/PA Photos

Havin' a laugh: Cipriani Restaurant, New York, May 2005.
Photo courtesy of H. Carreno/Rex Features

Robert Plant & The Strange Sensations at Somerset House, July 2006.
Photo courtesy of Zak Hussein/PA Photos

With Alison Kraus on the *Today* TV show, New York, October 2007.
Photo courtesy of NBCU-photobank/Rex Features

Chains had opinions to express and social issues to discuss; just as punk had done to 1970s classic rockers, grunge bands metaphorically attacked 1980s hair metal bands like Poison and Bon Jovi. Even Guns N' Roses – whom *Kerrang!* had declared 'the most dangerous band in the world – were seen as an enemy of grunge bands.

Plant had very little time for the likes of Mötley Crüe but was surprisingly attracted to US alternative rock bands. It's reasonable to claim that one can sense a whiff of frustration when Plant throws rants into the air about his dislike and distrust of heavy metal and all its sub-categories.

Interviewed by *Kerrang!* in 1993 he exclaimed: "[If] this embryonic Seattle stuff which began and had finally developed into Nirvana and Pearl Jam, questions the whole pompous hard rock/heavy metal shit, then that's great! That's all I ever wanted, 'cos I think that the majority of heavy metal is a farce! I mean, Soundgarden and Nirvana – that's not heavy metal any more than Led Zeppelin was."

He handpicked some favourites from that era as he told *Kerrang!* in 1990: "People like Faith No More and Prong and Jane's Addiction and Soundgarden – they are to me what is important about aggressive music … I think [Faith No More's] first album is absolutely stunning. I think their first album caught, they just rode two styles and the two styles fucked each other to such a degree it worked perfectly. It was great to hear. More than that, it was a shock."

More local to Plant, the North West of England was enjoying a regeneration of music around 1990-91. Manchester had spawned the likes of The Stone Roses, Happy Mondays and soon-to-be bad boys Oasis.

Ecstasy and acid were the drugs of choice at the time but for Plant his drug-taking days were over and done with. "I don't do drugs now at all, so I can't comment on the effect of today's drugs on the music," Plant explained to *Raw* magazine's Sylvie Simmons in 1990. "But if I did, I think I'd still be relating to the things that fired me up in the beginning. If I went to an Acid House party, I'd listen to the music, trying to figure out where they stole the bass line from, analysing the whole thing and then dancing like mad!"

Besides, he still cherished other ambitions: "I thought I would have been playing football for [the] Wolves by now."

★ ★ ★

1991 flew by quickly after Plant took a break following the previous couple of hectic years. On April 20, 1992 he performed at the Freddie Mercury Tribute concert at a sold-out Wembley Arena. Televised globally, Plant performed with the remaining members of Queen: guitarist Brian May, drummer Roger Taylor and bassist John Deacon. Dressed in a flamboyant blue shirt, black trousers and lots of jewellery, he was in an energetic and fiery mood as he sang a couple of lyrics from 'Thank You' before bursting into Queen's hillbilly rock number 'Crazy Little Thing Called Love'. He also sang the epic 'Innuendo' which included bits of 'Kashmir' in the middle part; however, he unfortunately had mic problems for the first few lines of the song. It was Plant's biggest gig since Live Aid back in 1985.

Plant had further appointments to fulfil in his diary for 1992: he made a guest appearance at a Fairport Convention gig in Banbury in August, prior to playing with the band during their encore at the Cropredy Festival on August 14. Other than that he was occupied writing songs and gearing up for yet another new studio album.

★ ★ ★

Recording of his sixth full studio album – to be titled *Fate Of Nations* – commenced at the end of '92. Yet again, Plant formed a new band: Phil Johnstone, Doug Boyle and Charlie Jones continued to work for him but he hired guitarist Kevin Scott MacMichael previously of Cutting Crew, guitarist Francis Dunnery formerly of It Bites, plus drummers Peter Thompson and Michael Lee, formerly of The Cult.[52]

Fate Of Nations also featured a number of session musicians and guest appearances, most notably from violinist Nigel Kennedy, Clannad singer Moya Brennan, ex-Fairport Convention guitarist Richard Thompson and Nigel Eaton playing the hurdy gurdy.

The album was produced by Robert Plant and Chris Hughes, engineered by Michael Gregovich and mixed by Tim Palmer and Michael Gregovich. It also featured several second engineers: Henry Binns, Danton Supple, Jacquie Turner, Pete Lewis, John Cornfield, Ross Cullum and Mark O'Donoughe.

Chris Hughes: "Robert had played various tracks in various states of completion to his A&R man David Bates. I understand they both agreed that the tracks were not quite right. David suggested Robert and I should meet. We met along with Charlie Jones at Olympic Studios in Barnes, London. We listened to some tracks and I offered my opinions. We started recording fairly soon after that."

Plant was very particular about which studios he wanted to record in, as Hughes elaborates, "Sawmills [in Cornwall] and Monnow Valley [in south Wales] were studios Robert had been working in before I got involved. The bulk of the album was recorded at RAK [in London.] I think Robert was looking for a place with a good atmosphere where instruments would sound natural and strong. RAK is one of those robust rooms."

Chris Blackwell was credited as co-writer on some of the songs. He writes on his official website *www.chrisblackwell.co.uk*: "[I] wrote 'Calling To You' ... and 'Network News' with Robert before deciding to jump ship. Strange politics came into play – [very] interesting time for all concerned. Robert decided the band had run its course and sadly we parted company. [I] didn't play drums for six years after this. Lost interest ... [*Fate Of Nations*] did well but I felt strangely disconnected from it."

To shed some more light on the foundation of the lyrics, Chris Hughes explains: "Robert had lyrics in varying states of completion. I saw him come up with things on the spot and I saw him with lyric books. One thing he did quite often was to pop in a new line [and] drop in a new bit of singing in order to try out a newer lyric. He liked to update his lyrics from time to time."

In terms of the songs, did Plant have any notions about how he wanted the album to sound? Hughes: "It's quite difficult to talk about the sound of the album or any album for that matter. It's a lot easier *listening* to sound. I dare say we wanted the songs to rage at times and be reflective at other times. I think we got a fair amount sounding right. Robert is about performance. Performance is the first and most important aspect when trying to express emotion in music. You can have the most amazing sounding backing track in rock history, but if Pinky and Perky are handling the vocals ..."

Hughes recalls a creative recording process with only moments of tension: "*Fate Of Nations* had its stressful moments, but not by The Troggs standards. Often in studios you have technical faults which means everything can grind to a halt. This can be frustrating at the best of times and can lead to tension. Robert, however, had a knack of being piss funny when he could see frustration rising in others. When an artist can see the funny side of things, that's an immense help. I guess Robert – being a strong character – could whip up or disperse tension with ease.

Purely from a production point of view, some things could have turned out better. When you're recording, sometimes the tracks have a life span [which] you can't always gauge. If you rush them and don't pay enough attention to detail they can end up under-developed and immature; if you spend too long on them they can die right in front of you. Hitting that balance inside 'the recording whirlwind that is Robert Plant' wasn't always easy, but well worth having a crack at. He once told me he'd desperately wanted to have another go at singing 'Kashmir' but either there wasn't time or the first vocal was deemed good enough. You get to learn that something you find personally disappointing works just fine for someone else."

As shown on some of Plant's previous solo endeavours, he did enjoy having guest appearances and *Fate Of Nations* was no exception. Hughes: "I spent a lot of time with Kevin Scott MacMichael. He was a fine musician and a great guitarist. He was a quiet spoken and very patient man. I valued his opinions and help with arrangements, etc. We jammed in the studio a few times, I liked his playing … I guess Robert did too.

Moya Brennan used to come with Clannad to record at The Woolhall Studios where I used to work. We became friends and so it was a delight to have her come sing with Robert. She is a fabulous singer … Recording the Indian musicians was fun [and] recording Lynton Maiff's string arrangements was also rewarding."

Moya Brennan: " [Robert] had an idea of what sound he wanted on these two specific tracks. He wanted my 'ethereal, haunting voice.' Jokingly, I did check he knew what he was asking for because normally I don't do rock and he has one of the best known voices in rock history … [Robert and Chris] were brilliant, [they] let me do my own thing within their guidelines and apparently were thrilled with the results. As I say, I was a bit nervous but it was very exciting.

I was releasing a solo album in the USA shortly afterwards on Atlantic and when I walked into their offices in New York, one of the top guys came up to me and said, 'You never told us you were on the Robert Plant album!' So it was nice to know people recognized my voice even on a rock album! And I made loads of new friends in the company! The cherry on the cake was being sent a gold disc for my contribution which I'll always value."

Robert Plant was very taken with Nigel Kennedy, as he told *Kerrang!* in '93: "I think he's possibly the most refreshing individual I've come across in years. It's fantastic! … leave him to his own devices and let the conversation develop, and his knowledge of the better music that comes from the hard rock genre … he knows exactly what it's all about."

The great beast was occasionally the topic of discussion during the recording of *Fate Of Nations*. Hughes: "Robert spoke about Zep – as he referred to them – once in a while [but] always in the context of music and how they approached things, rarely (if ever) in the context of the sociology of the group. He didn't openly invite other people's speculations about Zep's approach to music. I remember having a difference of opinion with him once about some aspect of what we were doing, and he said, 'In Zep we used to do such and such …' and I said: 'How come you can bring up Led Zeppelin to support your argument but no one else can?' I continued: 'Let me tell you something about Zeppelin, you'll never ever know about and that's what it's like to be fifth row, centre, at the Albert Hall [in] 1970 [and] being blown away by an unstoppable raging 'Whole Lotta Love'. You've no idea what that's like, but I have.' He laughed, point taken. I think he may have even bought a round that evening."

Despite Plant's reputation as sometimes being a challenging man to work with, Hughes felt privileged to add the album to his curriculum vitae both as a producer, and at the request of Phil Johnstone and Plant, as a session drummer too. Hughes contributed his talents as a sticks-man to a number of tracks. "Robert's sense of humour is all pervasive," he enthuses. "He made me laugh so many times ... Robert is not a slow worker, he likes action [and] he likes results. But he is prepared to listen to other points of view, which inevitably might slow things down. He can spot a good idea coming at him when he hears one. In general, he would like his musicians quickly 'tuned in' to the idea and 'ready' for the song to come intuitively."

Recording was completed in early 1993. Hughes says, "I can't remember how long it took exactly, however ... I vividly remember my extremely pregnant wife coming to the studio to drag me off to hospital on the very last day of recording [on] February 6, 1993 ... Mixing came later."

After months of recording at three different studios during 1992/93, Hughes must have accumulated a number of opinions about what it was like to work with such a revered and literally untouchable rock singer. Indeed, his thoughts have not left him despite the passing of over ten years.

Hughes: "His knowledge of music is encyclopaedic; he can draw reference with great skill. He can get the basics of a track up and running in no time. He'll know if something is a bluff, instantly. I learned at close quarters what an amazing artist – not just a phenomenal singer – he is.

He was quite capable of walking into the room in seven-foot-viking mode ready for a battle; a battle of wits more often than not. He'll roast you if you take your eye off the ball. Seeing the artist at work was often exciting. His ability to create a situation from next to nothing or to raise the 'bar' on a track was always amazing ... [It was] an honour and a great opportunity – I got to work with a hero; he even let me play drums on a couple of things."

As engineer this time around, Phil Johnstone recalls: "I had a history of working with Robert and I also had a history of working with [his A&R man] Dave Bates. I'd mixed many projects for ... bands like Big Country, Texas, James, The Mission and House Of Love, lots of different types of music so it was good because Dave felt I could understand what he had to say and Robert also knew that he could trust me because we'd worked together a lot so it was quite useful for that record. As I was brought into mix it, I really didn't know much about the recording of it; we spent about three weeks at a studio called Westside, mixing away at the album. One of my favourite tracks was called '29 Palms' [and] I also really liked 'Calling To You'. I think that that's a fantastic record, *Fate Of Nations*; I really like it a lot. I think they managed to take Robert back into a more familiar territory, sound-wise, of the guitars and the organic sounds because it's sort of come full circle. Robert had gone through all this experimental stuff and then started to see the beauty in some of the stuff he did when he was younger ... I felt it was a very strong record."

★   ★   ★

As Plant was gearing up for the release of *Fate Of Nations* in March, 1993 Geffen Records released a hard-blues rock album called *Coverdale-Page* which featured Jimmy Page with former Deep Purple and Whitesnake main man David Coverdale. *Kerrang!* declared in its review of the album: "Who needs a Led Zep reunion? Planty must be seething."

Was Page looking for the kind of success with Coverdale that he'd achieved with the similarly looking and sounding Robert Plant? Coverdale confessed to a *Kerrang!* scribe Paul Elliot in 1993 that he was aware of Plant's lack of enthusiasm for him and despite reports to the contrary said he had met Plant a number of times going right back to his tenure in Deep Purple in the 1970s. Evidently his relationship with Jimmy Page was far warmer!

Despite having a Top 10 hit in the US *Billboard* Top 200 Albums with their only record, the Coverdale–Page project did not properly lift off the ground after tickets refused to shift at the speed the label wanted, so after some dates in Japan the project folded before Christmas, '93.

Coverdale and Page went their separate ways despite showing huge promise with their studio work. Coverdale formed another line-up of Whitesnake for the disappointing 1997 album *Restless Heart* and Page teamed up with an old collaborator after signing to Trinifold Management run by Bill Curbishley ... but more on that in the next chapter.

★   ★   ★

Fate Of Nations was released on May 1, 1993 in the UK and managed to climb to gold status by December 1. In the UK, Plant distributed his album through Phonogram/Fontana and in the States via Es Paranza/Atlantic. A Top 10 hit in the UK, *Fate Of Nations* failed to take off with the same gusto in the States, reaching Number 34 but staying in the charts for a respectable fourteen weeks. It also achieved Top 20 status in Sweden and New Zealand.

Fate Of Nations spawned the UK Top 20 single '29 Palms' which was named after a small Californian town but was about Plant's alleged relationship with Canadian singer Alannah Myles. However, despite their quality, 'I Believe' and 'If I Were A Carpenter' failed to ignite strong sales.

The critics were passionate in their praise for the album with many rightfully declaring it his best release since *The Principle Of Moments*. Deborah Frost wrote in *Rolling Stone*: "He's searching for more viable and eloquent means of expression ... Plant's always incredible voice finds a new temperature for sex ('29 Palms' – have mercy!) and plumbs new dimensions of strength and of sorrow. Plant's technical achievements alone attest that some of rock's greatest performers are, like any legendary vintage, only improving with time."

Billboard: "*Fate Of Nations* is rock 'n' roll arranging of a high order, redolent of early experimentalists like the Incredible String Band or Moby Grape on their first album, with Plant's vocals recalling the deep-soul entreaties of James Carr." *Entertainment Weekly:* "... [a] wonderfully textured and mature solo album, his best ever ..." *Musician:* "Having tired of the post-modernism that pervaded *Now And Zen,* Plant shifts gears and turns to ... hippie music? Well, sorta. Although the thrumming acoustics and Celtic modality hark [back] to *Led Zep III,* Plant's approach has less to do with nostalgia than emotional intensity ..."

Q Magazine included it in their list of 'The Best 50 Albums Of 1993' and enthused: "... this generously proportioned magic carpet ride over some varied, though well-signposted, terrain should be regarded as another notable notch on the belt ... the venerable vocalist's most ambitiously constructed album to date."

Fans and critics appreciated of Plant's back-to-basics approach. He has reportedly claimed that album's lighter folk and acoustic mood provided an escape from the carnage of the Gulf War in 1991; seeing such images on the television and in the newspapers on a daily basis disgusted him and he wanted to make a more organic and natural album. Melodic rock singer and Robert Plant fan, Tony Harnell, believes, "the vibe in all of his work is very organic and fresh and not over produced and I think that makes him sound real and connects him to the listener on a very deep level."

Fate Of Nations starts with the mature and melodic 'Calling To You' which features violinist Nigel Kennedy.[53] 'Down To Sea' weaves Moroccan influences with folk and acoustic melodies. 'Come Into My Life' features sultry backing vocals by Moya Brennan and evocative guitar work by Richard Thompson; Plant's voice is brooding and emotional. 'I Believe' is certainly one of the album's stand out tracks; it's an indelible and carefully composed song. '29 Palms' is a fantastic track with an allure that is infectious as it is undeniably charming. 'Memory Song (Hello Hello)' is one of the lamer songs on the album but 'If I Were A Carpenter' is completely absorbing and is especially moving because of the finely crafted string arrangements. 'Promised Land' is a heavier affair with Plant sounding forceful and energetic; there's also a pretty good electric guitar solo that's worth a mention. 'The Greatest Gift' is an over-sentimental ballad while 'Great Spirit' is very laid-back and moody with momentary flourishes of electric guitar. 'Network News' finishes the album in an upbeat and thirsty mood.

Fate Of Nations is an expertly and passionately orchestrated and composed album that remains possibly Plant's best solo endeavour to date. It's far removed from his preceding albums and thankfully some distance away from the pop electronics that had occupied him previously.

In 2007, *Fate Of Nations* was reissued in remastered and expanded form by Rhino Entertainment[54] and the reviewers were more than favourable with their choice of words. *All Music Guide* (*www.allmusic.com*): "At first, *Fate of Nations* seems so light and airy that it slips away through the layers of acoustic guitars, violins, and keyboards. Upon further listenings, more textures appear, and the album gains a calm sense of tension and reflectiveness."

Armed with a superlative album, Plant was ready to hit the road again. For this tour, Plant's band included guitarist/keyboardist Phil Johnstone and bassist Charlie Jones from his previous touring band, with guitarists Kevin MacMichael and Francis Dunnery and drummer Michael Lee.

The *Fate Of Nations* world tour began in Europe with the first gig in Rome on May 1, 1993. On May 14 and 20 they played the King's Head pub in Fulham, West London and billed themselves as the Band Of Joy. Declaring it 'Gig Of The Year', *Kerrang!* reviewed the second King's Head gig: "Bob was obviously enjoying himself, punching away the hot sweaty air, and continuously pushing back his golden locks … If anything Percy's voice has smoothened over the years, giving him far more range these days … he has a hell of a band behind him … the best Plant performance since Led Zep at Earl's Court 1975!"

The European dates ran through to August. It was Plant's biggest tour and surprisingly he even supported Lenny Kravitz on some dates as well as playing solo shows and recognised festivals such as Glastonbury in the UK, Midfyns in Denmark and Parkpop in Holland.

By the time Plant hit the States in September, there was some discontent in certain quarters of the band – guitarist Kevin MacMichael later quit and was replaced by the blues player Innes Sibun.[55]

The North American leg of the tour began in Florida on September 15. Innes Sibun: "I remember [touring America] being a real thrill; being a blues guitarist it was great visiting all the places where the blues started. When we played in Chicago, Robert got Buddy Guy and James Cotton to come to the gig and hang out, and James Cotton got up and played a couple of blues songs with us. Buddy is such a hero so just to talk with him made my day.

When we played in Austin, Texas we went down to Antone's Blues Club after the show and it turned out to be Clifford Antone's birthday party so everyone was up there jamming; I got to play with Tommy Shannon and Chris Layton from Stevie Ray Vaughan's band. Chris Duarte and all these other Texan blues guys; Don Henley from the Eagles was there too.

Another time was in Vancouver; we went to a club after the show and Robert and I played guitar with the guys from Bryan Adams's band and the singer from Mötley Crüe [Vince Neil] sang [with us] – that was fun.

We played two nights at the Orpheum Theater in Boston and on the first night I could see this guy at the side of the stage wearing a white scarf but as it was dark I couldn't make out who it was. Then Tim, my guitar tech, bought out my change of guitar [and] told me to play well as Jimmy Page was watching! It was a bit like being caught in bed with someone else's wife knowing that Jimmy was there watching Francis and me playing Led Zep songs with Robert! Jimmy was really cool about it though; he is a lovely guy. After the show we all went to the House Of Blues for a drink and people were going crazy to see Robert and Jimmy walk in together … the place went mad!"

Sibun has many fond memories of touring American with Robert Plant, he enthuses: "When we had a day off in Kansas, Robert, Charlie and myself got a cab and set off to find Vine, the street that is mentioned in the song 'Kansas City'. We found the sign in the middle of a park where the street used to be. Robert is so enthusiastic about music and I learned a lot from him." The guitarist also remembers the diverse set list which constantly changed. We played nearly everything off *Led Zeppelin II*: 'Babe I'm Gonna Leave You' and 'Your Time Is Gonna Come' from *Led Zeppelin*. [Also] 'Going To California' and 'Rock And Roll' from *Led Zeppelin IV* [and] 'Black Country Woman' from *Physical Graffiti*.

There was 'Set A' and 'Set B' which had been decided on before I joined the band and they were a mixture of songs from *Fate Of Nations*, other songs from Robert's solo albums and the Zeppelin songs. We also did some acoustic stuff like 'Bluebird' which is a Buffalo Springfield song. Robert gave us plenty of input into the songs. He is a really witty guy, very good fun to be with. We pretty much had free rein to play what we wanted to as long as it was within the framework of the original stuff."

The *Fate Of Nations* North American tour finished in New York on December 1. Plant played at the Paramount Theater, along way from his more glamorous days in Led Zeppelin when they enjoyed multiple sold-out nights at Madison Square Garden.

After the North American road jaunt, Plant headed back over the Atlantic to play some more dates in Europe before Christmas. Sibun: "I remember we had a really bad flight over the Alps from – I think it was Paris to Zurich – so we decided to travel by train for the rest of the European dates, which was good fun. The two dates in the UK were fun too: Wolverhampton Civic Hall and Brixton Academy where some of the road crew dressed up in a pantomime camel suit and ran across the stage as it was a few days before Christmas."

In early 1994, Plant ventured to South America where he and the band played gigs between January 15 and January 29 in Sao Paulo, Buenos Aires, Santiago, Rio de Janeiro, Caracas and Mexico City. Innes Sibun: "South America was an amazing experience; we started in San Paulo, Brazil where we played the Hollywood Rocks Festival with Aerosmith and Whitney Houston headlining the other two nights. We then did Hollywood Rocks in Rio which was wild, we had armoured car escorts from the hotel to the stadium and cops on motorbikes with rifles stopping all the oncoming traffic to let us through – it was crazy! We also played in Argentina, Venezuela and Mexico where we rushed straight from the show to do a TV programme called *En Vivo* which apparently went out to 300 million viewers. We mimed 'If I Were A Carpenter' and I ended up having a sitar to mime with and got a fit of the giggles; the whole programme was mad and unorganised but a great laugh."

The entire tour was an amazing experience for the guitarist: "I only toured for six months for the *Fate Of Nations* album ... [The gigs] were all great; I was bought up listening to Led Zep so to be on stage with Robert night after night playing Zep songs was a dream come true! He was a really easy person to work for and a great laugh too."

The *Fate Of Nations* album and tour was a total triumph but it was also the closing chapter of another phase in Plant's perpetually evolving career.

WALKING BACK TO
LED ZEPPELIN:
THE PAGE & PLANT YEARS
1994–1998

*"Jimmy and I wanted to go forwards rather than backwards.
I've wanted to play with Jimmy again for some time, but the idea
of rolling out the barrel with another drummer seemed obsolete."*
Robert Plant speaking to *Kerrang!* in 1994

It was Bill Curbishley – a legend in the business – who achieved what most would consider to have been a near-impossible task; having been Robert Plant's manager since 1986, he became Jimmy Page's manager in 1994 and with lots of behind-the-scenes discussions and persuasive talk, he finally got the pair to collaborate with each other again. Page always wanted to reform Led Zeppelin while Plant wanted to move on with his solo career, but that didn't mean they couldn't work together under their own names as Page had done with David Coverdale. Thus Page & Plant was born ...

Yet again blues guitar legend Alexis Korner played an integral role in the next important phase of Plant's career, even if it was from beyond the grave: on Sunday, April 17, 1994, Robert Plant, Jimmy Page and a host of other performers took part in a benefit concert at the 900-capacity Buxton Opera House in Derbyshire in memory of Korner, who influenced and aided so many blues artists of the 1960s including the Rolling Stones. Aside from some jamming, Page and Plant performed 'Baby Please Don't Go', 'I Can't Quit You Babe' and 'Train Kept A Rollin'.' They were joined by drummer Michael Lee and bassist Charlie Jones.

Of course, more rumours of a Led Zeppelin reunion flew around the press like a whirlwind but Plant was having none of it; he did, however, agree to form a new partnership with Jimmy Page for an MTV special to coincide with the then-popular *Unplugged* series. Plant spoke to *Kerrang!* in 1994 about the concept: "I couldn't envisage doing these songs again without Jimmy. *Unplugged* is a tired medium, so we decided to use a bit of grey matter and write some new songs. It was either that or give up, go home and watch the Wolves!"

Throughout August '94, they got together with an array of musicians and made a film of their performances with the intention of airing the footage on the successful music channel MTV. To give one a sense of the sheer size and spectacle of the production, the film featured, in total, the following musicians: Charlie Jones (bass guitar and percussion) Michael Lee (drums and percussion) Ed Shearmur (keyboards and organ, piano) Porl Thompson (guitars and banjo) Nigel Eaton (hurdy gurdy) Najma Akhtar (vocals) and Jim Sutherland (mandolin and bodhran).

The Egyptian Ensemble: Hossam Ramzy (percussion) Ali Abdel Salem (duf and bendir) Farid Khashab (bendir and reque) Farouk El Safi (duf and bendir) Ibrahim Adbel khaliq (bendir, merwas and finger cymbals strings) Wael Abu Bakr (soloist) Bahig Mikhaeel (strings) Hanafi Soliman (strings) Amin Abdel Azim (strings) Bashir Abdel Al (Nay – Egyptian bamboo flute) and Abdel Salam Kheir (oud).

Musicians in Marrakech: Brahim El Balkani, Hassan El Arfaoui, El Mahjoub El Mathoun and Abdelhak Eddahmane.

London Metropolitan Orchestra: Rosemary Furness (violin) David Juritz (violin) Rita Manning (violin) Elizabeth Layton (violin) Ian Humphries (violin) Perry Montague-Mason (violin) Mark Berrow (violin) Pauline Lowbury (violin) Clare Thompson (violin) David Ogden (violin) Peter Hanson (violin) Jeremy Williams (violin) Cathy Thompson (violin) Ed Coxon (violin) Anne Lorlee (violin) Harriet Davies (violin) Andrew Brown (viola) Rusen Gunes (viola) Andrew Parker (viola) Bill Hawkes (viola) Jane Atkins (viola) Nichalas Pendlebery (viola) John Jezard (viola) Caroline Dale (cello) Ben Chappell (cello) Cathy Giles (cello) Jonathan Tunnel and Stephen Milne (cello).

Hossam Razmy: "I was contacted by a few executive members of the team organising the recording of the album. I got a call from Mr. Rex King of Trinifold Management. Later on, I understood from Mr. Bill Curbishley – the director of Trinifold Management – that they were given my contacts by Real World Records, Peter Gabriel's company with whom I worked for several years. I also got another call from Ed Shearmur, the musical director and keyboardist of the project. And finally I got a call from Robert himself. They had all been searching for someone to do the Arabian and Middle Eastern arrangements for some of the songs. I did not believe the idea originally as I received so many phone calls over the same subject, I thought it was a hoax. But then I was very pleasantly surprised when I found out that it was for real!"

Hossam Ramzy was integral to the success of the project: "My role was originally as a helper to Ed Shearmur with the arrangements and percussion ... Then I realised that I needed to bring my own band and musicians. Then [I] became an organiser for them as well and then [I] became responsible for the whole Egyptian Middle Eastern side of it. And that was a tough job for me. It was not easy at all. The learning experience was much stronger than I ever imagined."

How did the rehearsals go?

Ramzy: "Ed [Shearmur] and I spent a lot of time together trying various ideas and sounds, rhythms and grooves and then we would test them at his home studio. I brought various musicians whom we had to listen and tried various modes and feels to the songs. Then Ed would present these ideas to Robert and Jimmy. Then we would bring my Egyptian musicians to a rehearsal with Robert, Jimmy, Charlie [Jones] and Michael [Lee.] We would try the idea live and see how it gelled together between us all. Some of the genres of sounds that I was experimenting with worked really well and were accepted immediately. Some were a bit hard to swallow but I kind of knew that this would happen.

Then we had to find the common ground for those types of arrangements until I personally had a realisation. It dawned on me that I [did] not [need to] change what I originally wanted as an arrangement. Arabian music and rhythms 'rock' in their own way. So does this music I am working with. I just needed to find the pivoting points between my rhythms and the rhythms of the songs. It was like a nova of delight when I presented the idea of the rhythms to the song 'Kashmir.' I realised that the best way for melting together these seemingly foreign cultures and styles of artistic creativity is to actually put the pure versions in the same bed and lay them next to each other without any watering down or even a single word of apology for being there."

The first filming sessions where held in Marrakech in Morocco on August 9 and 10. Those location shots on the streets of the city with the public looking on featured special guest musicians from the region. Ramzy was surprised by the amount of location filming that took place, as he explains: "Robert and Jimmy were doing some kind of musical pilgrimage or going back in time over their history and tracing back their roots of where they'd previously journeyed and where their trails of earlier experiences took them. You see, I personally saw and felt that the music of Zeppelin had so many influences of very diverse genres of music that fused together and became a sound of its own kind. You couldn't say this came from here or that came from there. It was what it was ... in all honesty and openness, they wanted to let the people see where and how they became who they were and who they are today and giving their audiences a chance to understand where their influences came from and introducing their personal likes and tastes. Allowing more of the colour to shine through and manifest."

After filming wrapped in Morocco, they travelled to Wales where Led Zeppelin had worked extensively in the 1970s. A week after the filming sessions in Morocco, Page & Plant and their entourage shot some more footage in Snowdonia and locations near Bron-Yr-Aur. Following on from that on August 25 and 26 they recorded live studio performances at London TV Studios on the South Bank by the River Thames. The London performances included a guest appearance by the London Metropolitan Orchestra.

Ramzy: "What I recall of the recording of the album was that it was very professionally done and so well organised that my personal fears about it being a live unplugged recording were disappearing moment by moment. I was very conscious of the fact that this is it. It had to be done on the day and no repeating and no over-dubbing. We had to be well and truly rehearsed and very tight as a band. So we spent the maximum time in rehearsals, discussions and meetings until we felt comfortable that all the members of the band were ready for the day. Of course this included Robert, Jimmy, Charlie Jones, Michael Lee, Ed Shearmur, Porl Thompson, Nigel Eaton, myself and my Egyptian Orchestra as well as the whole crew, sound and light engineers, not forgetting the tech crew as well. We were all prepared for it. I was particularly impressed with how the management arranged all of these points and all of these people and made us all ready for day. We had only two hours for live recording and that was our shot at it. And here you have it: an amazing album that truly changed the face of music in this world!"

As well as a set list of Zeppelin classics with a Middle Eastern flavour, they also performed their new song 'Wonderful One'. Producer Kevin Shirley, who later worked as a mixing engineer on the *No Quarter: Jimmy Page Robert Plant Unledded* DVD in 2004 told *Blog Critics Magazine* (*www.blogcritics.org*) that "I think those two guys really enjoy the flavours of the more exotic and indigenous instruments around the planet. I think that's always fired them up, even in Zeppelin, way back when."

Despite the magnitude of the concept, Ramzy recalls that Plant did make time to have conversations with his guest musicians: "We talked a lot and later on we became friends and discussed various musical ideas and suggestions. Robert also speaks some Arabic and I always encouraged him to speak it with me."

Of course, fans and critics wanted to know if Page and Plant were comfortable working with each other so intensely after more than a decade since the Led Zeppelin airship sank to the ground. Ramzy remembers a musically stimulating environment with no arguments.

Ramzy: "No. Unless if you call someone saying 'I think we should [use] that particular rhythm or arrangement instead of this rhythm or that arrangement,' a disagreement. But we all thought the same way. I suggested things. Some things were liked by Robert and Jimmy [and] some [things] were liked by only one of them. Some were not liked by Ed; some were hated by all, including myself. This doesn't make a disagreement. It is just the work of making amazing music."

Ultimately, the film united Western rock with traditional Middle Eastern music with electric and acoustic instruments. *No Quarter: Jimmy Page Robert Plant Unledded* was aired on MTV in the States on October 12, 1994 and on October 17 in Europe. A rockumentary on Led Zeppelin followed the UK transmission and included interviews with Page and Plant. The set list for the performance was: 'No Quarter', 'Thank You', 'The Battle Of Evermore', 'Gallows Pole', 'Nobody's Fault But Mine', 'City Don't Cry', 'Yallah', 'Wah Wah Wonderful', 'Since I've Been Loving You', 'Friends' and 'Kashmir'.

The 90-minute film was such a ratings success it even eclipsed Eric Clapton's 1992 *Unplugged* performance which rejuvenated the ex-Cream guitarist's career. To promote the film and its forthcoming CD and video, Page and Plant appeared on television together right up until the end of the year giving interviews and guest performances; they even visited as far away places such as Japan and Australia.

However, the film was not a hit with everyone, especially not John Paul Jones who joked that Page and Plant must have lost his phone number. He was also allegedly annoyed that the ex-Led Zeppelin pair decided to name the album *No Quarter,* a song which he co-wrote. He is reported as saying in *Kerrang!* in 1994: "They never asked me to do it, to be honest. The first time I heard it, I read it in the papers and I really haven't had any communication with them."[56]

No Quarter: Jimmy Page Robert Plant Unledded was given the full music business treatment and released on CD as simply *No Quarter* on October 14, 1994. The album was issued via Atlantic in the US and Fontana in the UK; by December it had gone gold and platinum having reached the Top 10 in both countries.

Only a few months later in 1995, the performance was issued as *No Quarter: Jimmy Page Robert Plant Unledded* on video; it included extra footage from the two MTV performances whereas the 14-track CD version merged songs from both nights as though it was one continuous gig. The originally released album and video was produced by Robert Plant and Jimmy Page and engineered by Mike Gregovich.

The critics were completely divided in their opinions of the album; some reviewers felt the Eastern flavours added an ambience and interesting texture to the Zep songs while others felt the reworkings did nothing but tarnish memories of Led Zeppelin's enduring legacy.

Anthony Decurtis wrote in *Rolling Stone*: "The album's closing track, 'Kashmir', also achieves an irresistible momentum as African, Indian and pure rock and roll motifs collide in a frenzy and shake the song to an ecstatic climax. It's a fitting end to a boldly imagined, thoroughly sensual musical journey."

Regardless of the critic's views, one of the record's main contributors, Hossam Ramzy, says, "The album became a milestone for the world of 'World Music Fusion'. It changed the lives of many musicians in the world and gave them the guidelines and licence to go off and experiment with various musical modes and scales. It gave the world a certain truth and gave the lovers of the old Led Zeppelin a chance to open yet another dimension in the warp to which they have travelled in the past with their music. And it is an incredible album to listen to."

The album gave birth to a trio of single releases in the UK: 'Gallows Pole' with 'Thank You' and 'City Don't Cry' with 'The Rain Song', and 'Four Sticks' with 'What Is And What Should Never Be' – all issued throughout December '94. Steffan Chirazi reviewed 'Gallows Pole' in an issue of *Kerrang!* and gave it a joyous review: "A classic song given some classic treatment," he wrote.

Most of the album's material was taken from Led Zeppelin's semi-acoustic third album *Led Zeppelin III,* which was hardly greeted with enthusiasm by most music journalists on its release. *No Quarter* begins with the mellow 'Nobody's Fault But Mine'[57] before the compelling 'Thank You' is played; Plant's voice is in fine shape and Page gives an equally satisfying performance. 'No Quarter' is delicately handled even though Plant's vocals are a little fuzzy while 'Friends' is haunting yet seductive. 'Yallah' is tenderly approached as is 'City Don't Cry'; perhaps it is the song which makes best use of the Egyptian musicians and backing vocalists. 'Since I've Been Loving You' has not lost any of its unmistakable supremacy. 'The Battle Of Evermore' is emotionally charged and simply the best song on the album; again, the Egyptian musicians augment the song's classic status and Najma Akhtar's vocals are outstanding. 'Wonderful One' lacks excitement and nerve but 'Wah Wah' is a quirky little number. 'That's The Way' is a highlight of the album, Plant sounds like he is at his most serene. 'Gallow's Pole' is a frenetic delight while 'Four Sticks' is another song with character and panache. Unfortunately, the string arrangements and orchestral work on 'Kashmir' hinder the strength and sheer pounce of the original; it suffers because of a lack of a central bass line but it's a bold attempt nonetheless.

Not every song on *No Quarter* works as well as anticipated but it's a worthy album and a genuinely passionate display of Page and Plant's love of music in all its guises.[58]

★ ★ ★

The famed South African-born producer Kevin 'Caveman' Shirley, who is renowned for his work on Iron Maiden's recent albums, remixed the original tapes of *No Quarter: Jimmy Page Robert Plant Unledded* in stereo and 5.1 surround sound for its first DVD release in 2004 to celebrate its tenth anniversary. He spoke to *Blog Critics Magazine* (*www.blogcritics.org*) in 2004 about the difficulty of the project: "Technically, it was very difficult," he explained, "there are edits in the program, and there were no notes about where the edits were. So it was very complicated – and actually, so complicated that I think you'll find that some of the versions of the songs are quite different from some of the original versions ... None of them had any relation to the old mixes."

Surprisingly, Page and Plant took a back seat and let Shirley work his magic as he told *Blog Critics Magazine* (*www.blogcritics.org*): "They were involved in the listening process; I think that Jimmy was very much behind me doing my thing for it ... [They] definitely didn't baby sit the whole program."

When the DVD was reviewed in *Classic Rock*, Paul Henderson wrote: "Lauded and lambasted in various quarters upon its release, the audio recording can be seen at the same time as a musical triumph, and a memory-shattering disappointment, and a reminder that, over time, although the song may indeed remain the same, the way it is heard and the performing of it does not. So whatever else you might expect from this *No Quarter: Unledded* DVD, don't expect Led Zep."

Edward B. Driscoll, Jr. enthused in *Vintage Guitar* magazine: "Throughout the DVD, percussion and strings frequently appear out of the rear channels, enveloping the viewer into the sound ... If you enjoyed last year's Zeppelin DVD, you'll enjoy *Unledded*."

The popular online magazine *musicOMH* (*www.musicomh.com*) were more enthusiastic about the DVD: "The pair [Page and Plant] clearly bonded deeply with the culture they encountered and it's a chance to see them not as rock gods but as people humbled and appreciative of other musicians ... what a breath of fresh air this half-musical travelogue, half-live concert DVD is."

One reviewer wrote on the website *DVD Movie Guide* (*www.dvdmg.com*): "While the show offers a restrained visual presentation, it didn't eliminate hard electric rock from the equation ... the program features a strong band and fares nicely in musical ways. Plant's voice isn't what it used to be, but he sounds very good during these shows. The band holds up their end of the bargain as well ... Page & Plant make sure that they do more than simply present emasculated versions of their songs. It's a strong show."

★　★　★

In 1995, after the success of the album, it was almost inevitable that the pair would hit the road for a tour of some sort, but it came as a welcome surprise at how lengthy the jaunt was going to be. Indeed, as soon as the tour began, sales of *No Quarter* hit the one million mark, which is a robust figure (albeit not nearly as healthy as the sales of any of Led Zeppelin's albums circa 1971–1975).

Labelled the 'Jimmy Page/Robert Plant World Tour', and using the headline 'The Evolution Of Led Zeppelin Continues ...' the marketing of the tour was a blatant reference to Led Zeppelin's legacy, much to the anger of dedicated Zep fans and indeed John Paul Jones.

The touring line-up was basically what Page & Plant used for their MTV performances: guitarist Porl Thompson, drummer Michael Lee, bassist Charlie Jones, keyboardist Ed Shearmur with Nigel Eaton playing the hurdy gurdy and percussionist Hossam Ramzy, who was accompanied by his group of Egyptian musicians called the Egyptian Ensemble. A local orchestra was added to most shows but not all; obviously the logistics of organising such an endeavour could not always go according to plan.

Hossam Ramzy: "I don't think that you will have enough time, ink or paper to put all the memories [from that tour] down. But I can tell you that it was like being born into a new world that I could only look at from the outside and imagine that it existed. I toured a lot in the past with various artists and with my own band. But this was something else ... You just don't believe it is happening to you or you are actually experiencing this.

The difficult part was to stay in touch with the reality of the real world and not get sucked into the magical mystery of this delicious universe of total stardom. You had to keep your feet firmly on the floor. Do the job at hand. Think of the past, present and future as well as have fun and savour the moment.

Also, leading seven other Egyptian musicians and dealing with their experience of the same thing was quite a job in its own right. But again, I thank Bill [Curbishley] and Rex [King] for helping me through my learning experience with that ... They helped me deal with it all and taught me many things about the business of touring and managing that I started taking each day as it came."

The American leg of the Page & Plant world tour began at the Pensacola Civic Arena in Florida on February 26, 1995. During the sold-out dates, *Kerrang!* reported that during one of two consecutive nights at the Palace of Auburn Hills in Michigan, Jimmy Page was almost stabbed by a crazed fan who got right up close to the guitarist when he was playing 'Kashmir'. It was claimed that there was a satanic link and the 23-year-old fan "hoped to banish the spirits he 'saw' circulating around Page!" Page was unaware of any incident and the fan was later imprisoned.

After playing in Detroit, they hit States such as Pennsylvania and New Jersey like the proverbial storm. Author and rock writer Neil Strauss reviewed one of the two shows Page & Plant played at the Meadowlands in East Rutherford, New Jersey in *The New York Times*. He wrote: "[They] focused on the dynamics that made Led Zeppelin's music distinctive instead of the heaviness that made it influential. The visually sparse, sixteen-song concert, in front of a sold-out crowd of 19,558, was structured to provide a fair retrospective of Mr. Page's and Mr. Plant's careers ... Though Mr. Page's guitar was often turned down too low and Mr. Plant couldn't hit all the high notes he used to, Mr. Page's exacting, effective guitar solos and Mr. Plant's preternatural moan made their songs about possessing women and being obsessed with them, about obsessing on blues songs and being possessed by them, seem relevant even when separated from the vigour of youth."

Before hitting California, they played in Massachusetts, Ohio, Indiana, Illinois, Wisconsin, Minnesota, Missouri, Colorado, Arizona and Colorado. A review of Page & Plant's gig at the 14,000-capacity San Diego Sports Arena on May 13 was published on the e-zine *Vintage Rock* (*www.vintagerock.com*): "From the opening notes of 'Thank You' to the final crescendo of 'Kashmir', Page, Plant and a consortium of support musicians that backed them, kept the pace alive and exciting, yet never predictable ... What is most interesting about this 'reunion' is that the songs are not being recycled for purposes of easy satisfaction ... In San Diego, the fans would have been just as receptive had the songs remained the same."

The US tour finished at The Gorge Amphitheatre in Washington on May 27. After touring America quickly, Page and Plant – along with their entourage – hit Europe in June playing France, Italy, Netherlands, Germany, Sweden, Denmark, Spain and Switzerland before arriving in their native country for an arena tour. During the tour of mainland Europe they also squeezed in a performance at Glastonbury Festival on June 25.

Hossam Ramzy: "[Plant] has a magnetism that only he is in charge of. He knows how to use it on and off stage. He commands the masses and he loves performing for the few. Giving that same energy to 120,000 people and presenting the same flow [of energy] to an audience of 500. This is a quality of a genius."

The Madrid Philharmonic Orchestra joined the band for several songs at the Madrid Palacio de Deportes on July 5, which was extensively reviewed in *The Music Box* (*www.musicbox-online.com*): "The show began with a bouncy medley of 'The Wanton Song', 'Bring It On Home', and unfortunately an abridged version of 'Whole Lotta Love'/'Dazed And Confused', perhaps the most explosive and gut-wrenching song in Zeppelin history. This night, they gave us a diluted two-minute tease of their thunderous hallmark, as though trying to format the track for AM radio. It was a colossal disappointment … no black magic, no pubescent, no fish-stuffed vaginas, but the Horned One himself, surely in attendance that night, had to be smiling as he watched the mighty airship Zeppelin take to the clouds once more."

The UK tour kicked off in Scotland on July 12 and finished with two dates at Wembley Arena on July 25 and 26; in between they also played dates in Birmingham, Dublin, Cornwall, and Poole.[59]

Following on from the UK tour, they journeyed back over the Atlantic Ocean, playing their first dates in Mexico on September 23 and 24. The second leg of the US tour finished with two sold-out nights at New York's Madison Square Garden on October 26 and 27. Touring-wise, that was it for 1995 but they returned the following year for a tour of South America in January followed by a road jaunt around Japan in February which included five nights at the Budokan Hall in Tokyo. By this point, there had been a change in the band; Porl Thompson had left so Page went completely solo. Furthermore, they travelled to Australia where they played shows in Sydney, Brisbane and Melbourne. The last date on the touring calendar was March 1.

Hossam Ramzy: "There is only one thing that always makes me laugh whenever I remember it: after our last concert in Melbourne, Australia in March, 1996, we were all hugging and kissing and just could not believe that it was all over. Robert came and hugged me, put his left arm over my right shoulder, looked at me and said, 'Hossam … Ya Sahby' which means, 'Hossam, my dear friend in Arabic.' I said, 'Yes Robert?' with tears in my eyes. He said, 'Having been together on this project for at least two and a half years, I want you to know that no matter what happened on or off the road, no matter who said what to whom or who did whatever, no matter who thought what and no matter what problems we faced together in this tour … I still think you are a bastard!'

"And I suppose, knowing Robert very well, this was his own way of saying 'I love you' to me. Come to think about it … this was better than many 'I love you's' that I have ever been told before."

The pair sparked a long lasting friendship: "We are very connected and he calls me almost regularly about all sorts of things with his music and I also call him to ask [for] his opinion about various things … on some of my songs. Robert also invites me to the rehearsals and tours and I do the same. He came to see my band's concert in Bristol in September, 2006.

Also, we are connected in another familiar way. His daughter, Carmen, is one of the great Egyptian Middle Eastern Dancers who has also studied with my wife and myself [at] our Egyptian Dance School in the UK. Carmen danced with us in Bristol and another amazing thing is that her husband, Charlie Jones ... was the Best Man at my wedding ... I met my wife Serena, who is from Sao Paulo, while we were on tour in Brazil!"

★   ★   ★

It may have been the end of the world tour but it was not quite the end of the Page & Plant collaboration. The pair made the unlikely decision of recording a full-length studio album together, their first since Zeppelin's last album *In Through The Out Door*.

The album was christened *Walking Into Clarksdale*, a reference to the legendary city which sits in the Mississippi Delta; the genesis of the blues can be traced back to Clarksdale, it's the place where Robert Johnson allegedly sold his soul at the crossroads in exchange for mastery of the blues guitar and the popularly recognised Delta Blues Museum is based there. It was obvious that they were revisiting their past and the music that had inspired them to learn their respective crafts in the first place.

Remarkably, *Walking In Clarksdale* took just 35 days to record at the famed Abbey Roads studios in London; sure, it's a long time compared to the short breaths it took Led Zeppelin to carve out their first few albums, but it's also incredibly short in comparison to some standards (perhaps the most obvious example being Guns N' Roses as yet unreleased opus *Chinese Democracy* has taken close to a decade to make at the cost of several million dollars).

Walking In Clarksdale was produced by Page & Plant and co-produced and engineered by Steve Albini who gave the album a modern touch. Based in Chicago, Albini had by that point – late '97 – worked wonders on albums by PJ Harvey, Cheap Trick and Bush. Page and Plant were both impressed by Albini's production of PJ Harvey's *Rid Of Me*. "Well, we were looking around at all the people who could be at the desk while we were on the studio floor," Plant informed *Yahoo! Music* in 1998. "Despite England having a revival of guitar music ... we were under the impression that most of the engineers out there work in a very sterile way ... So we contacted Steve ... and we thought he was so conscientious and really right on the ball that we talked to him on the phone and that was it."

Indeed, it was integral for Page and Plant – two older, legendary rock stars, highly revered in many circles – to hook up with a young, hip producer to give them a modern, polished sound.

In Britain especially, straight-forward rock and roll bands were seen in vogue. Oasis, Blur and Pulp spearheaded the major mid-1990s cultural

149

movement known as 'Britpop'. With influences ranging from Slade, Led Zeppelin via The Who to The Clash, the Sex Pistols, The Smiths and The Stone Roses, those bands became the epitome of what was termed 'Cool Britannia'. 1997 also saw a change in British government; fed up with the high taxes and strikes under Conservative leadership, Tony Blair led 'New' Labour into power for the first time since Harold Wilson's Labour Party took victory in 1974. And for the first time since the 1960s, Britain became universally popular for producing a spate of top rated bands. Although not strictly Britpop, politically minded rock bands like Radiohead and The Manic Street Preachers also achieved notable success in the period.

On the other side of the pond, angst-ridden grunge music had by now imploded. The suicide of Nirvana's troubled lead singer Kurt Cobain brought a sad end to that controversial era. A less intellectual genre of music known as nu-metal – a fusion of rap and metal – dominated the US charts in the mid-to-late-1990s with moronic bands like Limp Bizkit achieving bafflingly high album sales although two other more talented bands, namely, Korn and Linkin Park, would go on to outlive the fleeting high profile of that genre.

Clearly Page & Plant had to prove that they could still make interesting music if they were to be taken seriously and make it into the Top 10 in both Britain and America. And if they could sell themselves in those two countries the rest of the world would surely follow suit.

No Quarter was a very ambitious undertaking but *Walking Into Clarksdale* was considerably low-key in comparison. The album featured the following musicians: Charlie Jones (bass and percussion) Michael Lee (drums and percussion) Timothy Whelan (keyboards) Ed Shearmur (programming, string pads) and Lynton Naiff (string arrangements).

Plant told *Yahoo! Music* at the time of the album's release: "This one [*Walking Into Clarksdale*] is Jimmy and I, the power writers in the band [Led Zeppelin.] It's just another day in the life of us as songwriters. You can only tell when you've got a lot of distance between yourself and the music."

★ ★ ★

Released in the UK on April 11, 1998, the single 'Most High' preceded the release of the album and was a Number 1 hit on the US *Mainstream Rock Charts*.[60] 'Shining In The Light' was also released as a single later in the year but there was little fanfare, although it did make it into the Top 10 in the US *Mainstream Rock Charts*. Also, 'When The World Was Young' was issued as a promo in the States, which saw a congratulatory nod from *Billboard*: "The production is magnificent. You feel that you're in the room with the guys, watching them jam up a little history. The live sound of the cut, and its ambling, spontaneous feel, are pure pleasure …"

Walking In Clarksdale was released via Mercury in the UK (Atlantic released the album in the States) on April 21, 1998 and was certified gold as early as May. It was a Top 10 hit in both the US and UK and went into the Top 10 in France, Sweden, Russia and the Czech Republic and even reached the top spot in Bulgaria. It achieved Top 20 status in Sweden, Germany, New Zealand and Canada. But similarly to *No Quarter*, sales of the album were expected to be even higher considering the involvement of both of Led Zeppelin's chief songwriters.

On the whole, the major music critics appeared to like the album, giving it a reasonable review: Josef Woodard wrote in *Entertainment Weekly*: "Plant's Moroccan-blues swagger and Page's unmistakable, scruffy-smart guitar touch come together beautifully. This song set sounds both vintage and, thanks to the lingering Zep craze, of the moment."

Tom Doyle wrote in *Q*: "Page & Plant's first complete studio album together in the nineteen years since *In Through The Out Door* may well have been perfect. Instead, perhaps, mercifully, by the grace of the mighty Thor, *Walking Into Clarksdale* is less second coming, more second honeymoon."

On the other hand, some major music websites and online fanzines were more eager to voice their obvious complaints: Stephen Thomas Erlewine wrote in the *All Music Guide* (*www.allmusicguide.com*): "Much of the album disappears under its own mass, since there are no well-written songs, catchy riffs, or memorable melodies to support the sound. And that's what makes *Walking Into Clarksdale* so frustrating – you can hear the potential, and even enjoy the album on the musical surface, but there's nothing to make you return to the album once it's finished."

The Daily Vault (*www.dailyvault.com*): "The difficulty with *Walking Into Clarksdale* isn't the lack of crunchy Page solos … It's not that *Walking Into Clarksdale* is a bad album, but knowing the history these two musicians have with each other – and there's the danger of comparing this to Led Zeppelin coming to the forefront again – it doesn't hold up as well. It still turns out to be a very entertaining album, especially when given a real chance with repeated listenings."

Salon Entertainment (*www.salon.com*): "All told, the album doesn't rattle as much as hum … and neither Page nor Plant has the same talent for arrangement as their old Zeppelin mate, John Paul Jones. Still, some drippy lyrics not withstanding, the pair succeeds in demonstrating that grown-up guitar rock needn't be a contradiction in terms."

Walking Into Clarksdale commences with the laid-back semi-acoustic 'Shining In The Light' which would have fitted comfortably on *Led Zeppelin III*. 'When The World Was Young' is a reflective, sombre opus almost miserable but brilliantly played. 'Upon A Golden Horse' includes some string arrangements but unfortunately it fails to ignite much interest. 'Blue Train' is the heaviest song thus far into the album but it lacks confidence and esteem. 'Please Read The Letter' plods through the motions but 'Most High' is an imaginative song with some wonderful Middle Eastern influences; Ed Shearman lays down the strong pad and programming parts and Tim Whelan plays the oriental keyboard – it's quite easily one of the album's better songs. 'Heart In Your Hand' is slightly tiresome but the excellent title track has some of the ingredients of early Zeppelin and one can sense Page's guitar screaming to break free under tight restraint. Plant sounds especially poetic on 'Burning Up' and Page's guitar flourishes quite remarkably. 'When I Was A Child' is a thoughtful but slightly mawkish tune and 'House Of Love' is a dull drone but 'Sons Of Freedom' picks up the pace with both Messrs Page and Plant sounding suitably fiery and energetic.

Inevitably, *Walking Into Clarksdale* does not hold up against the quality of Zeppelin's first few masterful albums – too much time had elapsed and the spark that ignited so much creativity between Page and Plant had disappeared into the pages of rock history. Fundamentally, the album lacks the electric powerhouse riffs of Jimmy Page and the wailing vocals of a young Robert Plant, which everybody expected it to have in abundance. "When it comes to recording new material, I want to try new material," Plant told *Yahoo! Music* in '98. "I don't want to be a guy who's singing notes that only attract dogs and strange wild animals."

Sure, *Walking Into Clarksdale* represents where Page & Plant were at the end of the twentieth century; two middle-aged storytellers who wanted to express themselves differently, albeit in a more mellow and melodic mood. However, context set aside, one can't help feel it was an anti-climax.

Were Page & Plant ready for another world tour? Surprisingly, yes. The major difference between the 1998 world tour and the one they did to promote *No Quarter* was how small the stage and the band seemed in comparison; it was a significantly stripped down show. The duo stuck with the services of drummer Michael Lee, bassist Charlie Jones and keyboardist Phil Andrews but disbanded everything and everyone else, which effectively gave more power to the Led Zeppelin songs.

The tour initially commenced in Croatia on February 21, 1998. Then they played Hungary, Czech Republic, Poland, Romania, Bulgaria and Turkey before coming back to the UK in March for two special nights at the relatively small Shepherd's Bush Empire in west London. They also found time for some promotional activities, making appearances on two popular but now defunct programmes, *Top Of The Pops* and *TFI Friday*. They also flew to France to appear on TV and play a show at the La Cigale in Paris.

The North American leg of the tour kicked off in Florida on May 19. After touring the South, they moved up to the Mid-West and then played a show at the Molson Amphitheater in Toronto on July 4. The gig was reviewed by Greg Oliver on the Canadian entertainment website *Jam Music!* (*http://jam.canoe.ca*): "On stage, the magic was still there. Plant, flowing locks blowing with the wind, bounding around stage like a kid, making jokes with the audience and cheering on his guitarist. In lieu of an intermission, the aged rockers did two acoustic songs while seated. A terrific version of 'Going To California' led nicely into 'Tangerine', the stage bathed in appropriate orangey tones."

They then toured the East coast which included an evening at a packed Madison Square Garden in New York on July 16, just a short few days before the end of the American leg. Richard Skanse reviewed the Madison Square Garden gig in *Rolling Stone*: "The songs remained the same and Page & Plant made no apologies for it ... the evening's best moments were 'Babe I'm Gonna Leave You' and the new 'Most High' ... although the whole *of Physical Graffiti* could have been played in the time it took the band to leave the stage after their extended display of waving and bowing to the crowd. Such stadium rock indulgence is their due, though – and more power to them – but it was hard not to feel short changed by the time they finally left and the house lights came on."

After touring the US, they flew back to Europe for some important festival performances including a heart-stopping gig at Reading Festival in England on August 28.

Then, it was back to North America yet again, beginning in Vancouver, Canada on September 5. Before coming back to the UK in October they ventured to such states as California, Nevada, Texas, Arizona, Tennessee and Louisiana. Troy J. Augusto reviewed their gig at the Hollywood Bowl, California on September 19 in the US entertainment paper *Variety*: "The show, which included plenty of close-ups on two large video screens, was a good mix of well-known, straight-ahead tracks ... [The] concert peaked mid-set, during a long reading of the bluesy 'How Many More Times' from Zeppelin's first album in 1969."

The surprisingly short UK tour began with two shows at the SECC in Glasgow on October 30 and November 2. From there they played the huge *Manchester Evening News* Arena on November 3 and then they journeyed down south for two final dates at Wembley Arena. Giving their performance nine marks out of ten, Dave Ling reviewed the first night for *Classic Rock* magazine and concluded his glowing review by saying, "how good it was to hear Plant hitting all the notes, and the audience threatening to drown him. And what else but 'Black Dog' and 'Rock And Roll' to seal a magnificent performance? They've still got it, and don't let anyone tell you otherwise..."

Magnus Mills reviewed the same gig in *The Independent*: "What of the Plant voice, patented in 1969 and imitated ever since? ... Robert yodeled comfortably along, surfing easily on Page's guitar-generated waves. Yes – the same voice. Stools were produced for 'Going To California', which apparently started the 'request' section of the gig. There were moments during this song when the guitar and vocal parts actually became indistinguishable … Page & Plant look as if they're heavily into this new stuff, performing with much more seriousness than when they lapse into the 'easy' songs, for example 'Whole Lotta Love'."

The rest of the '98 touring schedule concentrated exclusively in mainland Europe playing, amongst other countries, France, Germany and Italy. The final gig was held at the Palais Omnisports in Paris on December 10.

Despite the critical acclaim, by the end of 1998 Plant had grown disenfranchised with the live set list and was becoming less enamoured with the whole Page-Plant collaboration. He was increasingly uncomfortable playing the same Zeppelin songs night after night in different countries. "The reality is that Page is a very clever, talented guy who has a particular slant on music," Plant confessed to Chuck Klosterman at *Spin* magazine in 2002, "and I was always his sidekick who had a different slant on music."

Reportedly, Plant decided to abruptly break off the collaboration even though Jimmy Page appeared happy to continue touring. Tours of Australia and Japan scheduled for 1999 should have followed. No one really knows why Plant decided to move to pastures new. Spending months on the road clearly forced Plant to revise his thoughts but he was clearly a little hasty when he prematurely told *Yahoo! Music* that he was a happy chap: "I can't put it into words, really. Perhaps we're more tolerant than we used to be with ourselves and with everybody else. We can now predict the tempo of how we work … This is a new chapter; we spend a lot more time together. We do a lot of laughing now – mostly at ourselves, I think."

After more than a decade since the end of Led Zeppelin and of being at the helm of his own career, Plant was uncomfortable in the present status quo. He didn't want another artist – especially such an ex-colleague as Mr. Page – effectively having such a fundamental role in his career; the only option as far as he was concerned was to leave the project.

Jimmy Page was interviewed by Nick Kent for a *Q Special Edition* issue on Led Zeppelin and asked about the demise of the Page & Plant collaboration. He said: "I wanted to keep working but Robert wouldn't hear any of it. Also, I wanted to eventually bring in John Paul Jones, but it was hard enough getting two of us together, never mind three."

Perhaps Plant felt that he'd worked too hard to gain credibility as a solo star and didn't want to lose that? Perhaps he felt that with the Page & Plant project, he'd lost momentum and wanted to pick up where he left off? Whatever his reasons, he moved back to the Midlands to recharge his batteries and ponder the future of his career.

Certainly, with Plant walking away from his collaborator, yet another nail had been hammered in the coffin of any potential Led Zeppelin reunion. "Everyone has their own agenda," Page confessed to Nick Kent. "Maybe, at this point in time, it's just too late."

Yet another chapter was closed …

Surely there was no hope for a reunion now?

BACK TO BASICS:
THE PRIORY OF BRION
1999–2000

"It's a long way from the king of cock rock."
Robert Plant speaking to *Folk Roots Magazine* in 2000

At the beginning of 1999, Robert Plant was 50-years-old and in the mood for reflection.

It was obvious that Robert Plant needed some breathing space from the large arenas that he'd been performing in and filling up with Jimmy Page as well as from the bright glare of the media spotlight – even as a successful solo artist, he was not that familiar with having so much coverage on television, radio and in the newspapers and magazines so, to circumvent his frustration, he formed a brand new back-to-basics band peculiarly called the Priory Of Brion.

Where does this odd name derive from? Plant's interest in mystics, religion and history filtered through yet again into his music and with typical humorous style: Priory Of Brion is an odd amalgamation of the highly-controversial French secret society Prieuré de Sion (Priory Of Sion in English) and the Monty Python classic comedy film *The Life Of Brian*. Drummer Andy Edwards says, "I think Robert liked the Monty Python film as the character gets mistaken for the Messiah when he was just a normal bloke."

Since the 2003 publication of *The DaVinci Code* by Dan Brown, interest in the Priory Of Sion has increased to enormous levels but Plant had already familiarised himself with the controversial group which according to Brown was founded in 1099. "When we looked into the history of the

Priory of Sion," says Edwards, "I think one of its leaders was a Monsier Le *Plant*ard so that was another funny connection."

For another reason, the Priory Of Brion was also a special project for Plant in that he teamed up with his ex-Band Of Joy colleague, guitarist Kevyn Gammond. "Kevyn's my best pal," he told *Folk Roots Magazine* in 2000. "We've always been friends although there was a gap in the middle of about fifteen or twenty years when I went mad."

Edwards: "I was teaching with Kev at Kidderminster [College] on the music course ... I taught music there between 1994 and 1998. At the time, Kev was just a lecturer there, he wasn't head of music. It was a joint music and drama course and Kev and I did some really quite avant-garde performances ... I had met Robert a few times too. I can remember being asked to rehearse at Kidderminster College one weekend and Robert turned up and we started playing ..."

Joining Plant and Gammond was fellow West Midlanders bassist Paul Wetton, drummer Andy Edwards and keyboardist Paul Timothy. Edwards: "[The] one thing that has always annoyed me is that The Priory was [reported variously to be] made up of 'local' musicians who weren't that great. In actual fact, these guys [Wetton and Timothy] are *incredible* players, both with a heavy jazz background. And although we weren't possibly that right for a project like The Priory, there is no doubt in my mind that these guys could play as good as anyone else who has passed through Robert's bands in the past."

The seeds of the project were actually grounded in 1997 when they played a gig at Brewley Tennis Court. "Robert asked Kevyn if he would like to play a little charity gig for his local tennis club," recalls Andy Edwards. "I got my mate Mark Hartley to play bass and we formed a little band. It wasn't really a Priory gig [as such] but it was [us] playing 'Morning Dew' and stuff like that. We did the gig playing old cover versions and Robert really enjoyed [it] and we kept on playing, even though the gig had happened. So it was definitely the beginning of the idea of doing that. On the night, I remember thinking I probably wouldn't get to play with Robert again so I tried to make the most of it. But at the time Robert was doing the Page & Plant thing and I think he had to go away and do that. Obviously the idea stuck in his head because in '99 I got [a call] from Kev saying Robert wanted to do something similar."

Similarly to The Honeydrippers (Plant's first post-Led Zeppelin project), the Priory Of Brion was an entirely therapeutic experience for him. What marked Priory Of Brion out from any other Plant solo endeavour was that Plant never intended them to record an album together which, as he told *Folk Roots Magazine* in 2000, gave the project "a kind of purity." Nor did he want them to play any Led Zeppelin material. "We actually went into the studio twice and recorded a total of about six songs," explains Andy Edwards. "Some of these recordings were reworked and appeared on some of the compilation CDs put out by Kevyn Gammond and his Mighty Atom Smasher[61] project which he runs at Kidderminster College."

The project was simply a return to Plant's roots; he wanted to go back to his 1960s youth and re-live those years via the blues, folk and R&B that inspired him, indefinitely. In other words, his aim was to play material by Moby Grape, The Youngbloods, Tim Rose, Tim Buckley, Buffalo Springfield, Jefferson Airplane and, of course, one of his favourite bands ever – Love. Speaking to *Folk Roots Magazine* in 2000, Plant refused point blank to label The Priory's music rock but "folk rock. Or perhaps we should call it 'frock'."

Not only did the Priory Of Brion give Plant the impetus to reacquaint himself with his childhood and adolescent idols but also his fans; in an arena packed with thousands of screaming people each voice can get lost amongst the sound of the band and the more over-zealous, hysterical fans. The band spent the first few months of 1999 rehearsing and arranging material for the modest-sized tour.

Edwards: "We tried to not turn up to sound checks if we could and Robert was seldom there. I remember the rehearsals to be really enjoyable. Robert would bring in a bunch of old records, all sorts of things. As well as the stuff we did like Moby Grape and Love, we tried out stuff by Dionne Warwick, Mel Torme, Joni Mitchell, etc. Then Robert would often usually leave us and we would start working an arrangement out between us, often changing the mood of the song quite dramatically. Then Robert would return and either like it or hate it. Often Robert would have a guitar and we would jam with that. Sometimes we would just be jamming and Robert would come in and start jamming a song over the top of what we were doing. He is very good at that! I think it's fair to say Robert likes to get involved in all aspects of the process, he was interested in my drum sound, the type of fills and solos we did, everything really." Inevitably, with such a thirst for classic popular music, there was an immense back catalogue of other artist's music to trawl through.

Edwards: "Robert pretty much decided the set list and, usually, just before we went on stage. If you ever see a Priory set list you will see they are handwritten, usually by me just before playing! Robert used to say that these were the songs behind the songs so I think the set was designed to cover all the strands that had informed his and Kevyn's development as musicians, so there was a fair selection covering stuff from the 1950s and 1960s, i.e. psychedelic, folk, garage, soul, R&B, blues, etc. Basically, all the stuff that was in the melting pot of Robert's formative years."

Of course, the Priory Of Brion was Plant's brainchild but exactly how much creative input did the other members have? "There was nothing stopping us suggesting songs for The Priory," says Edwards, "but Robert's and Kev's knowledge was so much greater than ours of these genres we didn't really have much to add. I think this was actually a barrier to the development of the band."

Clearly Edwards, Paul Timothy and Paul Wetton were much younger than Plant and Gammond, so it took them a great deal of practice to become acquainted with the songs.

Edwards: "Our influences were a lot different to Robert's and Kev's. This was actually a surprise to me as Zep was one of my favourite bands and had opened the door to so much music when I was a kid, music on the whole that Robert really disliked! I had come up in the post-punk New Wave era so that had an influence. I was also into a lot of jazz and fusion too. Robert was really open to this, however, I remember dragging him to see Billy Cobham, my idol, and he watched intently and had a lot of positive things to say. Also, I must say that The Priory did open me up to so much stuff and now I'm older I get what Robert was trying to do a lot more. I get country music now! So, no, we didn't have that much input into the song choices. I suggested playing the song 'Sunny' which I think we played once or twice and the middle section of our version of 'White Rabbit' was kinda taken from 'Bitches Brew' by Miles Davis, so our influences did creep in. I always felt the best thing we played was 'Darkness, Darkness' where we really got to show our influences as a band."

Touring began almost immediately after rehearsals, playing their first shows in various pubs and clubs in the summer of 1999; however, Plant's name was not initially attached to the project because he wanted to stay anonymous although there were many whispers and rumours amongst zealous fans that Plant was behind the project. Andy Edwards says, "The Priory may have been one of the first bands to really use the internet as the only way anyone could find out about it was through the fan sites like *Tight But Loose* and on various forums."

As reported in *Classic Rock*, Plant even joked to the adoring crowd about the absurdity of doing just a low-key and financially unsound project. He reportedly said: "This is a career suicide tour, which is the best thing that has happened to me. Who would have thought we'd have ended up as a Van Morrison covers band ... At least it's not a Zeppelin covers band! My manager doesn't understand why I'm doing this. I could be at the NEC ... but this is why!"

Each member of the band except Plant adopted stage names to avoid the press, as Andy Edwards recalls: "I don't actually know [we did it.] Robert named us on the first Priory gig at Bishops Castle [in Shropshire on July 23]. He did it on stage without us knowing. I think the idea was that The Priory was a hiding place for Robert, away from the big stadiums and rock and roll hoopla. And so it became a secret society and we were its secret members ... I think each name sort of pointed to stuff in Robert's past – I became 'Aleister Crowley' because it referred to mythology of Zep, in some way. Kev was 'Carlisle Egypt' which was his stage name in the Band Of Joy. Also, Paul Timothy was 'Owen Glyndwr' [who] was the Welsh king that fought the English ... and Paul Wetton was 'Eric Bloodaxe', a Viking who also fought the English!"

It was a fundamentally thrilling project for all concerned and while it was an eye-opening experience for the three relative novices Wetton, Edwards and Timothy, it was a nostalgic trip back to the past for ex-Band Of Joy musician Gammond. "Kevyn has got quite an avant-garde approach to guitar," explains Edwards. "I think with The Priory, Robert didn't want to refer to Zep, and Kev is about as far from Jimmy Page as you can get, stylistically. So this really helped Robert get away from the Zep thing. But Kev was like a musical terrorist, always trying to pull the songs apart, which wasn't always Robert's intention [but] I don't think that caused friction. Also, they are best mates so if Robert had a criticism then it was sometimes awkward having to have a go at his friend. But I think Kev had another take on the material that was exciting, and on stage he was a lively performer and he created another focus for us."

Ultimately, it was a refreshing and exciting period for Plant who had almost forgotten what it was like to be at arm's length with an audience and not have a security barrier and burly guards separating him from his paying fans. "If it all gets too rock 'n' roll again, I'll just turn my back and go off to Morocco for a couple for months," he told *Folk Roots Magazine* in 2000. Yet again, Plant was proving that his iconic, rock star status was not going to obstruct him from doing what he thinks best even if there's little or no money to be made. The irony is, of course, the project actually gave him some of the best press he'd had in his career thus far, with plenty of coverage in all the major rock magazines.

Edwards: "Obviously I had never played such big venues until I played with Robert. It has often been said we only played small venues but this isn't true. In the UK we played a lot of little venues but in Europe the gigs were a lot bigger. But to be honest the smaller gigs were more enjoyable. Robert would talk about the songs we were playing and tell stories so it was quite intimate and I think the audience got a kick out of this ... I always felt Robert felt as at home in the little venues as the big ones. But I think Robert has always played little venues too, before and after The Priory."

In August he took his project to the Jazz & Roots Club in Shrewsbury and they had a spot on the Bridgnorth Folk Festival on August 28. In September they played a date at the Kings Hotel in Newport and at the tiny Boardwalk in Sheffield. Another festival date was booked on the calendar when they played at the National Forest Folk festival on

Halloween evening. Looking at the set list, one can see there are songs by Donovan and Van Morrison's former band Them, plus blues legends Big Joe Williams and Ray Charles. Plant was more than happy with his voice; while the days of screeching alongside a huge rock riff have long since passed, he can sing with more meaning, depth and emotion.

In November, Plant took the band to closer to home in places like Stourbridge, Litchfield and Kings Heath in Birmingham. Certainly playing small gigs in Britain sparked many memories of the early years of Led Zeppelin and Plant was never too coy when it came to conversing with people about those times.

Edwards: "[He told] us lots of funny stories about 'the old band'. Robert told me a number of times that his memories of Zep were mostly of happy, fun times and he was saddened that since then in various publications it has been portrayed as a dark and troubled time. To me it seemed that Jimmy was like the keeper of the Zep flame where as Robert, although aware of his influences, wants to make new music and progress. I think this is shown by the choice of solo projects by both of them. This, however, obviously makes a magical working relationship which has been hard to replicate perhaps outside of that band."

They played the Oakengate Theatre in Telford on November 26 and the Central Station nightclub in Wrexham the following evening. The Telford gig was reviewed in an issue of *Classic Rock*: "Clearly Robert Plant is back on top form, as his magnetic persona and unique voice breathe renewed life into the classics he has chose[n] to share with us ... hat's off to you, Robert ..."

On December 8 a storming set was played at the Stourbridge Town Hall.[62] To finish off the year in low-key style, they journeyed to Oxford to play the popular music venue The Zodiac and back home to the West Midlands to bring the roof down at the Regis Hall in Cradley Heath on December 23, right in the heart of the Black Country. And to celebrate the festive period, they added 'Santa Claus Is Coming To Town' to the set list, bringing a cheery end to those December gigs.

★ ★ ★

Plant was still in the mood to pursue his Priory Of Brion project, so 2000's incredibly hectic touring schedule began in the first week of February with a gig at the Sugarmill in Henley, Stoke-on-Trent. It was certainly a big difference from the more glamorous and lucrative North American tour Jimmy Page undertook with The Black Crowes in September of the same year.

The Priory's touring diary for 2000 was announced to the press with immediate effect; now, Plant was keener for people to know he was the leader of the project hence 'The Priory Of Brion (Robert Plant And Friends)'.[63]

Still sticking to pubs and clubs, in March, they played shows in Wales, Liverpool, Nottingham and Northampton. Plant had made some minor changes to the set list and included a version of the Ben E. King and James Bethea song, 'We're Gonna Groove.'[64] With The Priory, it was Plant's aim to celebrate other artists' music and give them due credit for inspiring him way back in his youth.

Easily the most publicised shows of 2000 were the many festival appearances The Priory undertook in Britain and overseas. Some of the more revered festivals in Europe included the Nice Jazz Festival in France, the Dranouter Folk Festival in Belgium, the Enzimi Festival in Rome and the Ole Blues Festival in Norway. In Britain, they even played a well-received set in the Acoustic Tent at the Glastonbury Festival on June 23, Britain's most famous annual festival which celebrates all types of music from rock to jazz to blues to folk. "The most memorable gig for me," recalls Andy Edwards, "was when we played Glastonbury. Up until then we had been playing only to the converted Zep fans. I think Robert was quite nervous about doing the gig. We had a camera ban, so because there was no TV coverage everyone had packed in to see it. But we played really well and we were well received. It was quite emotional."

And, of course, Plant is no stranger to the Cropredy Festival, organised by his old friends Fairport Convention, and as well as that gig he took his band to the Cambridge Folk Festival on July 30. For Andy Edwards, Paul Wetton and Paul Timothy, the tour dates outside of the confines of their native country were especially memorable.

Edwards: "Robert was just one of the lads. He travelled with us in some quite uncomfortable conditions. I remember touring Ireland [in June] in a little minibus and Robert's back was playing up. He could have bailed out any time but the idea never even came up. We had this driver and he just happened to be an expert in Irish history and started giving us a running commentary [of] the scenery and history of where we were travelling. In the end I think Robert paid him just to drive us for the whole tour because his commentaries were so interesting. It became like a holiday, stopping off at various abbeys and beauty spots. That's what it was like touring with Robert, like being on holiday!"

After more than twenty concert dates in the UK and Ireland, they concentrated mostly on mainland Europe between mid-June and November, playing festivals and selected headlining solo shows in some quite big venues.

Edwards: "I remember the gigs abroad were less 'secret' and so it felt more like playing for 'Robert Plant' rather than in some weird, secret band. I'd never really toured like that back then, so the whole experience was new to me. And I think Robert enjoyed being out on tour with people who had never done that before. I think he felt our excitement and enjoyed that."

Outside of the UK, the band flew to Finland, Italy, Portugal, Switzerland, France, Belgium, Sardinia, Holland, Brussels, Luxembourg and Greece. Edwards: "The stuff that sticks in my mind is the surreal things. I remember playing Naples [on September 24]; it was an open-air event in the middle of the city. They had closed the centre of the city off. There was one toilet in a cafe for about 10,000 people. As the gig approached, we realised there was no way of getting out of the event as our bus was in the middle of [these] crowds. At the end of the gig, Robert was smuggled out and we acted as a decoy and had to make a run for the bus with half the audience chasing after us. Some of the fans followed our bus for about two [to] three hours in their cars. Robert's fans never ceased to amaze me with their fanaticism. More then once I saw fans drop to the floor after meeting him."

However, despite the business of flying around Europe, they did find time to come back to the UK to play three shows in the south of England; Bristol, Coventry and Milton Keynes. Respected rock author and journalist John Tucker attended The Priory's gig at The New Trinity Community Centre in Bristol on October 04.

Tucker: "I'd seen Plant a handful of times previously, but in larger venues which had showcased the event rather than the man. Two dates on the 1990 *Manic Nirvana* tour (supported by Alannah Myles at Birmingham in the summer and Colin James at Newport a few days before Christmas) had been impressive and expansive shows, with a handful of Zeppelin numbers sprinkled among a set of Plant's strongest solo material to date. And, of course, for sheer spectacle the 1995 UK Page & Plant tour was breathtaking in both scope and size. But all that was topped by the intimacy of the Trinity Centre. A former church, now arts centre, in one of the less desirable parts of town, it was the ideal venue for Plant's latest venture, the relatively short-lived Priory Of Brion.

Plant was relaxed and in fine form, and in such an informal setting it was almost like having your best mate's band playing in your front room. A number of times during the evening he remarked on the fittingness of the venue for an evening such as this, and at the end of one song, during which he'd perched on a stool, he picked it up and moved it to the back of the cramped stage, remarking to great amusement from the audience as he returned to the microphone that 'A year ago, I'd have had someone to do that for me!'

The set that Plant and his band played was largely composed of songs that had influenced the singer as a young man, although many of them had been cleverly reinterpreted, reinvigorated and/or reworked till they were almost unrecognisable. Amongst them were 'Hey Joe', 'Morning Dew' and

'Darkness, Darkness', all of which went on to figure on the *Dreamland* album a couple of years later, as well as a storming version of 'Gloria'.

It was one of those gigs that stays with you forever. To say that there was magic in the air is now an unimaginable cliché, but that's exactly the way it was. It seemed to me that it was a time of transition for the singer too, from having to conform to people's expectations of what he should do as the former Led Zeppelin vocalist to being able to perform exactly what he wanted, which I guess was the essence of The Strange Sensation – the band into which Priory Of Brion evolved. Four or five people were openly and unashamedly bootlegging the set that night, and I'd love to hear it now."

As the year drew to a close, Plant was feeling pressure from his record label to record some new material for the following year's calendar. Edwards: "In the beginning, it was interesting because the gigs were small and secretive. But as the band progressed, to make it work it began to play under Robert's name and on bigger stages so it became just another project but without an album behind it. I think there was a lot of pressure from certain quarters for Robert to play with 'name' musicians in a 'proper' project or even better, do something with Page. This was a real pressure on the band and in the end it stopped being fun. I remember there was a bit of a row between us all at Athens airport [in November] and after that it didn't seem the same."

That's certainly the way Plant felt as he informed *Folk Roots Magazine* in an interview taken during the summer: "I don't want the Priory Of Brion to get any bigger. It' supposed to be as far removed from that rock and roll thing as possible ... The thing about doing what I'm doing now is that we don't really know what is going to happen. The venues are not tried and tested gigs."

The year finished with three small gigs back home in the Midlands: on December 14 they played at the tiny Victoria Community Centre in Crewe, on December 17 at the Darwin Suite in the Assembly Rooms in Derby and finally on December 21 they finished the year off with a gig at the Wulfrun Hall in Wolverhampton. On the final night of the tour, Plant finally gave in to pressure from his fan base to include Led Zeppelin material in his set list and so The Priory played 'Thank You' at the Wolverhampton gig while they also excited the audience by including a segment of 'Houses Of The Holy' during 'As Long As I Have You'.

Speaking now, Edwards reflects on that two-year project with great energy, but he can clearly see Plant's reasons for doing something that very few popular artists could get away with – or indeed have the nerve to undertake in the first place. "I think that Robert's original idea for The Priory was inspired but it got diluted as time went on. The Priory was about looking back and celebrating the golden age of rock and roll and showing how cool that stuff was. We were never that polished or rehearsed but neither was the music to which we referred. I think for a long time Robert and Kev had thought about doing something like The Priory. It must have been exciting for them at that time, just on the cusp of success but still not there. And having us guys in the band must have made it feel like it had the same vibe. Perhaps Robert should have got some *really* young guys in but they might not have got it at all ... I don't know!"

And so at the (perhaps understandable) behest of his label and managers, Plant dissolved the Priory Of Brion and began work on a new album with a new group of musicians. Everybody went their separate ways: Paul Wetton joined a group called the Gwyn Ashton Band who even managed to tour Europe, but then he left and joined a hip hop outfit called Cantaloop. Paul Timothy got a job as a DJ and producer of dance music; he has released various remixes and records since 2000. Also, he formed a group called Soul Central and they had a Top 10 UK chart hit with a track called 'Strings Of Life.' Andy Edwards joined the progressive rock band IQ in 2005 and they released a DVD in 2006 called *Stage*. These days Edwards stays exclusively within the prog/jazz field, having also joined the revered Jem Godfrey prog rock band Frost in 2006.

THE STRANGE SENSATION:
A NEW SOUND,
A NEW BEGINNING
2001–2007

" [In] the 1960s, people moved towards Ravi Shankar and the whole Indian thing. People were looking for something more tangible and less cynical. So I think there is a little avenue for this music to open up in a natural way."
Robert Plant speaking to the *Afropop Worldwide* website in 2003

For his next project, it was a case of going back to the drawing board. Due to commercial pressures, getting a new band and project together had to be a hasty process, one that was much quicker than the near three year gap between *Shaken 'n' Stirred* and *Now And Zen.* Plant assembled a group of young, talented and professional musicians in one of the most serious and hard working line-ups of his career.

Bassist Charlie Jones was already a familiar face. As a producer and accomplished guitarist, Justin Adams had collaborated with Jah Wobble for eight years – brought up in the Middle East, his love of world music, jazz, punk and reggae clearly impressed Plant who always strives for new ideas, especially ones that merge varying styles of music and moods. In an interview with the online world music magazine *Global Village Idiot* (*www.globalvillageidiot.net*) Adams spoke of his luck at getting a job working for Robert Plant: "He knows where I'm coming from and lets me do my thing – and it's well paid! There have been moments in my career when I thought I'd have to do other things to pay the bills."

Bath-based drummer Clive Deamer had previously recorded music with Portishead, Van Morrison, Roni Size and Hawkwind. Deamer had suggested keyboardist John Baggott who is known for collaborating with the seminal Bristol band Massive Attack and Porl Thompson had previously played in The Cure and joined Page & Plant for their first world tour in 1995. There is an obviously commercial aspect to Plant's choices of musicians; combine their CVs and one can see a list of some of the very best contemporary artists. It's exactly what his record company (Universal) had hoped for. To be fair to them, the entire project was a shrewd move and one which would bring him strongly back into the public eye. Speaking in 2002 to *USA Today* about the energy and commitment he had for his latest band venture, Plant said, "They come from amazingly diverse corners, which is part of the thrill for me. I didn't want to revisit a tired and tested area."

The nostalgia and renewed sense of compassion that led Plant to pay homage to his heroes in the project Priory Of Brion stayed with him as he hit the road in a blaze of glory with his new band. Interviewed by Dan Ross in *Record Collector* in 2002, Plant was aware of the similarities: "The band [Priory Of Brion] had dozed into a coma, and rather than blow the gigs out, I thought it would be a good idea to try it in a different form."

Robert Plant and The Strange Sensation first appeared on stage together in front of the paying public at the Train in Aarhus, Denmark on April 22, 2001. The choice of songs was not too dissimilar to those played by his previous band the Priory Of Brion. After Denmark, they travelled around various parts of Europe and then on to America which was Plant's first road jaunt there since 1998; those dates took the band straight through to the end of August, also paying welcome visits to Sweden, Norway, Boston, Pennsylvania, Washington D.C., New York, Ontario, Michigan, Illinois, Poland and Switzerland.

The date in Montreux, Switzerland was certainly one of the year's highlights; after being introduced by Ahmet Ertegun, Plant – joined by Jimmy Page, Bill Jennings and Mike Watts – performed a rockin' feast of songs at the Montreux Festival to celebrate the now legendary Sun Records. After gigging in Switzerland, they ventured to Estonia, Greece, Finland, Belgium and France.

★　★　★

Robert Plant and The Strange Sensation began work on their first album together during the final few months of 2001; it would be titled *Dreamland*.[65] Only a couple of years before, Plant stated in an issue of *Classic Rock* that he would never write any new material again. Needless to say, he spoke too soon and had actually written a total of seventeen songs for his new album. Produced by Plant and co-produced and engineered by Phil Brown, *Dreamland* was recorded mostly at Moles Studio, which is based on the first and second floors of an eighteenth century Georgian house in Bath. Recording had also been conducted at Church Studios and RAK in London with assistance by Raj Das, Dan Austin and Graham Domily respectively at those studios. Plant was not too keen to work at Peter Gabriel's Real World Studio near Bath; he jokingly told *Classic Rock*, "I've worked out there quite a bit. But ever since Peter beat me at tennis I thought I'd put my money elsewhere!"

The album was mastered by Denis Blackham at Country Masters. Besides his core band, the album features special guest appearances by backing vocalists Raj Das, May Clee Cadman and Ginny Clee.

The music that Plant and his new band – and indeed the Priory Of Brion – had been playing on stage filtered through into the new album, which features a hefty amount of covers, paying tribute to artists such as Bukka White, Tim Rose, Bob Dylan, Tim Buckley, Jimi Hendrix, Robert Johnson, John Lee Hooker and Arthur 'Big Boy' Crudup. The initial idea was to include just three covers: Jimi Hendrix's 'Hey Joe', 'Morning Dew' by Tim Harding and 'Song Of The Siren' by Tim Buckley. "It really comes from an envy of American music," Plant explained to *Entertainment Weekly* upon the release of *Dreamland*. "I can't find anything in English music that [is] actually half as seductive or relevant."

Evidently his latest album would hear Plant in a dream-like daze, simply in awe of the material that he'd handpicked. It was a trip down memory lane, and perhaps it was also a road of enlightenment and discovery for this young group of musicians who had not lived through some of the periods of popular culture that Plant had witnessed first-hand and – in some cases, such as the British Blues Boom of the 1960s – been an integral part of. It would turn out to be a testament to his love of music, akin to Eric Clapton's blues album *From The Cradle*, David Bowie's *Pin Ups*, Bob Dylan's *Self Portrait* and John Lennon's 1975 tribute to his idols, *Rock 'N' Roll*.[66]

★   ★   ★

Before the release of *Dreamland*, Plant played two warm-up dates: the first performance was at Bristol University on February 5 and then at London's prestigious Royal Albert Hall on February 9 where Plant took part in the yearly Teenage Cancer Trust Charity organised by Roger Daltrey of The Who.

In May it was announced that Plant would make a brief guest appearance playing harmonica on the track 'The Lord Is My Shotgun', for

Primal Scream's album *Evil Heat*. Singer Bobby Gillespie informed *Blabbermouth*: "Robert lives near our studio and we're always having a chat. I asked him, 'Would you like to blow some harp on a psychedelic blues song we've got?' and he said: 'What key's it in?'"

The world tour had actually preceded the release of *Dreamland* with three dates in Portugal arranged for May 22, 23 and 24.[67] Always one to prefer an intimate show, Plant had scheduled two low-key dates at Bangor University and Liverpool University at the end of May. In his review of the gig in *The Guardian*, journalist Dave Simpson wrote: "Plant has lost neither his hair nor his voice, which has all the range it did on *Led Zeppelin I*. When he lets fly with the first Valhallic wail, pints are spilled. The atmosphere is part-mystical, part-humorous … every time the band rock out, the spirit of Zeppelin isn't far away – but Plant has repeatedly proved that there is life after the 1970s."

After the Liverpool date, Plant performed a short set at the famous Isle Of Wight Festival on June 3, which included a stomping version of 'Hey Joe' and the Zeppelin tracks 'Four Sticks', 'Celebration Day' and 'Going To California'.

On June 6, a special performance was recorded at Westway Studios in London for VH1's ever-popular series, *Storytellers*. Artists are invited on the show to perform a short set in front of a small assemblage of fans who are given the opportunity to ask the guest artist a question. Elton John, Billy Joel and Meat Loaf have also taken part in the series; the latter even undertook a tour of North America using the same format and released a DVD and CD from his initial VH1 performance.

Before a trip to the States, a gig at London's Astoria took place on June 10. James Halbert enthusiastically reviewed the gig in *Classic Rock*: "It's all very endearing, and a reminder that, at heart, the Golden God is just another music fan who wants to sit you down and force you to listen to his favourite records."

One reviewer wrote on the online magazine *New Horizons* (*www.elrose.demon.co.uk*): "The band can play too, producing a very effective wall of sound for the heavier tracks and showing admirable restraint on the more reflective material, allowing ample space for Plant's vocals to work their magic."

Dreamland was released via Mercury Records on June 16, 2002 in the UK and although it charmed the critics, it only peaked at Number 20. In the States, it was issued by Universal and was an even smaller success, reaching Number 40; the album followed a similar pattern around the world. The switch in record labels brought renewed vigour and zest for the ageing singer, as he told *USA Today* in 2002: "It's nothing personal, but I was beginning to feel like an heirloom. A lot of things had changed lately, from the people I was working with to my ideology. I've been around for a long time."

Despite some decent airplay due to a set of white releases for broadcasters, 'Darkness, Darkness' entered the US *Mainstream Rock Charts* at a barely adequate Number 27. The album spawned three singles in the UK: 'Morning Dew', 'Song To The Siren' and 'Last Time I Saw Her'.

Dreamland was the first album by Robert Plant and The Strange Sensation, although it is titled exclusively as a solo opus, which was probably with the intention that the 'Robert Plant' brand name would win back some of the fans that he may have lost since releasing his previous solo album way back in 1993. His band had co-authored all the album's original material (four songs out of the complete ten).[68] "You can probably hear the great future for this band lurking on the fade-outs of the tracks," he told *Universal Music Canada* (*www.umuisc.ca*) in upon the album's release.

Critics and fanzine reviewers were overwhelmed with *Dreamland*. Dave Lewis wrote in *Classic Rock*: "There are few, if any, Led Zeppelin trademarks, and few of the vocal heroics that have characterised his solo work. His voice is all the better for it, and in great shape here, displaying a determination to engage every listener throughout, while cleverly reworking his style ... *Dreamland* will be perfect late-night listening for your own summer schedule of love. As the singer once put it: if you listen very hard, the tune will come to you at last."

Dan Ross concluded his review in *Record Collector* by saying: "Ultimately, *Dreamland* is no substitute for an album of new material, but Plant has intimated that reworking these classics has inspired him to pen many new lyrics."

Dreamland opens with an adaptation of the Bukka White-inspired song 'Funny In My Mind (I Believe I'm Fixin' To Die)'; Plant adds a world music texture to the Mississippi Delta blues song, making it more contemporary. His version of Tim Rose's 'Morning Dew' is a highlight of the album – sultry and dignified. 'One More Cup Of Coffee' is a soothing version of the Bob Dylan original and the flamenco guitar courtesy of Clive Deamer is a nice touch. 'Last Time I Saw Her' is a smart contemporary pop song with strumming indie guitars and eccentric sound effects. Plant treats Tim Buckley's 'Song Of The Siren' with the tenderness and reserve it deserves; it's a beautifully composed and wishful song, delivered in sensual and thoughtful tones and the finely played Arabian strings add more food for thought. An imaginary trip to the Mississippi Delta in 'Win My Train Fare Home (If I Ever Get Lucky)' is a clever creation, merging sounds from Messrs Arthur Crudup, Robert Johnson and John Lee Hooker. 'Darkness, Darkness' is a mellow acoustic song that's moody and indelible. Despite being an original song amongst a set of cover versions, 'Red Dress' fits into the proceedings magnificently but it's a confident and sturdy cover of 'Hey Joe' which remains one of the album's more secure songs; it's a brilliant re-construction of the song which Jimi Hendrix made universally famous. Lastly, 'Skip's Song', written by Alexander Lee Spence, is as far away from his screeching, wailing Zeppelin days as Plant could get; interestingly there is certainly a latterday Beatles vibe in the choruses.[69]

To promote his pending tour of America, Plant performed 'Darkness, Darkness' on *The David Letterman Show* in New York, one of the country's top-rated entertainment shows. Later on in the year, he also performed 'Morning Dew' on *The Jay Leno Show* in LA.

The singer's stay in the US lasted until mid-September where Plant and his band supported The Who on a tour of large venues across the States. On the itinerary, no less than four dates at New York's Madison Square Garden were scheduled from July 31 to August 4. It was a chance to show larger American audiences that his band The Strange Sensation was one of the highlights of his career. Speaking to Chuck Klosterman of *Spin* magazine, Plant was not in agreement that those who saw his band on stage were necessarily fans of heavy metal – a genre Led Zeppelin had helped create. "I've been playing festivals in Europe for the past year, and I find those audience want the sensitivity, too," he explained.

On September 15, they recorded a special performance for the Austin City Limits series at KLRU Studios in Texas. The producer of the show Terry Lickona told *Public Service Radio* (*www.pbs.org*): "I was blown away by the Middle Eastern influence, by the adventurousness of what he does as opposed to going into familiar patterns or expectations. I've got respect for him doing that … He's still doing the kind of music he believes in."

Prior to a UK tour of small venues during the latter half of 2002, Plant was interviewed on a German radio show on October 7. The UK tour kicked off at Exeter University the following day and proceeded through to the end of the month having visited Norwich, Birmingham, Leeds, Manchester, Newcastle, Glasgow, Sheffield, Portsmouth, Bristol and Hammersmith.

On November 5 a brief tour of mainland Europe commenced in Copenhagen, Denmark. From there they travelled to Norway, Sweden and Finland before finishing up with two nights in Russia; the first night was at the Ice Palace in St. Petersburg on November 12 which was followed by a gig at the Olympics Stadium in Moscow.

★ ★ ★

2003 was yet another hectic year on the annual planner; Plant learned that he had been nominated for a prestigious Grammy award under the 'Best Rock Album' category alongside Bruce Springsteen.

On January 6, 7, and 8, Plant performed at the second Festival In The Desert in Essakane, Mali, Africa with his guitarists Justin Adams and Skin Tyson and the bassist/percussion player from the French band Lo-Jo. The festival also featured such celebrated world musicians and singers as Ali Farka Toure,[70] Oumou Sangare, Tinariwen and Tidawt. Plant himself explained to *Afropop Worldwide* (*www.afropop.org*) that the festival "is phenomenal, the location is stupendous, but in real terms, where are we? I mean this is fantastic to find out. But my impressions are that there is a lot [of] gasoline being used here and this is an incredibly poor country. I think the political means to an end must far outweigh any of our musical filtrations."

Festival In The Desert is a celebration of world music, bringing together tribal nomads from all over the Sahara Desert called Tuareg who are also known as Tamashek. Plant told *BBC News*: "I was attracted by the Tuareg lifestyle. The music reminded me of why I sang in the first place – it is not commercialised."

The festival is one of a kind; there are very few festivals, anywhere in the world, that unite such an eclectic and varying type of music. Speaking to the *National Public Radio* (*www.npr.org*), Plant was keen to explain the connection between Africa and America and the creation of blues music. "I'm not an anthropologist," he said, "but I just have to say that what was going down musically and the mood of it all sounded like some kind of primeval connection with what you would call the blues…"

Guitarist Justin Adams wrote about his love for Mali and its music in an article titled 'Sahara Blues In Mali With Robert Plant' for *The Times*; he describes one little anecdote with pleasure: "We got straight into rehearsals [and] were half way into a version of 'Whole Lotta Love' with acoustic guitars and hand drums in our tent, when our next door neighbours, a group of Tuareg girls, stunning in indigo and gold, gatecrashed our rehearsal. The way they started to move to the rhythm made the distance between tribal dance and rock 'n' roll disappear. Later, after they had disappeared, a group of young camel riders pulled up to our tent. 'Where are the girls?', they demanded. 'Elles sont parties,' we managed, and they galloped off."

Before touring resumed proper, Plant made time to perform on the BBC3's *Recovered* programme at Riverside Studios in Hammersmith as well as a performance on BBC2's *Live Floor* programme. Robert Plant and The Strange Sensation then played a handful of gigs in Norway which commenced with a performance at the Ole Blues Festival on April 26.

Plant took his band to Italy to play a series of shows which were interrupted by a performance at the Ashton Court Festival in Bristol on July 19. The festival celebrates local musicians and tickets were sold at an implausible £5 each; clearly there was a high demand and it was reported that Plant had to gain special permission from the local council to extend his set to ninety minutes.

By this point, the most significant facet of early 2003 was the departure of Plant's son-in-law, bassist Charlie Jones, which clearly resulted in another minor shake-up of The Strange Sensation. He was replaced by Billy Fuller who was then working in a record shop in Bristol as well as playing bass in the renowned local band Fuzz Against Junk.

After their sojourn in Italy, Plant and The Strange Sensation played exhilarating gigs in France, Denmark, Estonia, Latvia, Belarus, and Ukraine before coming back to England to play at the Canterbury Fayre on August 23.

In November 2003, to commemorate Robert Plant's lengthy solo career, Atlantic issued a compilation called *Sixty Six To Timbuktu*, which includes some of his most recognised solo material as well as selected obscurities. Naming an album after the poor Egyptian city in an area of Mali known as the Tombouctou region, proves that Plant's love of African culture has reach a near-zenith. A note worthy inclusion is 'Red For Danger', which Plant had recorded with guitarist Robin George back in 1988. Plant explained to music writer Barney Hoskyns: "I went down to Taunton and spent many hours with mastering engineer John Dent trying to match different periods. Some of it was too brittle."

Unfortunately despite some good reviews, the two CD set failed to achieve high sales; it reached Number 27 in the UK charts and Number 134 in the US *Billboard* Top 200. Fans also bemoaned a lack of material from *Manic Nirvana* and *Pictures At Eleven* and The Honeydrippers EP on the first disc.

However, the second disc of rarities certainly pleased archivists: it features 'Road To The Sun', an out-take from *The Principle Of Moments* and the Dave Edmonds (of The Crawling King Snakes) and Roland James (former guitarist with Jerry Lee Lewis) song 'Philadelphia Baby.' 'Louie Louie' was recorded in Texas in October, 1993 during the US *Fate Of Nations* tour and featured on the soundtrack to the smash hit comedy *Wayne's World 2*. The Arthur Alexander song, 'If It's Really Got To Be This Way', was included on a 1994 tribute album to the R&B legend while 'Rude World' was recorded with Jimmy Page at RAK in London in 1997, during their collaborative years. The Skip Spence song, 'Little Hands', was conceived at NAM Studios in Wiltshire in 1999 after the Page & Plant project came to a highly-publicised end. 'Life Began' was recorded in 2001 with Afro Celt Soundsystem, the avant-garde group who – hence the name – merge African and Celtic sounds together. The R&B number 'Let's Boogie Woogie Roll' was recorded with Jools Holland in 2002 with the Extraordinaire supplying backing vocals while 'Win My Train Fare Home' was recorded live on stage at the Festival In The Desert near Timbuktu in 2003 and featured Skin Tyson and Justin Adams from The Strange Sensation as well as various African musicians.

The critics were evidently overwhelmed. Adam Sweeting raved in *The Guardian*: "Look at it this way: if Zep hadn't bitten the dust, we would never have heard most of this amazing music." John Metzger wrote on *The Music Box* (*www.musicbox-online.com*): "The result is that, in retrospect, many of his own works lack the timelessness of his forays with Led Zeppelin, if only because his solo tunes sometimes became overburdened with keyboards and drum beats that now seem out of place ..."

David Chiu wrote on the online music magazine *New Beats* (*www.newbeats.com*): "It is apparent that Plant's favourite solo album is *Fate Of Nations* because a certain fair amount of the album's cuts are on here ... Die hard fans might quibble about some omissions ... but the second disc of rarities should make up for any disappointment."

The year ended on a high note with a performance at a Nobel Peace Prize concert at the Oslo Spectrum in Norway on December 11. It was a brief set which included 'Darkness, Darkness', 'Morning Dew', 'Going To California' and a version of John Lennon's classic 'Imagine', with a host of other performers who took part in the event.

★　★　★

2004 was a quiet year for the boys, opting to work on a new album behind the scenes. Plant did, however, make a few low-key live appearances: in March he joined Vanilla Fudge onstage at the Stourbridge Rock Café. The performance certainly brought back memories of the days in 1969-1970, when Led Zep use to support the cult Long Island band around the States.

October saw two collective impromptu performances by Robert Plant, blues guitarist Gary Moore, Greg Lake (formally of ELP) and Asia and Procol Harum founder Gary Brooker at two separate clubs in London. They declared themselves The RD Cruisers and the profits went to Roger Daltrey's charity, the Teenage Cancer Trust. Also, during that month, Plant and Jeff Beck guested starred on the track 'Look Out Mabel' for The Big Town Playboys on their album, *Roll The Dice*.

In the following month's live diary was a short slot at the Leadbelly Tribute Concert in Ohio. The Strange Sensation's Justin Adams joined Plant on stage as he sang a few songs. Most notably was a version of 'Where Did You Sleep Last Night?' with Alison Krauss; a highly-anticipated professional relationship would be conceived which will be discussed at the end of this chapter.

Work on *Mighty ReArranger* – the first fully titled Robert Plant and The Strange Sensation album – began in earnest in Snowdonia in 2004. It has been reported that Plant and The Strange Sensation had worked on various parts of the album alone before coming together as a collective. Plant decided to summon his muse in the ancient historical village of Avebury in Wiltshire where he devoured poetry and took inspiration from Stonehenge, the prehistoric circular standing stones that have been a great cause of interest for scholars, academics, fans and tourists for many years.

Sadly, it was during the making of the album that Plant's father – Robert Plant Senior – passed away. Plant was bereft but continued to work on his latest musical endeavour to help him over the loss. He told Sylvie Simmons at *The Guardian* newspaper in 2005: "There's no time to waste time."

The album promised to blend world music with progressive rock and varying layers of textures and sounds, and feature a whole range of eclectic instruments such as a Moog Bass, a Bendir, a Tehardant and a Lap Steel. The album was produced and mixed by Steve Evans at Riverside Studios, Batheaston in the south-west of England. Some mixing had also been completed at RAK Studios in London. "I have a band now that's consolidated a lot of north African musicality into a rock thing," he told one journalist at *BBC Berkshire* after the album's release. "It's all written already, it's just that we didn't know it. I'm not trying to be cosmic, it's just everything's on a roll …"

Prior to the release of the *Mighty ReArranger*, Plant and his robust band of musicians undertook some live dates in aid of their latest release. They began by playing both Tsunami Relief Benefits at the Carling Academy in Bristol on February 19 and 20. Following on from those gigs, which also included performances by the alternative Bristol based bands Massive Attack and Portishead, was a trip to the States for the first time since supporting The Who on tour in the summer of 2002. On March 17, Plant delivered an important speech at the South West Music and Media Conference in Austin, Texas. He even played live too which included some Zeppelin tunes such as 'No Quarter', 'Black Dog', 'Heartbreaker', 'Babe I'm Gonna Leave You', 'Whole Lotta Love' and 'When the Levee Breaks'.

After their American gigs, Plant flew back to the UK and on April 1 he played a set at the Carling Academy in the birth place of The Beatles, Liverpool. From there he travelled down to the Midlands to perform at the Students' Union at Warwick University and then it was arranged for him to perform at the annual Teenage Cancer Trust show at the Royal Albert Hall on April 4.

Adam Sweeting reviewed the show in *The Guardian* and wrote: "As he navigated his way through a selection of Zep classics and new songs, it was like watching a map of Plant's evolving musical interests unfold. There was primitive rock 'n' roll, folk and blues, and a whiff of psychedelia, but running through the show was a constant pulse of music from points further south and east ... Whatever Plant is paying [The] Strange Sensation, it's worth every penny, because they complement him immaculately."

Indeed the pace did not slow down, even for a man in his fifties: April to June saw dates in Berlin, Lithuania, Russia, Finland, Sweden, Denmark and Iceland. On April 27 he appeared on *BBC Radio 2* at the Scala Theatre in London.

By now, Plant had reassembled the Es Paranza label; its previous release was *Fate Of Nations* way back in 1993. The *Mighty ReArranger* was released through Sanctuary/Es Paranza on May 2, 2005 in the UK and May 10 in the United States.[71]

Might ReArranger has proven to be one of Robert Plant's highest rated albums in his solo repertoire and sales of the record proved quite lucrative in Britain, especially as it reached Number 4 in the UK Top 40.

In other territories, *Mighty ReArranger* also proved to be a reasonable hit: it was a Top 20 hit in Norway, Sweden and Italy and in the States the album hit Number 22 in the US *Billboard* Top 200. Plant was fairly chuffed with himself. Helped by the album's lead single 'Shine It All Around', which was a Top 20 hit in the US *Mainstream Rock Charts*, the record was a palpable mini-sensation.

In a three star review, Paul Rees wrote in *Q*: "*Mighty ReArranger* mixes *Led Zeppelin III*'s bucolic whimsy, [*Led Zeppelin*] *VI*'s heaving percussion and the Eastern infections of their latter period ... Plant can still strut with the vigour of a man half his age."

In a four star review Alexis Petridis wrote in *The Guardian*: " ... given the regard in which Led Zeppelin are held, none of it sounds like pastiche, possibly because these nods to the past are surrounded by music that fixes its gaze firmly forward."

Mighty ReArranger is littered with political references and although Plant does not go into too much depth – *a la* Neil Young – such thoughts do reveal his mindset at the time of writing. The album opens with the political tribal track 'Another Tribe'; it's a beautifully layered song and Plant sounds comfortable and content. 'Shine It All Around' has the feeling of a contemporary indie rock song; in fact, the simple riff could fit pleasingly alongside a set of Oasis songs. Indeed, the drum effects and layered vocals authenticate 'Shine It All Around', making it one of the album's stand-out tracks. 'Freedom Fries' is yet another song that is politically motivated; this time aimed at the Americans who criticised

France for not supporting them and their controversial war in Iraq. 'Tin Pan Alley' is Plant's jibe at his peer's and their obsession with the past; it's a strong and fiery song that builds up to a powerful crescendo of intelligent riffs. 'All The Kings' is a delicate ballad that is played at a snail's pace but Plant's voice is alluring; perhaps it's the closet that Plant will get to evoking the mood and emotion of a song by his beloved Joni Mitchell. 'The Enchanter' is a misty song that treads through the blues via modern digital technology with distinctive drum machine beats and a hidden but thumping bass line. The spiritual and hypnotic song 'Takamba' has occasional flourishes of Arabic sounds and the lead riff is precise and fluent. 'Dancing In Heaven' is a mid-paced acoustic song that articulately evokes Plant's love of Neil Young and the West Coast artists of the 1960s. 'Somebody Knocking' is less interesting than its siblings although a gritty blues guitar that opens the song promises something more inventive. 'Let The Four Wings Blow' is an inspiring guitar-based song that pays homage to the blues and the West Coast bands like Moby Grape *et al* that led Plant, like a magnet, towards Californian music of that ilk; the guitar even has touches of a less complicated Clapton circa 1974. 'Mighty ReArranger' is catchy song with a bluesy piano and an unforgettable chorus. The closing song, 'Brother Ray' is dedicated to rhythm and blues legend Ray Charles who died in 2004; it's a brief spot of jamming that would have made Charles smile.[72]

With a new album under his belt, Plant played to ecstatic audiences at two shows on the Isle Of Man and one date in Norway, prior to a full-length North American tour that commenced on June 15 in Rhode Island. Plant was very particular about the sound that he wanted to get across to the audiences. He explained to *Rolling Stone*: "I've really always had an idea to develop this melange of North African music and the Plant side of Led Zep – to push the two together."

Just like the old times in Led Zeppelin, Plant took his musicians around the length and breadth of the vast continent covering such states as Massachusetts, New Jersey, Pennsylvania, Connecticut, New York, Tennessee, Georgia, Virginia, Ontario, Minnesota, Illinois, Minneapolis, Colorado, Arizona, Nevada and California; the final date of the US tour was July 24 when Plant brought the proverbial roof down at Los Angeles Greek Theatre. Plant was just as keen to play the smaller venues with an intimate audience of just a couple of thousand people as he was playing to many more thousands at popular festivals around the world. His sound engineer of twenty five years, Roy Williams, said to the online music technology magazine *Mix* (*www.mixonline.com*) in 2005 that "he likes to hear it coming from the front, what the audience hears. He's very old-school; not afraid of technology at all, mind you."

After strong sets at the WOMAD Festival in Reading on July 31 and at the Festival de Mouros in Portugal, Plant took a well-earned break for a couple of weeks. Speaking about WOMAD, Plant was interviewed by a journalist at *BBC Berkshire*: "The reason I'm here is, I've got new work and I've got an elevated state now … I think [WOMAD] gives so much more of a window on the set lists of what music can do."

Yet those days of supposed relaxation flew by quick enough and it was time for appearances at the hugely successful V Festivals in Chelmsford and Staffordshire on August 20 and 21; those shows were followed by anticipated sets at the Rock en Seine in Paris. It is important for Plant and The Strange Sensation to play festivals because not only does it provide them with a larger audience than a solo tour, but such festivals bring together contrasting styles of music which is the essence of the band and their ambitions.[73]

In September, Plant took The Strange Sensation over to Canada to play a surprisingly extensive tour which included dates in Ottawa, Montreal, London, Winnipeg, Edmonton, Calgary, Vancouver and Victoria. And if the seven dates back in March and his tour in June and July wasn't enough to please eager Americans, further US dates had been added to the tour itinerary for the end of September through early October.

Frankie Banali – the drummer in the classic heavy metal band Quiet Riot – remembers catching Plant on stage in California: "It was on Sunday, October 2, 2005 at the Wiltern Theater, Los Angeles, as the guest of Ludwig Drums artists' relations representative Todd Trent, who is also a dear friend and knows Robert Plant through the Ludwig Drums connection. It was the first opportunity that I have had to see Robert Plant live since the Led Zeppelin days, purely because my own tour schedule makes it impossible to attend many shows, even those by one of my heroes. It really was wonderful to say a quick hello and chat about the show … and a thrill for me to have my picture taken with him. It's a treasured memory."

After the LA show, on October 5, Plant organised a special benefit concert with Seattle grunge rock legends Pearl Jam at the House Of Blues in Chicago. The evening was in aid of the victims of the devastating Hurricane Katrina, one of the worst natural disasters in US history, which had wreaked havoc in many southern states in August. Tickets cost $1000 and by the end of the evening $1 million dollars had been raised. Donations were also made to the Jazz Foundation Of America. Various Led Zeppelin songs were performed that night including the first live version of 'Fool In The Rain', plus 'Going To California' and 'Thank You'. They also performed a blistering cover of Elvis's 'Little Sister' and the 1959 Tamala Motown tune 'Money (That's What I Want)'. The evening was drawn to a close by a cover of Neil Young's 'Rockin' In The Free World'.

It was now time to play three dates in Britain beginning on October 27 at the Corn Exchange in Edinburgh. That night was swiftly followed by shows in Glasgow and Gateshead before yet another trip over to the continent from November 9 at the Olympia in the French city of love. The set list had been altered by now and included some old blues standards.

A lengthy road jaunt around France preceded a tour of Italy and then it was time to head back over to England to play at the Hammersmith Palais. *The Times'* resident music critic Lisa Verrico was at the London show and in her review she wrote: "The band ... can take some of the credit for the 56-year-old's fine form ... their energy invigorated him, his howl drove them on ... for a man who refuses to re-form his old group, no matter how many millions are on offer, he revisited his past with surprising enthusiasm."

After London, Plant flew to Dublin for a gig on December 9 and so the year finished with a homecoming gig at the Wolverhampton Civic Hall on December 12.

2006 began on a high note: Plant was nominated for two Grammy Awards – 'Best Solo Rock Vocal' for 'Shine It All Around' and 'Best Hard Rock' for 'Tin Pan Alley'.

Indeed, it was a year that carried on where the previous one had finished off – namely on the road. Robert Plant and The Strange Sensation performed what seems on paper like a random series of festival appearances and shows in obscure towns around the globe. The fact is that Plant *likes* to tour; it is part of his nature and the side of his personality that likes to soak up local cultures and eccentricities. Just like an explorer who looks for his next challenge, Plant looks for a town that he has not played before. Starting in February, Plant breezed through Mexico, Switzerland, France, Tunisia, Belgium and Holland.

A haphazard date in Italy was sandwiched between an appearance with ex-Whitesnake guitar player Bernie Marsden at the 60th birthday bash of the revered broadcaster Bob Harris in Oxfordshire.

Plant also appeared alongside the Ian Hunter Band and the New York Dolls at the Beacon Theater in New York for the Arthur Lee Benefit Concert. He played a full one hour set in NYC that began with 'In The Evening' and from there he sailed through covers of songs by Love plus Zeppelin's 'Ramble On' and 'Thank You', a version of 'Hey Joe' and the Elvis song 'I Can't Help Falling In Love With You'. Ian Hunter joined Plant on stage for covers of the Buffalo Springfield song 'For What It's Worth' and the Everly Brothers 'When Will I Be Loved'. At the time, Lee was suffering from acute leukemia and could not afford the costs of a bone marrow transplant – he died on August 3, 2006. Reviewing Plant's performance, David Fricke wrote in *Rolling Stone*: "A thrilling folk-rock gallop with Plant singing of those 'days of old, when magic filled the air' with the same excited, forward motion he heard as a teenager in Love's classic mid and late 1960s albums."

It was then time to head over to Switzerland, France, Belgium and Cork in Ireland before performances at the annual Cornbury Festival in Oxford alongside Deacon Blue and The Waterboys and at Somerset House in London. On July 12, Plant took his musicians to a hotter climate over in Calais to play at the Festival de La Cote d'Opale. Heading toward the end of July, Plant and The Strange Sensation made appearances at festivals in Italy, France, Austria, Czech Republic and Hungary. In terms of actual touring, his diary finished at The Porchester Halls in London.

The first week of November brought the welcome release of Plant's first ever solo music DVD, the aforementioned *Soundstage Presents Robert Plant And The Strange Sensation*. It's quite a remarkable example of just how energetic and creative he is despite his advancing years.

As well as the DVD, a superlative retrospective box set called *Nine Lives* was released in the UK on November 20 through Rhino Entertainment. Accompanied by a detailed booklet with colour photos, the extensive set does not feature any of the Page & Plant albums. It would be accurate to state that *Nine Lives* is a celebration of *his* solo career and any input from Page or Led Zeppelin would distract the listener from Plant's own creative pursuits. So the box set includes fully remastered and expanded editions of *Pictures At Eleven*, *The Principle Of Moments*, *The Honeydrippers: Volume 1*, *Shaken 'n' Stirred*, *Now And Zen*, *Manic Nirvana*, *Fate Of Nations*, *Dreamland*, *Mighty ReArranger* and a bonus DVD that contains a sixty minute documentary; it features interviews with Phil Collins, Roger Daltrey, Tori Amos, Ahmet Ertegun, Bobby Gillespie, Roy Harper, Nigel Kennedy, Lenny Kravitz and the former tennis champion John McEnroe.

What did the critics have to say about Plant's solo career and the way it was captured in one complete set?

Writing in *Uncut* magazine, Adam Sweeting made a very good point: "Good grief, has Robert Plant really made all these albums? More digestible is the *Sixty Six To Timbuktu* compilation, which cherry-picks the albums and adds a bunch of tantalising rarities."

The Canadian entertainment online magazine *Jam!* (*jam.conoe.ca*) stated: "You've got eye-catching packaging … It is exhaustive. And exhausting. Yet, amazingly, *Nine Lives* still fails to tell the whole story … We can understand Percy not wanting to muddy the waters of his solo work with Zep-related fare. But sound as his principles might be, on a practical level, *Nine Lives* suffers …"

Justifiably, Plant took some time to chill out before and during the Christmas period although his annual Boxing Day football shindigs also took place at his local village.[74]

★ ★ ★

Speaking to *Classic Rock* in 2004, Plant told editor Sian Llewellyn, "Is it about age? Is it about testosterone? Is it about male-ism? You know, are people just stuck in particular channels; can somebody who likes Jane's Addiction really get into Alison Krauss?"

As far as Plant was concerned, such a notion is entirely possible. Clearly Plant has expanded his musical tastes and progressed massively from his earlier blues-loving years and his next release was anticipated to be something vastly different from his previous studio work; having tackled blues, folk, rock, pop, world music and rockabilly, Plant's third post-Page & Plant foray saw him collaborate on an entire album with the revered American bluegrass country singer, acclaimed fiddle player and Grammy winner Alison Krauss. He promised that it would merge much of the music that inspired him. "I know I avoid things if I think they might be too difficult, because I never want to fail," Plant told *Uncut* in 2007. "With [the next album, with Krauss] *Raising Sand*, I finally wanted to visit the America I've always loved musically."

In 2000, Plant had reportedly made an entirely random phone call to Alison Krauss when she was at home in Nashville during which the former Led Zeppelin singer enquired about a possible collaboration. Fast forward to 2004 and the pair met in person for the first time at a tribute concert to the blues legend Leadbelly at the Rock And Roll Hall Of Fame in Cleveland. Plant was impressed with her performance during rehearsals and had it in mind that they should get a collaboration worked out.

However, both artists were busy with various projects of their own and it took them a couple of years before they could enter a studio together and make a full album; their collaboration was officially announced in October, 2006. Speaking in May, 2007, Krauss told the Nashville news site *WKRN Local News*: "[Robert Plant] suggested making a record together. I suggested [producer] T-Bone Burnett and he did a wonderful job of collecting material. We had a great time."

When they did manage to squeeze recording slots into their busy schedules, they worked on the album – *Raising Sand* – in Los Angeles and Nashville in just ten tight days. In a press statement that was reported on the music website *Live Daily* (*www.livedaily.com*) Plant said: "When we got 75 percent of the way down the line, I realised we'd created something that I could never have dreamt of."

Plant was not only working in the studio with Alison Krauss but he was also keen to lay down vocals for a Fats Domino tribute album for Vanguard Records alongside other such esteemed artists as Paul McCartney, Elton

John, Tom Petty, Willie Nelson and B.B King. Teaming up with some local musicians known as the collective Lil' Ban O' Gold, Plant worked on the songs 'It Keeps Raining', 'I've Been Around', and 'Valley Of Tears'. A living blues legend, Domino's home in Louisiana was ruined when Hurricane Katrina ripped through many southern US states in August, 2005. As reported on *Blabbermouth*, Plant told the press: "I think the sentiment and rationale behind this makes absolute sense. I've been to [Domino's] house. You've got to rebuild and do it quick and get the community back in there before it becomes some major new development for something unholy. So, I think it's a good idea. I'm glad to be here. You have to be humbled when you see what people are having to deal with."

As well as recording, quite a few important live dates were sporadically laid out through the year. Perhaps the biggest live event of the year for Robert Plant was a show stealing appearance on the second day of the Dubai Desert Rock Festival at the Country Club. March 9 witnessed performances by the Indian band Junkyard Groove, Mastodon, In Flames, Stone Sour, The Prodigy and the heroes of British heavy metal, Iron Maiden. The second day of the festival saw The Bravery and Incubus perform prior to Robert Plant's entry on the stage. *Classic Rock*'s esteemed writer Geoff Barton attended the festival and wrote in his review: "Robert Plant – barrel-chested, goatee-bearded – put in a praiseworthy performance. There were plenty of songs from his old band ... hell, it was heart-stopping stuff."

It was reported on the news website *Blabbermouth* that Plant played an impromptu three songs with the South African group Soweto Gospel Choir on April 24 at the legendary music hall Tiptina's in New Orleans. Plant made further festivals appearances throughout the year including the Rockwave Festival in Greece in June, the Live Earth show in Romania on July 8 and the Wine And Blues Festival in Malta on July 18.

On August 18, Robert Plant and The Strange Sensation performed a set during a rainy evening at the Green Man Festival at Glanusk Park in the Brecon Beacons, Wales. Speaking to *Uncut* editor Allan Jones, Plant said his performance at the Green Man Festival was "appropriate."

These days Plant's personal life rarely gets written about outside of the music press. However in September, *The Times* reported that after years of living in a luxury fifteenth century converted farmhouse, Plant "has been spotted house hunting in Hampstead, north London. The singer has been seen out and about in the area with an agent from Foxtons ... Foxtons declined to comment."

As previously mentioned, the rest of the year's news was taken up by the Led Zeppelin reunion, originally scheduled for the end of November 2007, but then moved to early December due to Jimmy breaking a finger. For those who did not manage to purchase a ticket it was simply a case of waiting for the arrival of his eagerly awaited collaborative album with Alison Krauss.

Raising Sand was issued via Rounder and Decca (sub-companies of the massive entertainment corporation Universal) on October 29, 2007 in the UK; the same month saw new studio releases by some of Plant's fellow heavyweight singer-songwriters from the 1970s, such as The Eagles, Neil Young and Bruce Springsteen & The E Street Band. "It's like nothing I've ever done," Plant told *Uncut* weeks before the album's release.

Pleasingly, considering the fact that *Raising Sand* is a collection of covers and a duet with an American country singer, the album entered the Top 10 in Plant's native homeland in its first week of release and reached the Number 2 spot in the US *Billboard* Top 200. It was a *huge* hit.

In his perceptive review of *Raising Sand* in *The Sunday Times*, Mark Edwards raised a valid point: "My worry is that a return to rock 'n' roll superstardom would do irreparable damage to Robert Plant's solo career, which is turning into the most interesting home stretch since Johnny Cash's remarkable resurgence."

Incredibly, Plant received possibly the best reviews of his career post-Led Zeppelin; in fact, a negative review in the UK press could barely be found. As well as a full five star review in *Mojo* ("one of the best albums of the year") and a glowing write-up in *Q*, Bud Scoppa wrote in his succinct review in *Uncut*: "The spacious, burnished settings ... allow Plant to overwhelm without raising his voice above a near-whisper ... This crew definitely need to stick together."

Raising Sand was given a lead review by writer Carol Clerk in the November issue of *Classic Rock*; observing that the album is "devoid of cliché." Clerk also noted that Plant and Krauss "share things democratically." Clerk's positive review finished with the line: "Plant should be equally as proud of what he has achieved here."

Record Collector named *Raising Sand* as the 'New Album Of The Month' and awarded the album four stars out of five. Reviewing the album, the noted Led Zeppelin chronicler Dave Lewis enthused: "You won't have to be a bluegrass or country fan to appreciate this."

Raising Sand opens with the sultry, softly-spoken Li'l Millet song 'Rich Woman' before Plant and Krauss murmur their way gently through Roly Salley's 'Killing The Blues'. The Sam Phillips-penned number, 'Sister Rosetta Goes Before Us', is led by the blissfully sounding Krauss while Plant stays in the background. Gene Clark's 'Polly Gone Home' is treated with surgical delicacy with both singers sounding melancholy and wistful. 'Gone Gone Gone (Done Moved On)' – an Everly Brothers tune – is a joyous, entertaining trip back in time to 1950s hillbilly-rock and roll. A second Gene Clark song, 'Through The Morning, Through The Might', is another tender lead for Krauss's sensual vocals, while Plant quietly moans behind the scenes. Yet Plant takes control of the original Page & Plant song 'Please Read The Letter' from 1998's *Walking Into Clarksdale*; here the song has more of a yearning emotion, aided by some country strings. A lead song for Krauss, Tom Waits' 'Trampled Rose', is a curious, intimate and ambient tune. The Naomi Neville-written 'Fortune Teller' sees Plant going solo, so it's actually more jazz than bluegrass. 'Stick With Me Baby', initially written Mel Tillis, is a highlight of the album with both Plant and Krauss sharing vocals to glorious effect. 'Nothin'' by Townes Van Zandt sees Plant in a chilled-out introspective mood with delicate violin strings by Krauss and flourishes of electric guitar. The amalgamation of the blues and country on 'Let Your Loss Be Your Lesson' is an obvious playground for bluegrass-country girl Krauss who sings the song on her own. Plant and Krauss sing in unison on the final song, 'Your Long Journey', by Arthur Lane Watson and Rosalie Watson; it's a beautiful folk track that proves to be a fitting end to this fascinating album.

Raising Sand is, for most of the journey, a mesmeric and intoxicating ride which – aside from a little fuzzy guitar work – is Plant's most robust music composition since 1993s *Fate Of Nations*.

It seems that as Plant is approaching 60, he shows no signs whatsoever of slowing his work pace down. Creatively, it can be argued that he is at his peak and on stage he is still as energetic and watchable as ever. He's not a washed-up rock star like some of his peers but neither is he trying to imitate his past, again like some of his contemporaries; he's a professional artist, and akin to his non-musical heroes, he is an explorer and historian eager to devour the heritage of different countries and cultures.

Perhaps the last words should be those spoken by the man himself. During an interview in September, 2007 with Allan Jones of *Uncut* magazine, Plant was modest in his opinion of himself as an ageing artist: "Half the reason I continue at my age to sort of skim ... my way through my days singing is because I want to connect with the kind of feel that was there. The feel that comes when people congregate somewhere, with the music as a catalyst."

EPILOGUE
LED ZEPPELIN RISING

It's been a long time since they've rock and rolled ...

By the end of 2007, the world – or so it seemed – had gone Led Zeppelin crazy. Every major newspaper, tabloid and magazine was counting down the days to Led Zeppelin's reunion gig on December 10 at the O₂ Centre (previously the Millennium Dome) in London. The performance was in aid of the late Ahmet Ertegun, co-founder of Atlantic Records and a friend and mentor to the band. Messrs Robert Plant, Jimmy Page, John Paul Jones and Bonham's son, Jason, planned to make history. Bonham's boy being on drums somehow stamped this new 'reunion' with absolute authenticity.

With millions having applied for the 20,000 tickets, anticipation was high; the intensity of the pressure on the four band members must have been breathtaking, with some observers suggesting this was the most high profile reunion of all-time. Given that previous Led Zep 'reunions' had proved largely underwhelming, the spotlight was all the more white hot.

And it wasn't just about the gig – what would happen afterwards?

Leading up to the show, Jimmy Page offered enticing hints of future projects, informing Q magazine that he "would like to keep this moving," and that the band's "initial get-together was so exhilarating and fun ..."

Although Plant did little to fuel such gossip, he showed great enthusiasm for the forthcoming gig when interviewed in November by Mark Kermode on BBC2's arts programme, *The Culture Show*. Rumours of a full Led Zeppelin tour for 2008 were widespread in the weeks leading up to the gig, but with tentative plans for a spring tour with the American bluegrass singer Alison Krauss, Plant was understandably reluctant to speak about future Zeppelin projects. The heavy metal news website

Blabbermouth reported that Plant was waiting to see how the December 10 gig panned out before commenting on any future plans.

The band kept tight-lipped about the set list, although Page told *NME* that their initial 40-minute slot had to be extended because of the sheer length of tunes like 'Dazed And Confused' and 'Kashmir', which were famous for having extended jam spots by the band – Bonham and Page in particular. Page was also humble about his current state of health, adding, "There's no way I can take on playing three-and-a-half-hour sets now … because I just don't have that energy anymore. But I've still got enough in me to get through a two-hour set."

And what about Jason Bonham? The son of legendary Zep sticks-man John Bonham … well, Plant, Page and Jones were all keen to express their satisfaction with their new drummer. Could they have picked a better man for the job? As quoted on *Blabbermouth*, Plant informed *The Pulse Of Radio*: "When Jason was younger and more juvenile, he thought [playing in Zeppelin] was a hereditary situation. But now, Jason knows that not only is he the right guy for this but with his enthusiasm and prowess, he's changing it."

Armed with photo ID, thousands of lucky fans were able to collect wristbands from the O_2 Arena box office on Sunday, 9 December and Monday 10, amid some very tight security and incredible press coverage. The wristbands accompanied normal tickets in a bid to stop unscrupulous touts making a financial killing in the Christmas season. *BBC News 24* showed clips of fans sleeping outside the venue in the hours leading up to the heavily hyped gig.

The O_2 Centre was in a state of media frenzy on the actual evening of December 10. A couple of hours before the gig, rock stars such as Dave Grohl and Marilyn Manson rolled up in expensive cars; other famous guests included Roger Taylor from Queen, Liam Gallagher from Oasis and the television presenter Jeremy Clarkson. Paul Rodgers, Paolo Nutini, Bill Wyman and AOR giants Foreigner were also booked to perform but everybody knew this night was all about one thing and one thing only: the return of Led Zeppelin.

The lights went down around 21:00; an excerpt from 'The Song Remains The Same' was played on the single video screen at the back of the stage; the particular archive clip used in the film showed how Zeppelin broke The Beatles' attendance record for a Californian gig back in the band's heyday in 1973.

And then it was time for the mighty atom.

The noise was, quite literally, deafening.

Led Zeppelin came on stage to the thump and groove of the opening track from their self-titled debut album, released way back in 1969. Indeed, it was a nice touch of appreciation to allow Jason Bonham to start proceedings with the famous beat to 'Good Times Bad Times'. And it was a sensible choice for the first song – not too immediately demanding on Plant's voice, compared to a higher pitched song like 'Heartbreaker'.

Of course, times had changed and the internet was now a central part of the music world. Not surprisingly, real-time commentary on the gig – both by the media and fans – was rampant. *NME.com* posted a running commentary on the gig, offering immediate and detailed opinions on how each song was played. With an unmatchable atmosphere of excitement, the band burst into what *NME.com* called a "slow, bluesy" version of 'Ramble On' and the heavy rocker 'Black Dog', which was hit by "quite muddy sound." Allegedly, Page himself had commented before the gig that he saw the Rolling Stones at the O$_2$ Centre in 2007 and thought the sound was not up to scratch.

Fantastic photos by the famed rock photographer and friend to the band, Ross Halfin, were quickly made available on the internet from the pre-gig rehearsals and the actual show. It was a simple stage design and the band looked fit and very cool. Aside from a white shirt, Page was very elegantly dressed in a black suit and dark shades. Plant was comfortable in black shirt and trousers while John Paul Jones looked a bit more rock and roll in black shirt and jeans. Bonham was more casual as he hid behind a huge drum kit.

During the gig, *BBC News 24* aired regular updates. Reporter David Sillito was backstage and even got to check out the band on stage, albeit briefly. He said that the £125 was "well spent" and that they were on "extraordinarily good form tonight." Sillito even commented that Plant was in "such fine voice." It seemed that Zeppelin had proved sceptics wrong even as the gig was only just starting.

For the first time in the evening, Plant spoke to the crowd, before the band moved on to 'In My Time Of Dying'. Then one for the fanatics – 'For Your Life' from *Presence* was played live for the first time *ever*. Page even brought out a bottleneck guitar for the number.

Reports of the set list filtered into the news rooms and on to the internet at a startling pace. It was simply jaw-dropping stuff: 'Trampled Under Foot', 'Nobody's Fault But Mine' and 'No Quarter', which saw Jones play keyboards and bass; then it was on to a lengthy rendition of 'Since I've Been Loving You' and a ten-minute version of the famously lengthy and self-indulgent blues track, 'Dazed And Confused' from 1969's *Led Zeppelin*.

And yes, they even performed 'Stairway To Heaven'.

Reportedly when they finished this song – the one Led Zep tune that Plant had refused to perform for so many years – he said to the crowd: "Ahmet, we did it!"

'The Song Remains The Same' was played with the gusto it deserves but some reports suggested that the sound was a bit poor; then the classic rock track, 'Misty Mountain Hop', from the revered *Led Zeppelin IV* preceded 'Kashmir', one of popular music's most famous songs.

Then the main set was all over.

Led Zeppelin walked off stage to a thunderous applause ...

With such an unprecedented amount of hype and such a dedicated audience, the band was inevitably going to treat the crowd to an encore and what better song than an extended version of 'Whole Lotta Love', one of rock music's most distinctly recognisable and alluring electric riffs. Plant spoke for a minute, reminding the audience that the whole point of the gig was to remember Ahmet Ertegun.

The two-hour set was brought to a close with the sixteenth and final song of the night – 'Rock And Roll' from 1971's *Led Zeppelin IV*. Remarkably, it was as if Jason Bonham had been possessed by his incredibly talented father. Okay, they didn't play 'Moby Dick', 'Heartbreaker', 'Immigrant Song', 'Communication Breakdown' or 'The Battle Of Evermore'. But this didn't matter – besides for a band with such a legendary back-catalogue, the set list was always going to cause discussion, argument and debate. That was part of the appeal. Regardless of song choices, by now the adrenaline was spiralling exponentially and the lucky audience members were enjoying their moment in popular culture history; not since the heyday of Led Zeppelin and, before them, The Beatles, had there been such an insane amount of press coverage, fan interest and sheer hysteria over tickets.

As for the future? Well, who knows what it holds. Immediately after the show, reporters were seen scurrying around the venue, interviewing ecstatic fans, all begging for a full reunion tour. There was even talk of any potential world jaunt being the world's first *billion dollar* tour ...

But that's not the point – the point is that they gave older fans a chance to relive their childhood memories and handed new fans the opportunity to appreciate a unique live experience. On December 10, 2007, Robert Plant, Jimmy Page, John Paul Jones and Jason Bonham had quashed all bad memories of previous reunion attempts and proved to the world that they could still do it.

Facing one of the highest levels of expectation in the history of rock gigs, Led Zeppelin had actually pulled it off.

Rock 'n' roll has never sounded better ...

APPENDIX I:
THE BATTLE OF EVERMORE

*"Phillip K. Dick, I liked. Ray Bradbury. The Tolkien thing grabbed
an entire generation because it's so endearing. During the Vietnam War
it wasn't unusual to see 'Frodo Lives' daubed on walls."*
Robert Plant speaking to Q magazine in 2005

During Robert Plant's younger years, he acquired an almost unhealthy
fascination with Norse/Germanic mythology and folklore which had a
dramatic effect of his lyrics and even impacted on Led Zeppelin's song
arrangements; certainly it has waned over the years but it is still a source
of interest for Led Zeppelin aficionados. It's hardly a secret that Jimmy
Page has one of the world's most extensive private collections of Aleister
Crowley memorabilia, books and manuscripts and that he once owned an
occult bookshop in London called Equinox and even Boleskine House, an
estate in Scotland previously owned by the Great Beast himself. Yet Plant's
interest in Celtic history, mythology and fantasy in general appeared to be
mostly theoretical and historical, where as Page literally built an archive
dedicated to his occultist interest; the following chapter will briefly discuss
Plant's avidness for the field and how it has made a profound impact on
his music over the years, particularly in Led Zeppelin.

The late fantasy author J.R.R. Tolkien was unquestionably one of
Plant's more obvious inspirations which led the singer to voyage further
into the swords, sorcery and heroic type of fantasy.

Born in South Africa but raised in the West Midlands – where the
working-class industrial North gave him inspiration for parts of Middle
Earth and the Shropshire hills to the west fuelled his descriptions of the
landscapes – Tolkien's novels became hugely popular with the hippie

generation during the swinging 1960s even though his famous trilogy was published in the mid-1950s and its prequel, *The Hobbit*, was published as early as 1937. Yet Tolkien was not the only author whose popularity underwent a rebirth, a number of other science fiction and fantasy writers such as Robert Heinlein and his novel *Stranger In A Strange Land* also found a new fan base who enjoyed smoking pot and taking LSD as they entered unexplored fantastical worlds.[75] Plant was one of those young hippie's who became inspired by Tolkien and his mammoth trilogy of books during the swinging 1960s. Perhaps the first glimpse of Plant's taste for the mysterious was his pre-Led Zeppelin band Hobbstweedle, whose name was taken from Tolkien's epic trilogy of fantasy works *Lord Of The Rings*.

There are scholars, academics and knowledgeable fans who could dissect Led Zeppelin's work and find minute details and references to *Lord Of The Rings* and draw all sorts of far-fetched theories; indeed the internet has pages and pages filled with such ponderings but the average rock fan will be more intrigued to learn about the young Robert Plant and the inspiration behind his lyrics than how particular Led Zeppelin songs represent specific scenes in either *The Fellowship Of The Ring*, *The Two Towers* or *The Return Of The King*.[76]

The Tolkien-Led Zeppelin connection is at its most apparent between *Led Zeppelin II* in 1969 and *Houses Of The Holy* in 1973. One of the songs which can be argued is profoundly influenced by Tolkien is 'The Battle Of Evermore'. Plant's influence on the band's lyrics became more apparent after his CBS contract – which prevented him from contributing to their first album – was terminated. Clearly the young Mr. Plant found his muse in fantasy writings and mythology which filtered through into his lyrics: 'The Battle Of Evermore', from the band's *Led Zeppelin IV*, released in 1971, name-checks the most common traits of the fantasy genre such as a queen, a prince, a dark Lord, a castle, a valley and Avalon – the Arthurian imaginary island. Another famous song to feature fantasy references is 'Ramble On' from their 1969 sophomore album and evidently this song is most definitely inspired by *Lord Of The Rings* because Gollum – a famous character (known as a Hobbit) from the books – is quoted in the lyrics.

The *Houses Of The Holy* song 'Over The Hills And Far Away' is almost self-explanatory, the song could possibly be about the core group of characters – Gandalf, the Hobbit and Bilbo – in *Lord Of The Rings* who travel over the hills of Middle Earth in search of the ring and anybody who has seen Peter Jackson's magnificent cinematic version of Tolkien's books could easily make that comparison.

There are other references of this ilk in Plant's earlier work; the singer-songwriter even went so far as to name his dog Strider, a character from *Lord Of The Rings*. Tolkien's influence certainly waned on Plant's career during the latter days of Led Zeppelin to the point where it ground to an abrupt halt.

Tolkien was certainly one of the biggest literary influences on Led Zeppelin although the influence of other writer's also shone through to a certain degree. *Houses Of The Holy* has one of the most recognisable album sleeves in the annals of rock music. The cover of the 1973 album – an amalgamation of photographs taken by Aubrey Powell – was inspired by Arthur C. Clarke's wonderful 1953 science fiction novel *Childhood's End* which also coincidentally influenced progressive rock legends Pink Floyd and David Bowie during his Ziggy Stardust years. The cover features a group of naked children climbing a hill of some sort as sunset arrives, which reflects the climax of Clarke's ponderous novel as hundreds of thousands of naked children, who only resemble humanity in their appearance, have been transformed and possess paranormal abilities such as telepathy and telekinesis.

The unrealistic imagery that fantasy authors like Tolkien and Clarke conjured in their literature didn't just inspire a lyrical outpouring of strange and surreal ideas and landscapes but such notions also manifested themselves in the actual music which reflected Plant's appetite for the unusual.

Robert Plant also displayed an intellectual curiosity with mythology and folklore especially that of Scandinavian, Greek and Celtic origin. Plant has lived on the Welsh border literally all his life and with such a vast history, as a songwriter and bohemian, was obviously going to be encouraged by the Celts, Saxons, Anglos, Christians and Pagans. At the time of *Fate Of Nations*, Plant was interviewed by *Kerrang!* rock writer Neil Jeffries: "I've been going back to some of my old haunts in the Welsh Borders and the Black Mountains," he explained. "Rediscovering my roots in remnants of Celtic culture. I've been wandering the hills with an Ordnance Survey map, checking out a lot of the old Bronze Age camps where the Celts began to fight off the Saxons. Reading all that stuff again …"

Plant stimulated his muse when Led Zeppelin spent weeks at a time during the 1970s at the remote cottage Bron-Yr-Aur in Aberllefeni in Wales and wrote the lyrically incomprehensible yet utterly alluring 'Stairway To Heaven'. The song makes all kinds of seemingly random references to forests and songbirds that could quite possibly be about the beautiful Welsh countryside and even a philistine could detect the sounds of traditional Celtic music, folk, roots and blues in 'Stairway To Heaven'. Plant is also interested in Owain Glyndwr, a Welsh rebel leader who, in the 1400s, led a failed revolt against English rule over Wales and is portrayed in Shakespeare's *Henry IV*; Paul Wetton, Plant's band mate in the Priory Of Brion, used Owen Glyndwr as a stage name during their initial tour. The former Led Zeppelin singer also named his son Karac, a Celtic name derived from the Welsh warrior Karacas.

Plant was also influenced by the nineteenth century explorer Sir Richard Francis Burton, having read Fawn M. Brodie's 1967 biography of him, *The Devil Drives : A Life Of Sir Richard Burton* prior to the making of the wonderful *Fate Of Nations* opus. Burton travelled around Asia and Africa extensively acquiring knowledge and wisdom during his life; he was also a poet, translator and linguist.

The 'good versus evil' and deeply religious traditions of Viking mythology also featured heavily in some of Plant's most famous set of lyrics such as the track, 'No Quarter', from *Houses Of The Holy*, which references the bearded and muscular god of war and thunder, Thor, son of the mighty Odin. Perhaps the most heavily quoted line from a Led Zeppelin song that derives inspiration from Norse/Scandinavian mythology is from the classic track 'Immigrant Song' from *Led Zeppelin III*. The song features a famous vocal wail and with Plant's long hair and toned physique, it is not too far fetched to say that on stage in front of an audience of literally thousands, Plant vaguely resembled a character from Scandinavian mythology, with his swinging microphone as a weapon.

Written in memory of the ancient Icelandic explorer Leif Erickson, 'Immigrant Song' makes vivid references to Norse mythology and ancient Norse religion. The song's premise is simple; it is about the ancient Viking conquests and their exploration of the western world in search of new lands and cultures. 'Immigrant Song' quotes Valhalla, the 'Hall of Slain'; it is said that Valhalla was a type of heaven for Vikings who died during battle under Odin's command and thus would be brought back to life in the hall of Valhalla; those who did not die fighting on the side of Odin and the gods were banished elsewhere to a literal hell. The song features pounding beats and sound effects to summon the listener's imagination as if the Vikings were actually going to battle, travelling by sea on their boats, hearing the oars rush through the water in deep slashes and then, once on land, racing forward with their weapons. Stephen Davis' popular unofficial band biography, *Hammer Of The Gods*, derives its famous title from a line in the 'Immigrant Song'.

Black Sabbath may have influenced popular heavy metal bands with an pseudo-occult/satanic image – such as the black metal band Venom and US thrash metal titans Slayer – and even British metal heroes Iron Maiden and Judas Priest circa 1977 have played around with such imagery albeit in a firmly tongue and cheek fashion. Yet it was Led Zeppelin and Robert Plant's earlier enthusiasm for Norse mythology and the fantasies of author/academic Tolkien that primarily inspired the Viking-esque, 'swords and sorcery' style of heavy metal imagery as manifested in such bands as Dio, Manowar and the Swedish outfit Hammerfall.

APPENDIX II:
ENCORE:

STARRING ROLES

Here is a list of former collaborators and friends/acquaintances who have made appearances in Robert Plant's life and career and contributed to this book:

Al Atkins: His latest album is called *Demon Deceiver*, released in 2006 via Diesel & Glory. For information on Al Atkins and his band The Holy Rage, visit his official website *www.alatkins.com* and *www.myspace.com/alatkinsholyrage*

Frankie Banali: He is the drummer in the American heavy metal band Quiet Riot. He released a terrific Led Zeppelin tribute album in 2007 called *24/7/365: The Tribute To Led Zeppelin,* which featured contributions from Glenn Hughes, amongst many others.

Michael Davis: He is the bassist in the legendary Detroit rock band MC5 and can be contacted at *www.MC5.org*

Andy Edwards: He lives in the Midlands and teaches drums. For information, visit *andyedwardsmusic.blogspot.com* and *www.myspace.com/59729647*

Chris Hughes: He is a very successful record producer and can be contacted at *www.chughes.co.uk*

Tim Palmer: Now based in California, Tim is a revered producer, engineer and songwriter who has worked with Ozzy Osbourne, HIM and Pearl Jam. For information, visit *www.timpalmer.com*

Hossam Ramzy: He is a highly-acclaimed percussionist based in the UK but born in Egypt. Visit his official website for information: *www.hossamramzy.com*

Innes Sibun: Recognised as a guitar virtuoso, Innes can be contacted at his official website: *www.innessibun.com* and *www.myspace.com/innessibun*. His latest CD is called *Tail Dragger.*

Mark Stanway: He is the keyboardist in the revered Midlands melodic rock band Magnum. Visit *www.magnumband.co.uk*

Mark Stein: He is still in the classic rock band Vanilla Fudge and can be contacted at *www.mark-stein.com*

Dave Weckl: A highly respected session drummer specialising in Jazz, Dave can be visited at *www.davidweckl.com*

APPENDIX III:
TIMELINE

Here is a selective list of some important dates in Robert Plant's life and career.

1948

August 20: Robert Plant was born in West Bromwich, West Midlands in England

1966

November: Listen with Robert Plant released their only single 'You Better Run' – a cover version of song by The Young Rascals

1967

March: Robert Plant's first solo single – 'Our Song'/'Laughin', Cryin', Laughin'' – was released in the UK

September: Plant's second solo single for CBS 'Long Time Coming'/'I've Got A Secret' was released in the UK

1968

May: The third and final version of the Band Of Joy featuring Robert Plant split up

October 15: Led Zeppelin made their first live appearance at the University of Surrey, Guildford

December 26: Led Zeppelin made their first live appearance in the US

1969

March 28: Led Zeppelin was released in the UK

October 31: Led Zeppelin II was released in the UK

November 9: Plant married Maureen Wilson in London – Zeppelin also played at the Roundhouse, Chalk Farm in London

1970

October 23: Led Zeppelin III was released in the UK

1971

October: Plant and Page made trips to India and parts of East Asia

November 12: Led Zeppelin IV was released in the UK

1972

March: Plant and Page made some recordings in Bombay with the Bombay Symphony Orchestra. Plant was awe-struck by what he experienced

1973

January 2: Plant caught the flu after hitch-hiking to a gig in Sheffield after Bonham's Bentley broke down

March 26: Houses Of The Holy was released in the UK

1974

January: The band were re-signed to Atlantic Records

1975

February 24: A double-album, *Physical Graffiti* was released in the UK

May 26: Robert and Maureen Plant flew to Agadir in Morocco for a holiday – his trip influenced him to write 'Achilles Last Stand'

August 4: Robert and Maureen Plant were involved in a serious car accident on the Greek island, Rhodes

1976

January: Plant begun to walk without aid for the first time since his car accident

April 5: Presence was released in the UK

October 20: The Song Remains The Same was premiered in New York at Cinema I

October 22: The soundtrack to *The Song Remains The Same* was also released in the UK

1977

July 23: Led Zeppelin played the Day On The Green festival in Oakland, California

July 24: Led Zeppelin played their last ever US concert at the second Day On The Green festival

July 26: On tour in America, Plant was told his five-year-old son had died

1978

August: Plant joined Dr Feelgood on stage in Spain

November 1: Plant took part in an auction at the Golden Lion pub in Fulham, London

1979

January 21: Plant's third child, Logan Romero, was born

June 9: Plant gave his first interview in two years

August 20: In Through The Out Door was released in the UK

1980

September 24: John Bonham was found dead

October 10: John Bonham was cremated at Rushock Parish Church in Worcestershire

December 4: Page, Plant and Jones issued a press statement saying Led Zeppelin would not continue after Bonham's death

1981

March: Plant played some live dates in the R&B band The Honeydrippers

1982

June 28: Robert Plant's first solo album, *Pictures At Eleven*, was released in the UK

September: The single 'Burning Down One Side' was released in the UK

November 22: Led Zeppelin's final album *Coda* was posthumously released in the UK

1983

July 4: The single 'Big Log' was released in the UK

July 11: The Principle Of Moments was released in the UK

November: The single 'In The Mood' was released in the UK

1984

November 12: The Honeydrippers: Volume One was released in the UK
December 15: The Honeydrippers performed on *Saturday Night Live* in America, hosted by Eddie Murphy

1985

January 18: Plant and The Honeydrippers (performing as 'The Skinnydippers') played a benefit gig at Rolls Hall in Monmouth, south Wales
February 2: The Honeydrippers single 'Sea Of Love' was released in the UK
May: The single 'Pink And Black' was released in the UK
May 20: Shaken 'n' Stirred was released in the UK
July 13: Page, Plant and Jones 'reunited' Led Zeppelin with Phil Collins and Tony Thompson on drums for the *Live Aid* charity concert at JFK Stadium in Philadelphia
August 19: The single 'Little By Little' was released in the UK

1986

March: Plant and The Big Town Playboys played some dates at various UK universities

1987

August 9: At a festival in Oxfordshire, Plant joined Fairport Convention on stage for a joint encore

1988

January 18: The single 'Heaven Knows' was released in the UK
February 29: Now And Zen was released in the UK
April 11: The single 'Tall Cool One' was released in the UK

1989

January/February: Plant began recording his new album
February: A video collection called *Mumbo Jumbo* was issued in the UK
November: Another Zeppelin 'reunion' took place at Plant's daughter's 21st birthday party in the Midlands
December 23: Plant made an appearance at a gig by Out Of The Blue at The Swan Centre in Kidderminster

1990

March 19: Manic Nirvana was released in the UK
March 26: The single 'Hurting Kind (I've Got My Eyes On You)' was released in the UK
May: The single 'Your Ma Said You Cried In You Sleep Last Night' was released in the UK
October 15: Led Zeppelin Remasters was released in the UK
October 25: The Song Remains The Same was released on video in the UK
October 29: Led Zeppelin: Volume 1 box set was released in the UK

1991

January: Three rescheduled dates at the London Town & Country Club

1992

February 6: Completed recording of *Fate Of Nations*, Plant's sixth full studio album

April 20: Plant performed at the Freddie Mercury tribute concert at Wembley Stadium in London

August 11: Joined Fairport Convention on stage during their encore at the Mill Theatre in Banbury

August 14: Joined Fairport Convention on stage during their encore at the Cropredy Festival

November 18: The remaining members of Led Zeppelin and Jason Bonham accepted the Q Merit award at a ceremony in London

1993

May 1: Fate Of Nations was released in the UK

May 8: The single '29 Palms' was released in the UK

May 14: Plant premiered his new band in the UK at the King's Head pub in Fulham, London

June 25: Played Glastonbury Festival

June 26: Played at the Midtfyns Festival in Ringe, Denmark

June 27: Played at the Parkpop Festival in Den Haag, Holland

July 3: The single 'I Believe' was released in the UK

October 9: Led Zeppelin: Volume 2 box set was released in the UK

December 25: The single 'If I Were A Carpenter' was released in the UK

1994

January 23: Led Zeppelin: Complete Recordings was released in the UK

August: Filming took place in Morocco, London and Wales for the *No Quarter* film and CD

October 14: No Quarter (CD) was released in the UK

December: A trio of Page & Plant singles were issued in the UK: 'Gallows Pole'/'Thank You', 'City Don't Cry'/'The Rain Song' and 'Four Sticks'/'What Is And What Should Never Be'

1995

January 12: Led Zeppelin was inducted into the US Rock And Roll Hall Of Fame

January 30: Robert Plant, Jimmy Page and Jason Bonham collected the 'International Artist Award' at the American Music Awards

November 21: Peter Grant died of a heart attack

1996

February: Page & Plant played five nights at the Budokan Hall in Japan

1997

May 29: Plant, Page and John Paul Jones collected an award at the Ivor Novello Awards

August 29: Led Zeppelin's only CD single, 'Whole Lotta Love', was released in the US via Atlantic Records

November 29: Led Zeppelin BBC Sessions was released in the UK

1998

April 11: The Page & Plant single, 'Most High', was released in the UK

April 21: Walking Into Clarksdale was released in the UK

December 10: Plant played his last gig as a duet with Jimmy Page in Paris – their collaboration then came to an abrupt end

1999

July 23: Priory Of Brion played the Three Tuns at Bishop's Castle in Shropshire

December 8: Priory Of Brion played at the Town Hall in Stourbridge,

2000

April 1: Early Days: The Best Of Led Zeppelin Volume One was released in the UK

April 1: Latter Days: The Best Of Led Zeppelin Volume Two was released in the UK

April 27-28: Priory Of Brion played at the Ole Blues Festival in Bergen, Norway

June 5: The Song Remains The Same was released on DVD in the UK

August: Recorded a cover of the Sonny Burgess tune 'My Bucket's Got A Whole In It' with Jimmy Page at Abbey Road Studios for a Sun Records tribute album

2001

July 18: Robert Plant and The Strange Sensation played at the Pori Jazz Festival in Finland

2002

June 16: Dreamland was released in the UK

2003

May 26: The two disc DVD *Led Zeppelin* was released in the UK

June 7: How The West Was Won was released in the UK

July 23: A poll ranked *Led Zeppelin IV* as one of the top-four best selling albums in America with sales of 23 million

November 3: Sixty Six To Timbuktu was released in the UK

2004

March: Plant made a guest appearance at a Vanilla Fudge concert at the Stourbridge Rock Cafe

October 11: No Quarter: Jimmy Page Robert Plant Unledded was released on DVD in the UK

October: Recorded 'Look Out Mabel' with Jeff Beck and The Big Town Playboys for the latter's album *Roll The Dice*

2005

March 17: Plant delivered a speech and played live at the Southwest Music And Media Conference in Texas

May 2: Mighty ReArranger was released in the UK

September 16: Plant performed a set in Chicago for the popular PBS series *Soundstage*

2006

April 26: Plant performed an impromptu set at Bob Harris' 60th birthday party

November 6: The live DVD *Soundstage Presents Robert Plant and The Strange Sensation* was released in the UK

November 20: Nine Lives box set was released in the UK

December 23: The Honeydrippers played the Kidderminster Town Hall

2007

February 14: The Honeydrippers played JB's in Dudley

March 9-10: Performed at the Dubai Desert Rock Festival

March 20: A remastered and expanded CD of *Mighty ReArranger* was released in the UK

June: Persistent rumours of a Led Zeppelin reunion circulated on the Internet

June 25: An unofficial/bootleg DVD *Led Zeppelin: Live At Knebworth 1979* was released on DVD in the UK

June 29: Plant performed at Greece's Rockwave festival

July 8: Plant performed a gig at Live Earth in Romania

July 18: Plant played at Malta's Wine And Blues Festival

October 29: Raising Sand, Plant's album with Alison Krauss, was issued in the UK

November 12: Led Zeppelin collection *Mothership* was released in the UK

December 10: Remaining members of Led Zeppelin (with Jason Bonham) reunited for a gig at London's O2 Arena

APPENDIX IV:
SOME WORDS ON
ROBERT PLANT

At the time of writing, in 2007 the author spoke to various well-known people in the music business about Robert Plant and here's what they had to say about the rock icon:

Al Atkins (Ex-Judas Priest): *"Robert and myself were born in West Bromwich and we're both more or less of the same age. We were both heavily into music and ended up vocalists in local bands – Rob in the Band Of Joy and myself in The Bitta Sweet...Within a year he teamed up with Led Zeppelin and not long after that I formed Judas Priest in 1969. I remember him as a really nice guy with a great voice, his unique vocal range and style was admired and copied by most rock vocalists, including myself..."*

Frankie Banali (Quiet Riot): *"Robert Plant initially had a very difficult task to accomplish. That was to write lyrics and melodies for the music that Jimmy Page and Led Zeppelin as a whole created. The diversity of the music written could not just be viewed as a canvas for stock lyrical, melodic or vocal normality. As diverse as the music was, so were the lyrics, melodies and vocals. Each record that Robert Plant has released always has something special, something different, something broader to offer than many of his contemporaries. Robert Plant developed a writing and singing style that was, and still is, completely original and unique. Couple this with a magnificent vocal range, and a confident stage presence and you truly do have a national living musical treasure in him ..."*

Moya Brennan (Clannad): *"I love the album [Fate Of Nations] as a whole but I think I can be forgiven for enjoying my songs the most! He was extremely charming and a real gentleman ..."*

Michael Davis (MC5): *"Let me put it this way: what I see in Robert Plant is strength. I see strength and feeling; the two most important elements in all music. He exudes emotion and talent and skill. He is not afraid to experiment. And the motherfucker's experiments always seem to work."*

Kevin DuBrow (Quiet Riot): *"Robert Plant influenced me more than I ever knew. Being in a band with a drummer (Frankie Banali) who is the world's Number One Led Zep fan, Plant had to wear off on me. Plant's great ability in my opinion is vocal parts he wrote to really unusual backing music. He made what seemed like ad libs really great, well-written parts. Just listen to the end of 'Whole Lotta Love'. It could take months to come up with those parts, if ever. His tone, especially on the earlier albums, was like a blues wailing siren. Just amazing!"* (R.I.P., 2007)

Tony Harnell (Starbreaker): *"He was the first guy I can recall who was singing that high, for one thing, so that was, of course, an influence. But I remember my first band played a lot of Zeppelin so I sort of cut my teeth singing Zep early on. I have grown to appreciate him even more as I have grown as an artist ... I love where Robert has gone as an artist: back to his roots and very eclectic.*

He's a true artist; he doesn't sit back and rely on his glory days [in] Zep. He's still in there and still viable and that's very good for the young artists today to see. Experience is just as important as young rebellion in music, Robert still has something to say and I love that."

Chris Hughes (Producer): *"Robert is peerless as a singer, unique; influential beyond calculation. I would call him one of the founding fathers. He has a complicated, restless soul."*

Tim Palmer (Producer): *"I still keep in contact with Robert, not every day or anything like that but he's one of the few people of that stature that I've ever worked with who, when they come through Los Angeles, you won't hear something through a third party [instead] I'll get a phone call on my cell phone and it's, 'Hello ... it's Robert here, I'm playing a show, do you wanna come and see it?' It's just so nice of him to do that; he never forgets to call [and] he's always been a complete gentleman to me. I think there's every possibility I could work with Robert again; it's been long enough now as a gap. I think it would be fun [and] I feel as though I'm a different producer than I was back in the 1980s, I guess you have to be otherwise you may as well stop."*

Simon Phillips (Toto): *"I have always admired how Robert has always moved forward with his music – forming different bands and trying new things and working with young musicians. It seems like he always has a new idea or some goal he wants to pursue. It seems that age never gets in the way of his creativity – and that is a very healthy way to live!"*

Don Powell (Slade): *"Slade played Dallas, Texas in the 1970s, Zeppelin came to the show, unknown to us, and were armed with lots of fruit, and proceeded to pelt us, while we were on stage ... even though we were having a really good night. They came backstage after the show and we knew straight away it was them! We shouted to them: "You fucking cunts! It was you!" We all had a great after-show party that night, except when John Bonham wanted to kill [bassist] Jim Lea!"*

Hossam Razmy (Percussionist): *"Robert is a genius artist ... and has a cutting edge with rhythm and likes music to be raw and muddy, earthy and full of grind. He creates music that's ... diverse and he has no limit to where he is prepared to go with a sound. This is the kind of artist I prefer to work with."*

Innes Sibun (Blues Guitarist): *"Well, I was a huge Zeppelin fan from an early age so I've always admired him and still do. He does his own thing and hasn't jumped onto the nostalgia bandwagon like so many of his contemporaries; he keeps striving and moving forward, which is great. He taught me a lot about music and performing ..."*

Mark Stanway (Magnum): *"I have known Robert since the early 1980s but as a close friend for several years. For the last couple of years (in between our respective touring commitments), we have been in a pub quiz team together. He is a true pro and exceptionally talented, he plays very good guitar and blows a mean harmonica; he is a perfectionist but not contrived; he is a workaholic, a musical encyclopaedia. To cap: I suppose one could say he is a purist.' On a personal level, I am proud to have him as a close friend and find him very amusing, most entertaining, wonderfully* *generous and extremely well-read; a most down to earth bloke – well, as much down to earth as a living legend could be. A thoroughly nice guy and good friend ..."*

Mark Stein (Vanilla Fudge): *"Robert became the epitome of all front men; no-one in rock could come close to the power and command he had in front of an audience. When you talk about grace, sexuality and energy, Plant was all that rolled up into one. He had an amazing look and the magnetism – what he and Page portrayed was magic! As a singer, he reached notes that were in the stratosphere and his style and phrasing was unique!"*

Marc Storace (Krokus): *"When I first heard Led Zeppelin, I was already singing hard rock and deep into the new underground movement. My band Cinnamon Hades had a large following consisting mainly of local and foreign students who were the sons and daughters of British and American Forces servicemen stationed in Malta. Our repertoire included [many of] their songs. I was blown away by Robert Plant's high range and vocal flexibility and 'Since I've Been Loving You' really proved he was the master of emotions. On top of that, he wrote lyrics I could relate to. I particularly loved the bluesy, loose feeling of this very tight band and the ethereal communication which went on between Plant and Page was simply phenomenal."*

Joe Lynn Turner (Ex-Rainbow & Deep Purple): *"I think he did some stretching out after Zeppelin, which is really admirable. He put out some very credible stuff in the 1980s between The Honeydrippers and his solo material ... It would be impossible for him not to have an influence. Even today ... take a band like Wolfmother – totally influenced by Plant."*

Midge Ure (Ex-Ultravox): *"[His music is] very melodic ... great structure to his songs while remaining [with] his roots in blues and still exploring new influences in traditional music ... Africa, etc. Anyone who ever was, wants to be, or is in a rock and roll band owes a nod of recognition to Robert Plant!"*

Dave Weckl (Jazz Drummer): *"He is an icon in the industry. He has set in the history books a style of writing and singing that was the 'beginning' – the foundation for lots of rock bands still, to this day. Having said that, I really like him! [I] always have and was honoured to be on that recording [*The Honeydrippers: Volume 1 EP*] with him..."*

APPENDIX V:
BONUS TRACKS:

ROBERT PLANT – SELECTIVE SET LISTS

It is not plausible to print every set list Robert Plant has ever played (that would make a book of its own!) during his solo career, but it is possible to print one or two set lists from each of his solo tours, which show the diversity of his performances and the progression of his career. Set lists change all the time; artists get bored and tweak them here and there, adding a song or moving a track to a different section of the gig, so each set list will include the date when the songs were performed.

Special acknowledgement must be made to the excellent archive website the *Robert Plant Homepage* (*www.robertplanthomepage.com*) as well as *Kerrang!* and *Metal Hammer.*

ROBERT PLANT

1983

(August 27 – Performed at Wings Stadium, Kalamazoo in Michigan in support of Pictures At Eleven & The Principle Of Moments*)*
1. 'In The Mood'
2. 'Pledge Pin'
3. 'Messin' With The Mekon'
4. 'Worse Than Detroit'
5. 'Moonlight In Samosa'
6. 'Fat Lip'
7. 'Thru' With The Two Step'
8. 'Other Arms'
9. 'Horizontal Departure'
10. 'Slow Dance'
11. 'Mystery Title'
12. 'Wreckless Love'
13. 'Like I've Never Been Gone'
14. 'Big Log'
15. 'Burning Down One Side'
16. 'Stranger Here … Than Over There'

1984

(February 6 – Performed in Melbourne, Australia in support of The Principle Of Moments*)*
1. 'In The Mood'
2. 'Pledge Pin'
3. 'Messin' With The Mekon'
4. 'Fat Lip'
5. 'Thru' With The Two Step'
6. 'Mystery Title'
7. 'Horizontal Departure'
8. 'Wreckless Love'

9. 'Slow Dancer'
10. 'Like I've Never Been Gone'
11. 'Big Log'
12. 'Burning Down One Side'
13. 'Little Sister'
14. 'Treat Her Right'
15. 'Stranger Here ... Than Over There'

1985

(June 17 – Performed at the LA Forum, California in support of Shaken 'n' Stirred*)*
1. 'In The Mood'
2. 'Pledge Pin'
3. 'Pink And Black'
4. 'Doo Doo A Do Do'
5. 'Little By Little'
6. 'Thru' With The Two Step'
7. 'Slow Dancer'
8. 'Young Boy Blues'
10. 'Honey Hush'
11. 'See Of Love'
12. 'Easily Lead'
13. 'Big Log'
14. 'Kallalou Kallalou'

1988

(April 11 – Performed at the Hammersmith Apollo, London in support of Now And Zen*)*
1. 'Helen Of Troy'
2. 'Other Arms'
3. 'Little By Little'
4. 'Train Kept A Rollin''
5. 'In The Evening'
6. 'In The Mood'
7. 'Black Country Woman'
8. 'Big Log'
9. 'Heaven Knows'
10. 'Dimples'
11. 'Going To California'
12. 'Billy's Revenge'
13. 'Tall Cool One'
14. 'Custard Pie'
15. 'Ship Of Fools'

1990

(May 22 – Performed at the Palais des Sportes, Paris in support of Manic Nirvana*)*

1. 'Watching You'
2. 'Nobody's Fault But Mine'
3. 'Billy's Revenge'
4. 'Tie Dye On The Highway'
5. 'In The Mood'
6. 'No Quarter'
7. 'Liar's Dance'
8. 'Tall Cool One'
9. 'Nirvana'
10. 'Immigrant Song'
11. 'Hurting Kind (I've Got My Eyes On You)'
12. 'Misty Mountain Hop'
13. 'Communication Breakdown'

1993

(June 4 – Performed at the Sporthalle, Cologne in support of Fate Of Nations*)*

1. 'Calling To You'
2. 'Ramble On'
3. '29 Palms'
4. 'If I Were A Carpenter'
5. 'Going To California'
6. 'Promised Land'
7. 'What Is And What Should Never Be'
8. 'Tie Dye On The Highway'
9. 'Whole Lotta Love'

(July 14 – Performed at the Birmingham NEC, England in support of Fate Of Nations*)*

1. 'Tall Cool One'
2. 'Ramble On'
3. 'I Believe'
4. 'Thank You'
5. 'Bluebird'
6. 'If I Were A Carpenter'
7. 'Going To California'
8. '29 Palms'
9. 'Promised Land'
10. 'Calling To You'
11. 'What Is And What Should Never Be'
12. 'Ship Of Fools'
13. 'Hurting Kind'
14. 'You Shook Me'
15. 'Whole Lotta Love'

1994

(January 22 – Performed in Rio de Janeiro, Brazil in support of Fate Of Nations)

1. 'Babe I'm Gonna Leave You'
2. '29 Palms'
3. 'Ramble On'
4. 'Tall Cool One'
5. 'Thank You'
6. 'If I Were A Carpenter'
7. 'Going To California'
8. 'Black Country Woman'
9. 'In The Mood'
10. 'Calling To You'
11. 'Hurting Kind (I Got My Eyes On You)'
12. 'Whole Lotta Love'
13. 'Rock And Roll'

THE HONEYDRIPPERS

1981

(April 13 – Performed with The Honeydrippers at The Blue Note Club in Derby, England)
1. 'Little Sister'
2. 'Hey Mae'
3. 'Lotta Lovin''
4. 'Your True Love'
5. 'Deep In The Heart Of Texas'
6. 'Honky Tonk'
7. 'How Many More Years?'
8. 'Cross Cut Saw'
10. 'Bring It On Home'
11. 'I Can't Be Satisfied'
12. 'Sugar Coated Love'
13. 'Bad Love'
14. 'What Can I Do'
15. 'Tell Me How'
16. 'Queen Of The Hop'
17. 'She She Little Sheila'
18. 'Got My Mojo Working'

1985

(January 18 – Performed at the Rolls Hall in Monmouth, Wales)
1. 'Move It'
2. 'Jailhouse Rock'
3. 'Going Down Slow'
4. 'Every Little Bit Hurts'
5. 'Crosscut Saw'
6. 'All Your Love'
7. 'I Need Your Loving Every Day'

8. 'Your True Love'
9. 'Georgia On My Mind'
10. 'Mystery Train'
11. 'Born Under A Bad Sign'
12. 'Roll Roll Roll'
13. 'The Young Ones'
14. 'Save The Last Dance For Me'
15. 'Can't Be Satisfied'
16. 'Great Balls Of Fire'
17. 'Little Sister'

2006

(December 23 – Performed at the Kidderminster Town Hall, England)
1. 'Mess Of Blues'
2. 'Little Sister'
3. 'She Little Sheila'
4. 'It's Gonna Work Out Fine'
5. 'Black Magic Woman'
6. 'Keep On Loving Me'
7. 'Big Log'
8. 'Can't Be Satisfied'
9. 'Rattlesnake Shake'
10. 'Big Hunk Of Love'
11. 'Daddy Rolling Stone'
12. 'What I'd Say'
13. 'Silent Night/Santa Claus'

PAGE & PLANT

1995

(March 22 – Performed at the US Air Arena, Washington DC in support of No Quarter*)*
1. 'The Wanton Song'
2. 'Bring It On Home'
3. 'Celebration Day'
4. 'Thank You'
5. 'Dancing Days'
6. 'Shake My Tree'
7. 'Lullaby'
8. 'No Quarter'
9. 'Gallows Pole'
10. 'Nobody's Fault But Mine'
11. 'The Song Remains The Same'
12. 'Since I've Been Loving You'
13. 'Friends'
14. 'Calling To You'
15. 'Four Sticks'
16. 'In The Evening'
17. 'Black Dog'
18. 'Kashmir

(October 27 – Performed at Madison Square Garden, New York in support of No Quarter*)*

1. 'The Wanton Song'
2. 'Bring It On Home'
3. 'Heartbreaker'
4. 'Ramble On'
5. 'No Quarter'
6. 'Tangerine'
7. 'Gallows Pole'
8. 'Since I've Been Loving You'
9. 'The Song Remains The Same'
10. 'Going To California'
11. 'Babe I'm Gonna Leave You'
12. 'Whole Lotta Love'
13. 'Four Sticks'
14. 'In The Evening'
15. 'Black Dog'
16. 'Kashmir'
17. 'Rock And Roll'

1998

(March 5 – Performed in Istanbul, Turkey in support of Walking Into Clarksdale*)*

1. 'The Wanton Song'
2. 'Bring It On Home'
3. 'Heartbreaker'
4. 'Ramble On'
5. 'Walking Into Clarksdale'
6. 'No Quarter'
7. 'Going To California'
8. 'Tangerine'
9. 'Gallows Pole'
10. 'Most High'
11. 'Babe I'm Gonna Leave You'
12. 'How Many More Times'
13. 'Burning Up'
14. 'Whole Lotta Love'
15. 'Thank You'
16. 'Rock And Roll'

(November 28 – Performed at the Zenith in Toulon, France in support of Walking Into Clarksdale*)*

1. 'The Wanton Song'
2. 'Heartbreaker'
3. 'What Is And What Should Never Be'
4. 'Walking Into Clarksdale'
5. 'No Quarter'
6. 'When The World Was Young'
7. 'Going To California'
8. 'Tangerine'
9. 'Gallows Pole'

10. 'Heart In Your Hand'

11. 'Babe I'm Gonna Leave You'

12. 'Most High'

13. 'How Many More Times'

14. 'Ramble On'

15. 'Whole Lotta Love'

16. 'Rock And Roll'

PRIORY OF BRION

1999

(September 25 – Performed at the Boardwalk in Sheffield)

1. 'Season Of The Witch'

2. 'Morning Dew'

3. 'A House Is Not A Motel'

4. 'A Wondrous Place'

5. 'Girl From The North Country'

6. 'If I Were A Carpenter'

7. 'Darkness Darkness'

8. 'Think'

9. 'Early In The Morning'

10. 'We're Gonna Groove'

11. 'Baby, Please Don't Go'

12. 'No Regrets'

13. 'Gloria'

14. 'Trouble In Mind'

15. 'Evil Woman'

16. 'High School Confidential'

2000

(April 3 – Performed at The Roadmender in Northampton)

1. 'Season Of The Witch'

2. 'A House Is Not A Motel'

3. 'August'

4. 'Bluebird'

5. 'If I Were A Carpenter'

6. 'Darkness Darkness'

7. 'Early In The Morning'

8. 'Think'

9. 'We're Gonna Groove'

10. 'Baby, Please Don't Go'

11. 'As Long As I Have You'

12. 'Gloria'

13. 'Morning Dew'

14. 'Trouble In Mind'

ROBERT PLANT & THE STRANGE SENSATION

2001

(June 4 – Performed at the State Theater, Detroit in support of Dreamland*)*
1. 'If I Ever Get Lucky'
2. 'Morning Dew'
3. 'In The Light'
4. 'Season Of The Witch'
5. 'Sitting By The Window'
6. 'Hey Joe'
7. 'Four Sticks'
8. 'Bummer In The Summer'
9. 'Seven And Seven Is …'
10. 'A House Is Not A Motel'
11. 'Babe I'm Gonna Leave You'
12. 'In The Mood'
13. 'Whole Lotta Love'
14. 'Misty Mountain Hop'
15. 'Song To The Siren'

2002

(May 31 – Performed at Liverpool University, England in support of Dreamland*)*
1. 'If I Ever Get Lucky'
2. 'Seven And Seven Is …'
3. 'Down To The Sea'
4. 'Four Sticks'
5. 'Come In To My Life'
6. 'Hey Joe'
7. 'Going To California'
8. 'Morning Dew'
9. 'Calling To You'
10. 'Tall Cool One'
11. 'Celebration Day'
12. 'A House Is Not A Motel'
13. 'Song To The Siren'
14. 'Babe I'm Gonna Leave You'

2003

(July 24 – Performed at the Sonica Festival in Verona, Italy in support of Sixty Six To Timbuktu*)*
1. 'If I Ever Get Lucky'
2. 'Four Sticks'
3. 'Morning Dew'
4. 'Seven And Seven Is …'
5. 'Gallows Pole'
6. 'Going To California'
7. 'Girl From The North Country'
8. 'Hey Joe'
9. 'Ramble On'
10. 'Last Time I Saw Her'

11. 'Tall Cool One'
12. 'Babe I'm Gonna Leave You'
13. 'Darkness, Darkness'
14. 'Whole Lotta Love'

2005

(April 15 – Performed at the Icehall in Helsinki, Finland in support of Mighty ReArranger*)*
1. 'No Quarter'
2. 'Shine It All Around'
3. 'Black Dog'
4. 'Freedom Fries'
5. 'Darkness, Darkness'
6. 'That's The Way'
7. 'Tin Pan Valley'
8. 'Takamba'
9. 'Gallows Pole'
10. 'When the Levee Breaks'
11. 'Babe I'm Gonna Leave You'
12. 'The Enchanter'
13. 'Whole Lotta Love'

2006

(July 10 – Performed at the Somerset House in England in support of Mighty ReArranger*)*
1. 'Tin Pan Valley'
2. 'Seven And Seven Is …'
3. 'Black Dog'
4. 'Let The Four Winds Blow'
5. 'Going To California'
6. '29 Palms'
7. 'Friends'
8. 'Morning Dew'
9. 'The Enchanter'
10. 'Four Sticks'
11. 'Gallows Pole'
12. 'When The Levee Breaks'
13. 'Whole Lotta Love'

APPENDIX VI:
SELECTIVE DISCOGRAPHY (UK)

Robert Plant's discography is very complicated and extensive so the author has made it as easily digestible as possible by including only 'official' releases on all Led Zeppelin/Robert Plant related albums and singles. Each album listed here includes the original release date, label and a full track listing. Wherever relevant, the author has added bonus tracks that were included on any (CD) reissue. This is by no means a complete and authoritative list and the author has referred to UK releases only...

PRE-LED ZEPPELIN

SINGLES (LP)

Listen
You Better Run/Everybody's Gotta Say (1966 – CBS)

Solo Singles
Our Song/Laughing, Crying, Laughing (1967 – CBS)

Long Time Coming/I've Got A Secret (1967 – CBS)

LED ZEPPELIN

STUDIO ALBUMS

Led Zeppelin (1969 – Atlantic)
Track Listing: *Good Times Bad Times/Babe I'm Gonna Leave You/You Shook Me/Dazed And Confused/Your Time Is Gonna Come/Black Mountain Side/Communication Breakdown/I Can't Quit You Baby/How Many More Times*

Led Zeppelin II (1969 – Atlantic)
Track Listing: *Whole Lotta Love/What Is And What Should Never Be/The Lemon Song/Thank You/Heartbreaker/Living Loving Maid (She's Just A Woman)/Ramble On/Moby Dick/Bring It On Home*

Led Zeppelin III (1970 – Atlantic)
Track Listing: *Immigrant Song/Friends/Celebration Day/Since I've Been Loving You/Out On The Tiles/Gallows Pole/Tangerine/That's The Way/Bron-Y-Aur Stomp/Hats Off To (Roy Harper)*

Led Zeppelin IV (1971 – Atlantic)
Track Listing: *Black Dog/Rock And Roll/The Battle Of Evermore/Stairway To Heaven/Misty Mountain Top/Four Sticks/Going To California/When The Levee Breaks*

House Of The Holy (1973 – Atlantic)
Track Listing: *The Song Remains The Same/The Rain Song/Over The Hills And Far Away/The Crunge/Dancing Days/D'yer Mak'er/No Quarter/The Ocean*

Physical Graffiti (1975 – Swan Song/Warner)
Track Listing: *Custard Pie/The Rover/In My Time Of Dying/House Of The Holy/Trampled Under Foot/Kashmir/In The Light/Bron-Yr-Aur/Down By The Seaside/Ten Years Gone/Night Flight/The Wanton Song/Boogie With Stu/Black Country Woman/Sick Again*

Presence (1976 – Swan Song/Warner)
Track Listing: *Achilles Last Stand/For Your Life/Royal Orleans/Nobody's Fault But Mine/Candy Store Rock/Hots On For Nowhere/Tea For One*

In Through The Out Door (1979 – Swan Song/Warner)
Track Listing: *In The Evening/South Bound Saurez/Fool In The Rain/Hot Dog/Carouselambra/All My Love/I'm Gonna Crawl*

Coda (1982 – Swan Song/Warner)
Track Listing: *We're Gonna Groove/Poor Tom/I Can't Quit You Baby/Walter's Walk/Ozone Baby/Darlene/ Bonzo's Montreux /Wearing And Tearing*

COMPILATIONS/COLLECTIONS

Remasters(1990 – Atlantic)
Track Listing:
Disc One – *Communication Breakdown/Babe I'm Gonna Leave You/Good Times Bad Times/Dazed And Confused/Whole Lotta Love/Heartbreaker/Ramble On/Immigrant Song/Celebration Day/Since I've Been Loving You/Black Dog/Rock And Roll/The Battle Of Evermore/Misty Mountain Hop/Stairway To Heaven*
Disc Two – *The Song Remains The Same/Rain Song/D'yer Mak'er/No Quarter/Houses Of The Holy/Kashmir/Trampled Under Foot/Nobody's Fault But Mine/Achilles Last Stand/All My Love/In The Evening*

Led Zeppelin (Vol. 1)(1990 – Atlantic)
Track Listing:
Disc One – *Whole Lotta Love/Heartbreaker/Communication Breakdown/Babe I'm Gonna Leave You/What Is And What Should Never Be/Thank You/I Can't Quit You Baby/Dazed And Confused/Your Time Is Gonna Come/Ramble On/Traveling Riverside Blues*/Friends/Celebration Day/Hey Hey What Can I Do*/White Summer/Black Mountain Side*/*
Disc Two – *Black Dog/Over The Hills And Far Away/Immigrant Song/The Battle Of Evermore/Bron-Y-Aur Stomp/Tangerine/Going To California/Since I've Been Loving You/D'yer Mak'er/Gallows Pole/Custard Pie/Misty Mountain Hop/Rock And Roll/The Rain Song/Stairway To Heaven*
Disc Three – *Kashmir/Trampled Under Foot/For Your Life/No Quarter/Dancing Days/When The Levee Breaks/Achilles Last Stand/The Song Remains The Same/Ten Years Gone/In My Time Of Dying*
Disc Four – *In The Evening/Candy Store Rock/The Ocean/Ozone Baby/Houses Of The Holy/Wearing And Tearing/Poor Tom/Nobody's Fault But Mine/Fool In The Rain/In The Light/The Wanton Song/Moby Dick/Bonzo's Montreux*/I'm Gonna Crawl/All My Love*
* Exclusive tracks

Led Zeppelin (Vol. 2) (1993 – Atlantic)

Track Listing:

Disc One – *Good Times Bad Times/We're Gonna Groove/Night Flight/That's The Way/Baby Come On Home*/The Lemon Song/You Shook Me/Boogie With Stu/Bron-Yr-Aur/Down By The Seaside/Out On The Tiles/Black Mountain Side/Moby Dick/Sick Again/Hot Dog/Carouselambra*
Disc Two – *South Bound Saurez/Walter's Walk/Darlene/Black Country Woman/How Many More Times/The Rover/Four Sticks/Hats Off To (Roy) Harper/I Can't Quit You Baby/Hots On For Nowhere/Living Loving Maid (She's Just A Woman)/Royal Orleans/Bonzo's Montreux/The Crunge/Bring It On Home/Tea For One*
*Exclusive tracks

Complete Studio Recordings (1994 – Atlantic)

Track Listing:

Disc One **(Led Zeppelin)** – *Good Times Bad Times/Babe I'm Gonna Leave You/You Shook Me/Dazed And Confused/Your Time Is Gonna Come/Black Mountain Side/Communication Breakdown/I Can't Quit You Baby/How Many More Times*
Disc Two **(Led Zeppelin II)** – *Whole Lotta Love/What Is And What Should Never Be/The Lemon Song/Thank You/Heartbreaker/Living Loving Maid (She's Just A Woman)/Ramble On/Moby Dick/Bring It On Home*
Disc Three **(Led Zeppelin III)** – *Immigrant Song/Friends/Celebration Day/Since I've Been Loving You/Out On The Tiles/Gallows Pole/Tangerine/That's The Way/Bron-Y-Aur Stomp/Hats Off To (Roy Harper)*
Disc Four **(Led Zeppelin IV)** – *Black Dog/Rock And Roll/The Battle Of Evermore/Stairway To Heaven/Misty Mountain Top/Four Sticks/Going To California/When The Levee Breaks*
Disc Five **(Houses Of The Holy)** – *The Song Remains The Same/The Rain Song/Over The Hills And Far Away/The Crunge/Dancing Days/D'yer Mak'er/No Quarter/The Ocean*
Disc Six **(Presence)** – *Achilles Last Stand/For Your Life/Royal Orleans/Nobody's Fault But Mine/Candy Store Rock/Hots On For Nowhere/Tea For One*
Disc Seven **(Physical Graffiti)** – *Custard Pie/The Rover/In My Time Of Dying/House Of The Holy/Trampled Under Foot/Kasmir*
Disc Eight **(Physical Graffiti)** – *In The Light/Bron-Yr-Aur/Down By The Seaside/Ten Years Gone/Night Flight/The Wanton Song/Boogie With Stu/Black Country Woman/Sick Again*
Disc Nine **(In Through The Out Door)** – *In The Evening/South Bound Saurez/Fool In The Rain/Hot Dog/Carouselambra/All My Love/I'm Gonna Crawl*
Disc Ten **(Coda)** – *We're Gonna Groove/Poor Tom/I Can't Quit You Baby/Walter's Walk/Ozone Baby/Darlene/ Bonzo's Montreux /Wearing And Tearing/Baby Come On Home*/Traveling Riverside Blues*/White Summer/Black Mountain Side*/Hey Hey What Can I Do**
* Bonus tracks

Early Days: The Best Of Led Zeppelin Volume One (1999 – Atlantic)

Track Listing: *Good Times Bad Times/Babe I'm Gonna Leave You/Dazed And Confused/Communication Breakdown/Whole Lotta Love/What Is And What Should Never Be/Immigrant Song/Since I've Been Loving You/Black Dog/Rock And Roll/The Battle Of Evermore/When The Levee Breaks/Stairway To Heaven*

Latter Days: The Best Of Led Zeppelin Volume Two (2000 – Atlantic)

Track Listing: *The Song Remains The Same/No Quarter/House Of The Holy/Trampled Under Foot/Kashmir/Ten Years Gone/Achilles Last Stand/Nobody's Fault But Mine/All My Love/In The Evening*

Mothership (2007 – Atlantic/Rhino Entertainment)
Track Listing:
Disc One: *Good Times Bad Times/Communication Breakdown/Dazed And Confused/Babe I'm Gonna Leave You/Whole Lotta Love/Ramble On/Heartbreaker/ Immigrant Song/Since I've Been Loving You/Rock And Roll/Black Dog/When The Levee Breaks/Stairway To Heaven*
Disc Two: *The Song Remains The Same/Over The Hills And Far Away/ D'yer Mak'er/No Quarter/Trampled Under Foot/Houses Of The Holy/Kashmir/Nobody's Fault But Mine/Achilles Last Stand/In The Evening/All My Love*

LIVE ALBUMS

The Song Remains The Same (1976 – Swan Song)
Track Listing: *Rock And Roll/Celebration Day/The Song Remains The Same/Rain Song/Dazed And Confused/No Quarter/Stairway To Heaven/Moby Dick/Whole Lotta Love*

BBC Sessions (1997 – Atlantic)
Track Listing:
Disc One – *You Shook Me/I Can't Quit You Baby/Communication Breakdown/Dazed And Confused/The Girl I Love She Got Long Black Wavy Hair/What Is And What Should Never Be/Traveling Riverside Blues/Whole Lotta Love/Somethin' Else/Communication Breakdown/I Can't Quit You Baby/You Shook Me/How Many More Times/Immigrant Song/Heartbreaker/Since I've Been Loving You/Black Dog/Dazed And Confused/Stairway To Heaven/Going To California/That's The Way/Whole Lotta Love/Thank You*
Disc Two – *Immigrant Song/Heartbreaker/Since I've Been Loving You/Black Dog/Dazed And Confused/Stairway To Heaven/Going To California/That's The Way/Whole Lotta Love/Thank You*

How The West Was Won (2003 – Atlantic)
Track Listing:
Disc One – *L.A. Drone/Immigrant Song/Heartbreaker/Black Dog/Over The Hills And Far Away/Since I've Been Loving You/Stairway To Heaven/Going To California/That's The Way/Bron-Yr-Aur Stomp*
Disc Two – *Dazed And Confused★/Walter's Walk★/The Crunge★/What Is And What Should Never Be/Dancing Days/Moby Dick*
Disc Three – *Whole Lotta Love★/Boogie Chillun★/Let's Have A Party★/Hello Mary Lou★/Going Down Slow★/Rock And Roll/The Ocean/Bring It On Home/Bring It On Back*
★Medley

The Song Remains The Same (2007 – Atlantic/Rhino Entertainment)
Track Listing:
Disc One: *Rock And Roll/Celebration Day/Black Dog (including Bring It On Home)★/Over The Hills★/Misty Mountain Hop★/Since I've Been Loving You★/No Quarter/The Song Remains The Same/Rain Song/The Ocean★*
Disc Two: *Dazed And Confused/Stairway To Heaven/Moby Dick/Heartbreaker★/Whole Lotta Love (Note: The songs marked ★ were not included on the original release)*

ROBERT PLANT (POST-LED ZEPPELIN)

STUDIO ALBUMS

Pictures At Eleven (1982 – Swan Song)
Track Listing: *Burning Down One Side/Moonlight On Samosa/Pledge Pin/Slow Dancer/Worse Than Detroit/Fat Lip/Like I've Never Been Gone/Mystery Title/Far Post*/Like I've Never Been Gone (live)**
*Bonus tracks on the 2007 reissue released by Rhino Entertainment

The Principle Of Moments (1983 – Es Paranza)
Track Listing: *Other Arms/In The Mood/Messin' With The Mekon/Wreckless Love/Thru' With The Two Step/Horizontal Departure/Stranger Here ... Than Over There/Big Log/In The Mood (live)*/Thru' With The Two Step (live)*/Lively Up Yourself (live)*/Turnaround**
*Bonus tracks on the 2007 reissue released by Rhino Entertainment

Shaken 'n' Stirred (1985 – Es Paranza)
Track Listing: *Hip To Hoo/Kallalo Kallalou/Too Loud/Trouble Your Money/Pink And Black/Little By Little/Doo Doo A Do Do/Easily Lead/Sixes And Sevens/Little By Little (remix)**
*Bonus track on the 2007 reissue released by Rhino Entertainment

Now And Zen (1988 – Es Paranza)
Track Listing: *Heaven Knows/Dance On My Own/Tall Cool One/The Way I Feel/Helen Of Troy/Billy's Revenge/Ship Of Fools/Why/White, Clean And Neat/Walking Towards Paradise/Billy's Revenge (live)*/Ship Of Fools (live)*/Tall Cool One (live)**
*Bonus tracks on the 2007 reissue released by Rhino Entertainment

Manic Nirvana (1990 – Es Paranza)
Track Listing: *Hurting Kind (I've Got My Eyes On You)/Big Love/S S S & Q/I Cried/Nirvana/Tie Dye On The Highway/Your Ma Said You Cried In Your Sleep Last Night/Anniversary/Liars Dance/Watching You/Oompa (Watery Bint)*/One Love*/Don't Look Back**
*Bonus tracks on the 2007 reissue released by Rhino Entertainment

Fate Of Nations (1993 – Phontana/Es Paranza)
Track Listing: *Call To You/Down To The Sea/Come Into My Life/I Believe/29 Palms/Memory Song (Hello Hello)/If I Were A Carpenter/Colours Of A Shade/Promised Land/The Greatest Gift/Great Spirit/Network News/Colours Of Shade*/Great Spirit*/Rollercoaster*/805*/Dark Moon**
*Bonus tracks on the 2007 reissue released by Rhino Entertainment

Raising Sand (with Alison Krauss) (2007 – Universal)
Track Listing: *Rich Woman/ Killing The Blues/ Sister Rosetta Goes Before Us/ Polly Come Home/ Gone, Gone, Gone/ Through The Morning, Through The Night/ Please Read The Letter/ Trampled Rose/ Fortune Teller/ Stick With Me Baby/ Nothin'/ Let Your Loss Be Your Lesson/ Your Long Journey*

COMPILATIONS/COLLECTIONS

Sixty Six To Timbuktu (2003 – Mercury)
Track Listing:
Disc One – *Tie Dye On The Highway/Upside Down/Promised Land/Tall Cool One/Dirt In A Hole/Calling To You/29 Palms/If I Were A Carpenter/Sea Of Love/Darkness, Darkness/Big Log/Ship Of Fools/I Believe/Little By Little/Heaven Knows/Song To The Siren*

Disc Two – *You'd Better Run/Our Song/Hey Joe/For What It's Worth/Operator/Road To The Sun/Philadelphia Boy/Red Is For Danger/Let's Have A Party/Hey Jayne/Louie, Louie/Naked If I Want To/21 Years/If It's Really Got To Be This Way/Rude World/Little Hands/Life Begin Again/Let The Boogie Woogie Roll/Win My Train Far Home (live)*

Nine Lives (2006 – Rhino)
Track Listing:
Disc One **(Pictures At Eleven)** – *Burning Down One Side/Moonlight On Samosa/Pledge Pin/Slow Dancer/Worse Than Detroit/Fat Lip/Like I've Never Been Gone/Mystery Title/ Far Post*/Like I've Never Been Gone (live)**

Disc Two **(The Principle Of Moments)** – *Other Arms/In The Mood/Messin' With The Mekon/Wreckless Love/Thru' With The Two Step/Horizontal Departure/Stranger Here … Than Over There/Big Log/In The Mood/Thru' With The Two Step/Lively Up Yourself/Turnaround/In The Mood (live)*/Thru' With The Two Step (live)*/Lively Up Yourself (live)*/Turnaround**

Disc Three **(The Honeydrippers: Volume One)** – *I Get A Thrill/Sea Of Love/I Got A Woman/Young Boy Blues/Rockin' At Midnight/Rockin' At Midnight (live)**

Disc Four **(Shaken 'n' Stirred)** – *Hip To Hoo/Kallalo Kallalou/Too Loud/Trouble Your Money/Pink And Black/Little By Little/Doo Doo A Do Do/Easily Lead/Sixes And Sevens/Little By Little/Little By Little (remix)**

Disc Five **(Now And Zen)** – *Heaven Knows/Dance On My Own/Tall Cool One/The Way I Feel/Helen Of Troy/Billy's Revenge/Ship Of Fools/Why/White, Clean And Neat/Walking Towards Paradise/Billy's Revenge/Ship Of Fools/Tall Cool One/ Billy's Revenge (live)*/Ship Of Fools (live)*/Tall Cool One (live)**

Disc Six **(Manic Nirvana)** – *Hurting Kind (I've Got My Eyes On You)/Big Love/S S S & Q/I Cried/Nirvana/Tie Dye On The Highway/Your Ma Said You Cried In Your Sleep Last Night/Anniversary/Liars Dance/Watching You/Oompa (Watery Bint)/One Love/Don't Look Back/Oompa (Watery Bint)*/One Love*/Don't Look Back**

Disc Seven **(Fate Of Nations)** – *Call To You/Down To The Sea/Come Into My Life/I Believe/29 Palms/Memory Song (Hello Hello)/If I Were A Carpenter/Colours Of A Shade/Promised Land/The Greatest Gift/Great Spirit/Network News/Colours Of A Shade/Great Spirit/Rollercoaster/805/Dark Moon/Colours Of Shade*/Great Spirit*/Rollercoaster*/805*/Dark Moon**

Disc Eight **(Dreamland)** – *Funny In My Mind/Morning Dew/One More Cup Of Coffee/Last Time I Saw Her/Song To The Siren/Win My Train Fare Home/Darkness, Darkness/Red Dress/Hey Joe/Skip's Song/Dirt In A Hole/Last Time I Saw Her/Dirt In A Hole*/Last Time I Saw Her (remix)**

Disc Nine **(Mighty ReArranger)** – *Another Tribe/Shine It All Around/Freedom Fries/Tin Pan Valley/All The Kings Horses/The Enchanter/Takamba/Dancing In Heaven/Somebody Knocking/Let The Four Winds Blow/Mighty ReArranger/Brother Ray/ Shine It All Around (remix)*/Red, White And Blue*/All The Money In The World*/Shine It All Around (Girls remix)*/Tin Pan Valley (Girls remix)*/The Enchanter (Unkle Reconstruction)**

Disc Ten **(Nine Lives** DVD) – *Nine Lives+/Burning Down One Side/Big Log/In the Mood/Rockin' At Midnight/Sea Of Love/Little By Little/Pink And Black/Heaven Knows/Tall Cool One/Ship Of Fools/Hurting Kind (I've Got my Eyes On You)*

*Bonus tracks

+Documentary (The DVD contains music videos to the songs listed).

SINGLES

Burning Down One Side (1982 – Swan Song)

Big Log (1983 – WEA)

Heaven Knows (1988 – Es Paranza)

Hurting Kind (I've Got My Eyes On You) (1990 – Es Paranza)

29 Palms (1993 – Es Paranza)

I Believe (1993 – Es Paranza)

If I Were A Carpenter (1993 – Es Paranza)

THE HONEYDRIPPERS
(FEAT. ROBERT PLANT, JIMMY PAGE & JEFF BECK)

STUDIO ALBUMS

The Honeydrippers: Volume One (EP) (1984 – Es Paranza)
Track Listing: *I Get A Thrill/Sea Of Love/I Got A Woman/Young Boy Blues/Rockin' At Midnight/Rockin' At Midnight (live)* ★
★Bonus track on the 2007 reissue released by Rhino Entertainment

SINGLES

Sea Of Love (1985 – Es Paranza)

PAGE & PLANT
(ROBERT PLANT & JIMMY PAGE)

STUDIO ALBUMS

Walking Into Clarksdale (1998 – Mercury)
Track Listing: *Shining In The Light/When The World Was Young/Upon A Golden Horse/Blue Train/Please Read The Letter/Most High/Heart In Your Hand/Walking Into Clarksdale/Burning Up/When I was A Child/House Of Love/Sons Of Freedom*

LIVE ALBUMS

No Quarter: Jimmy Page And Robert Plant Unledded (1994 – Phonogram/Fontana)
Track Listing: *Nobody's Fault But Mine/Thank You/No Quarter/Friends/Yallah/City Don't Cry/Since I've Been Loving You/The Battle Of Evermore/Wonderful One/That's The Way/Gallows Pole/Four Sticks/Kashmir*
(NOTE: This album was reissued in 2004 with a different track listing)

SINGLES

Gallows Pole (1994 – Phonogram/Fontana)

Most High (1998 – Mercury)

ROBERT PLANT
& THE STRANGE SENSATION

STUDIO ALBUMS

Dreamland (2002 – Mercury)
Track Listing: *Funny In My Mind/Morning Dew/One More Cup Of Coffee/Last Time I Saw Her/Song To The Siren/Win My Train Fare Home/Darkness, Darkness/Red Dress/Hey Joe/Skip's Song/Dirt In A Hole*

Mighty ReArranger (2005 – Sanctuary/ Es Paranza)
Track Listing: *Another Tribe/Shine It All Around/Freedom Fries/Tin Pan Valley/All The Kings Horses/The Enchanter/Takamba/Dancing In Heaven/Somebody Knocking/Let The Four Winds Blow/Mighty ReArranger/Brother Ray/Shine It All Around (remix)*/Red, White And Blue+/All The Money In The World+/Shine It All Around (Girls remix) +/Tin Pan Valley (Girls remix)+/The Enchanter (Unkle Reconstruction)+*
*Hidden track
+ Bonus tracks on the 2007 remastered and expanded deluxe edition

APPENDIX VII:
SELECTIVE FILMOGRAPHY (UK)

There are far too many 'unofficial' Led Zeppelin DVD's to name here so I have included the more important ones, which are all 'official' titles. To avoid complications the DVD's listed here include the original release date on DVD rather than on any other format. This is not a complete list and the author has referred to UK releases only...

LED ZEPPELIN

The Song Remains The Same **(DVD)**
(2000 – Warner Home Video)

Led Zeppelin **(DVD)**
(2003 – Warner Music Vision)

The Song Remains The Same **(Deluxe remastered DVD with added features)**
(2007 – Warner Home Video)

PAGE & PLANT

No Quarter: Jimmy Page Robert Plant Unledded **(DVD)**
(2004 – Warner Music Vision)

ROBERT PLANT
& THE STRANGE SENSATION

Soundstage **(DVD)**
(2006 – Universal)

APPENDIX VIII:
SELECTIVE BIBLIOGRAPHY:
RELATED & RECOMMENDED
BOOKS ON LED ZEPPELIN

This is by no means a complete list of books on the band but the ones listed here are amongst some of the more worthwhile and important Led Zeppelin related titles, so they are definitely recommended. They are listed in alphabetical order according to the author's name. The author gratefully acknowledges permission to quote and use references from some of the books on this list. Every quote and reference taken from selected books is fully acknowledged in the main text.

However, it has not been entirely possible to contact every copyright holder but every effort has been made to contact all copyright holders and to clear reprint permissions from this list of sources. If notified, the publishers will be pleased to rectify any omission in future editions.

LED ZEPPELIN

Clayson, Alan.
Led Zeppelin: The Origin Of The Species – How, Why And Where It All Began.
(Chrome Dreams, 2006)

Cole, Richard & Turbo, Richard.
Stairway To Heaven: Led Zeppelin Uncensored.
(Harper Collins, 1992)

Cross, R. Chris & Flannigan, Erik.
Led Zeppelin: Heaven & Hell.
(Crown Publications, 1991)

Davis, Stephen.
Hammer Of The Gods: Led Zeppelin Unauthorised.
(Pan Macmillan, 1995) *(Revised – originally published in 1985)*

Epting, Chris.
Led Zeppelin Crashed Here: The Rock And Roll Landmarks Of North America.
(Santa Monica Press, 2007)

Godwin, Robert.
The Making Of Led Zeppelin's IV.
(Collectors' Guide Publishing, 1996)

Godwin, Robert.
Led Zeppelin: The Press Reports.
(Collector's Guide Publishing, 2005) *(Revised – originally published in 1997)*

Hoskyns, Barney.
Led Zeppelin IV: Rock Of Ages.
(Rodale Books, 2007)

Hulcett, Ralph & Jerry, Prochnicky.
Whole Lotta Led.
(Citadel Press Inc, 2005)

Lewis, Dave.
Led Zeppelin: A Celebration.
(Omnibus Press, 1991)

Lewis, Dave & Pallet, Simon.
Led Zeppelin: The Concert File.
(Omnibus Press, 2005)

Preston, Neal.
Led Zeppelin Portraits.
(Harpercollins, 1986)

Preston, Neal.
Led Zeppelin: A Photographic Collection.
(Vision, 2002)

Shadwick, Keith.
Led Zeppelin: 1968-1980.
(Backbeat, 2006)

Welch, Chris.
Led Zeppelin: Dazed And Confused: The Stories Behind Every Song.
(Thunder's Mouth Press, 2005)

Yorke, Ritchie.
Led Zeppelin: From The Early Days To Page & Plant.
(Virgin Books, 1999) *(Revised – originally published in 1974)*

JIMMY PAGE

Case, George.
Jimmy Page: Magus, Musician, Man: An Authorized Biography.
(Hal Leonard Publishing Corporation, 2007)

Friend, W Thomas.
Fallen Angel: The Untold Story Of Jimmy Page And Led Zeppelin.
(Gabriel Publishing Inc, 2003)

White, Juliann.
Jimmy Page: Past Presence.
(Xlibris Corporation, 2002)

JOHN BONHAM

Bonham, Michael & Deborah.
Bonham On Bonham: My Brother John.
(Icarus Publications, 2003)

Bonham, Mick.
John Bonham: The Powerhouse Behind Led Zeppelin.
(Southbank Publishing, 2005)

Welch, Chris & Nicholls, Geoff.
John Bonham: A Thunder Of Drums.
(Backbeat Books, 2001)

PETER GRANT

Welch, Chris.
Peter Grant: The Man Who Led Zeppelin.
(Omnibus Press, 2002)

SOURCES

In addition to the books listed in the bibliography, the following publications and multimedia sources have been imperative in writing this book. The author is indebted to them all. Special mention must be given to *Classic Rock* and the brilliant www.robertplanthomepage.com. The author gratefully acknowledges permission to quote and use references from this list of sources where it has been attained. Every quote and reference taken from selected sources is fully acknowledged in the main text.
However, it has not been entirely possible to contact every copyright holder but every effort has been made to contact all copyright holders and to clear reprint permissions from this list of sources. If notified, the publishers will be pleased to rectify any omission in future editions.

Music Biographies

Carson, Annette.
Jeff Beck: Crazy Fingers.
(Backbeat Books: London, 2001)

Holder, Noddy & Verrico, Lisa.
Who's Crazee Now.
(Ebury Press: London, 1999)

Music Reference

Betts, Graham.
Complete UK Hit Singles: 1952-2005.
(Collins: London, 2005)

Betts, Graham.
Complete UK Hit Albums: 1956-2005.
(Collins: London, 2005)

Hornsby, Laurie. (Edited by Mike Lavender)
Brum Rocked On!
(GSM Bestsellers, LTD: Sutton Coldfield, 2003)

Miscellaneous Music Books

Klosterman, Chuck.
Chuck Klosterman IV: A Decade Of Curious People And Dangerous Ideas.
(Faber & Faber: London. 2006)

Wall, Mick.
Star Trippin': The Best of Mick Wall – 1985-'91.
(M&G Publishing: London, 2006)

Magazines/Music Papers

Billboard, Classic Rock, Folk Roots, Kerrang!, Melody Maker, Mojo, The Music Box, Music Express, Musician Magazine, NME, Q, Record Collector, Record Magazine, Rolling Stone, Sounds, Spin, Top Pops & Uncut.

National/Local Newspapers (in chronological order)

Detroit News, July 25, 1982

Detroit News, September 2, 1983

The New York Times, April 8, 1995

The Independent, November 7, 1998

The Guardian, October 14, 2005

The Independent, November 25, 2005

Daily Express, September 28, 2007

Online Articles (in chronological order)

Lion Among Zebras: The Robert Plant Interview – 1976
(Writer unknown. *Circus,* 1976 – see *http://trublukris.tripod.com*)

Life After Led Zeppelin by John Hutchinson
(*Record Magazine,* September, 2, 1983)

Life In A Lighter Zeppelin by J.D. Considine
(December, 1983 – see *www.led-zeppelin.org*)

Stairway To Snowdonia: Rapping With Robert Plant by Barney Hoskyns
(*Rock's Backpages,* October, 2003)

Robert Plant Related Websites

www.robertplant.com (Official artist website)
www.robertplanthomepage.com

Led Zeppelin Related Websites

www.geocities.com/Athens/2406 (*Led Zeppelin & JRR Tolkien Relations Page*)
www.johnpauljones.com (Official artist website)
www.led-zeppelin.com (Official band website)
www.led-zeppelin.org (includes an extensive 1992 interview with ex-members of the Band Of Joy)
www.tightbutloose.co.uk (*TBL* is a magnificent tribute site run by the respected Led Zeppelin archivist Dave Lewis)
http://users.adelphia.net (an archive site called *Led Zeppelin Live: The Reviews*)

Music Websites

www.allmusic.com
www.artistdirect.com
www.blender.com
www.blogcritics.org
www.brumbeat.net
www.dailyvault.com
www.gactv.com
www.getreadytorock.com
www.globalvillageidiot.net
www.hairballjohnradioshow.com
www.harpmagazine.com
www.inmusicwetrust.com
www.livedaily.com
www.mfnrocks.com
www.melodicrock.com
www.metalunderground.com
www.mixonline.com
www.mp3.com
www.music.msn.com
www.music.yahoo.com
www.musicbox-online.com
www.musicomh.com
www.newbeats.com
www.rock-is-life.com
www.rocksbackpages.com
www.rollingstone.com
www.sputnikmusic.com
www.superseventies.com
www.therockradio.com
www.the-trades.com
www.treblezine.com
www.trublukris.tripod.com
www.2walls.com
www.vintagerock.com

Entertainment Websites

www.barnesandnoble.com
www.dvdmg.com
www.80sxchange.com
www.ew.com
http://jam.canoe.ca

www.theshrubbery.com
www.swaves.com
www.variety.com

Non- Music/Entertainment Websites

www.aboutmediakit.com
www.afropop.org
www.connollyco.com
www.salon.com

News Websites

www.bbc.co.uk
www.expressandstar.co.uk
www.guardian.co.uk
http://lifestyle.timesofmalta.com
www.npr.org
www.nytimes.com
www.pbs.org
www.timesonline.co.uk
www.usatoday.cm
http://wkrn.com/nashville

FOOTNOTES

[1] Although an edited version of 'Whole Lotta Love' was almost released in the UK with 'Livin' Lovin' Main (She's Just A Woman)' as a B-side, Peter Grant quickly stepped in and quashed any plans by Atlantic to issue the single.

[2] Two regions in the English Midlands.

[3] People born between July 23 and August 23.

[4] Plant still has close connections to the area and lives on a farm that lies on the Welsh Border near Kidderminster. He told *Circus* magazine in 1976 that he will "always keep a toe in the country."

[5] A 'rock and roll meets country' sound, which dominated the airwaves back in the 1950s.

[6] Eric Clapton is another student of Robert Johnson's school of blues; he even recorded an album of Johnson covers in 2004 called *Me And Mr. Johnson*, which was greeted with favourable reviews.

[7] Merseybeat is also known as the Liverpool Sound and the Mersey Sound.

[8] Simpson later managed a Midlands band by the name of Black Sabbath, previously known as Earth.

[9] Baldry died in Vancouver, Canada – his adopted home – in 2005.

[10] Although it should be noted that The Animals moved from Newcastle to the capital in 1964 at the time of the highly-publicised British invasion of America.

[11] Confusingly there were actually three line-ups of the band with Robert Plant between 1966 and 1968.

[12] Mitchell and Young are actually Canadian.

[13] The exact origins of the song have caused a great deal of debate but the Hendrix version was a cover of the Tim Rose folk version; it was recorded on the request of Hendrix's manager Chas Chandler, formally the bassist in The Animals. The very loose connection between Tim Rose and the Band Of Joy would spring up again in the near-future.

[14] It should be noted that some reports have suggested that Pete Robinson, who had previously been in an earlier line-up of the Band Of Joy, was also involved in the project.

[15] Al Atkins says that after Possessed, which featured both Mick Reeves and Vernon Perera, "they both got killed while returning from a gig at Carlisle in the group's bus."

[16] Presumably the death of Karac, Robert Plant's son, in 1977, more of which later.

[17] Included on Plant's 2003 compilation, *Sixty Six To Timbuktu*.

[18] A singer who is technically wedged between a tenor and a mezzo-soprano.

[19] Some recent reliable sources have suggested that they actually finished playing under the New Yardbirds moniker after a gig at Liverpool University on October 19. Either way it was certainly the second half of 1968 when they went ahead with the name change.

[20] The album had been recorded in October, 1968 at Olympic Studios in Barnes, south London.

[21] The Dixon song in question is 'You Need Love'; he has since been credited as a co-writer of the song.

[22] Plant later resurrected the song on his *Manic Nirvana* tour in 1990.

[23] An extended medley of 'How Many More Times' incorporated a number of other songs, namely, 'The Hunter', 'Boogie Chillun'', 'High Flyin' Mama', 'Down By The River',

'Travelling Riverside Blues', 'Long Distance Call' and 'The Lemon Song.' An organ solo was
also played mid-way through the set.

[24] Years later, the late Bon Scott and Angus Young of AC/DC would be perfect examples of
how well a guitarist and front man can work together on stage with such confidence.

[25] Page often enjoyed a bottle of Jack Daniels bourbon.

[26] Also see *Star Trippin': The Best Of Mick Wall – 1985-91.*

[27] On the subject of Robert Plant and Rob Halford – two West Midlands lads – it is worth
mentioning that in December, 2006 it was reported on the *Metal Underground* website
(*www.metalunderground.com*) that *Hit Parader* voted Robert Plant as the Number 1 heavy
metal singer in their survey of 'Heavy Metal's All Time Top 100 Vocalists.' Rob 'Metal God'
Halford arrived at Number 2.

[28] "My vocal was shot when I sang it … it is a complete imitation; light-hearted but clever in
some respects," he explained to *Record Magazine* in '83.

[29] Page himself was in Sicily where he was interested in buying a farmhouse once used by
Aleister Crowley before he was told to leave Italy by Mussolini.

[30] The film and accompanying soundtrack was released in October, 1976 to a mixed reception.

[31] "…my knowledge of Arabic music, although limited, is equally fanatical," he enthused to
Record Magazine's J.D. Considine in 1983.

[32] A similar compassion (and empathy) is felt on the Eric Clapton track, 'Tears In Heaven', a
song about his four-year-old son, Conor, who died in 1991.

[33] Lemmy loathes to call Motörhead a heavy metal band; they are a rare exception to any rule,
because they were loved by both the punk and metal fan bases.

[34] The names of such drummers as the Foo Fighters singer/guitarist and ex-Nirvana drummer
Dave Grohl have cropped up over the years.

[35] Plant returned to Rockfield in 2006 where he was reunited with Robbie Blunt and Jezz
Woodruffe for a 25th anniversary celebration of the release of *Pictures At Eleven*. He told one
journalist for the *BBC* (*www.bbc.co.uk*): "Rockfield was an absolute dream because it was
pastoral, funny and had a fantastic musical history … I really enjoyed my being in this
environment. I had lived in this goldfish bowl in Led Zeppelin … so it was fantastic to
come here and find this whole culture [of musicians] around Monmouth." Indeed, Plant's
enduring legacy and his relationship with Rockfield has left an indelible impression on
young rock musicians who aspire to record at the famed studios in south Wales.

[36] The live versions of 'Pledge Pin' and 'Horizontal Departure' were used as B-sides to 'In The
Mood' and others were used as bonus tracks on the 2007 expanded editions of each of his
solo albums.

[37] 'How Many More Times' was re-worked by Zeppelin on their first album.

[38] The reissue included a live version of 'Rockin' At Midnight' recorded on September 8, 1985.

[39] The tour ultimately provided live recordings for future use as bonus tracks and B-sides.

[40] Initially the album was called *Pink & Black.*

[41] Further Zeppelin references are found on 'Pink And Black' and 'Easily Lead.'

[42] The reissue includes a longer remixed version of 'Little By Little.'

[43] Reportedly Plant and Crash wrote eighteen songs together.

[44] Plant dislodged its initial title, the rather bland, *Wolves.*

[45] The 2007 reissue includes previously unreleased live versions of 'Billy's Revenge', 'Tall Cool
One', and 'Ship of Fools'.

[46] Plant also found time during the US tour to fly off and play a couple of rearranged gigs in Ireland in September.

[47] 'Your Mama Said You Cried In Your Sleep Last Night' was released later in the year in May and, like its sibling, barely made a dent in the singles charts on both sides of the Atlantic. No more singles were released off the album.

[48] The reissue features three bonus tracks: 'Oompa (Watery Bint)' 'One Love' and 'Don't Look Back'.

[49] Dome was far less kind to Myles, who allegedly had a relationship with Plant at the time which lasted around a year. He wrote: "Precisely why Plant chose this hopeless individual to support him remains a mystery."

[50] January 8, 9 and 10.

[51] For example, it's doubtful that he could have matched the thirty two sold out nights at London's Royal Albert Hall as Eric Clapton had in 1990/91.

[52] Reading the sleeve notes to the album and looking at how many musicians are given credits will explain the convoluted state of personnel at the time.

[53] The song gave Plant a Grammy Nomination in 1994 for 'Best Hard Rock Performance With Vocal'.

[54] The reissue features a few bonus tracks: 'Colours Of A Shade', an acoustic version of 'Great Spirit', the demo 'Rollercoaster' and the acoustic song 'Dark Moon'.

[55] Kevin MacMichael died in 2002 from lung cancer.

[56] In September, 1994, John Paul Jones released *The Sporting Life*, his album with Diamanda Galas.

[57] Itself a re-recording of the same-titled Blind Willie Johnson song.

[58] *No Quarter* was reissued on CD in 1994 with 'Yallah' being retitled as 'The Truth Explodes' while the US version contains additional tracks. Stephen Thomas Erlewine enthused in the *All Music Guide* (*www.allmusic.com*): "Nevertheless, the *Unplugged* setting did give the duo an opportunity to gracefully back away from the bombast that was assumed to be Zeppelin's stock-in-trade ... As good as much of *No Quarter* is, it isn't necessarily the kind of record that invites those repeated listens. At its core, it's an experiment, the sound of two middle-aged musicians looking back at their groundbreaking work ..."

[59] The Black Crowes were special guests at the gigs in Glasgow at Sheffield.

[60] 'Most High' won Page & Plant a Grammy award in 1999 for 'Best Hard Rock Performance'.

[61] In between the first bout of touring and the release of *Dreamland*, it was announced in 2001 that Robert Plant had become patron of a newly-founded West Midlands based record label called MAS (Mighty Atom Smasher) Records organised by Kevyn Gammond and Kim Tanser of Kidderminster College. The community label is also supported by students on the Music Industry Management course at Kidderminster College. Kim Tanser spoke to *BBC Hereford And Worcester* in 2003 about the project: "MAS Records has been set up to provide a framework of expertise and resources to support the development of music in our area."

[62] Surprisingly, it has been reported that Plant and his band even teased the audience with a segment of 'Stairway To Heaven' during the encore, which was the last of three songs listed.

[63] As Plant's name was publicly attached to the tour a wide number of bootlegs appeared on the market and are still readily available on the internet.

[64] Led Zeppelin covered 'We're Gonna Groove' in their live set list in 1970 but it didn't appear on record until the release of the 'odds and ends' album, *Coda*, in 1982.

65 The original title was *Heat First*.

66 During the time Plant had off the road in 2001, he didn't spend all his days working in the studio. He told *Entertainment Weekly* in 2002: "I've been quite happily doing nothing but improving my tennis game and flirting."

67 Around this time there was a minor change in the line-up of The Strange Sensation: guitarist Porl Thompson parted company from the band and was replaced by the capable talents of Liam Tyson, more commonly known as Skin. Tyson had made a name for himself as the lead guitarist in the Liverpool indie band Cast who achieved modest success in the latter years of the 1990s Britpop period.

68 'Funny In My Mind (I Believe I'm Fixin' To Die)' is credited as being an adaptation of the Bukka White number with input by Plant and his band. 'Win My Rain Fare Home (If I Get Lucky)' is an originally written song as is 'Red Dress' and 'Last Time I Saw Her'.

69 Two originally written bonus tracks – 'Dirt In A Hole' and 'Last Time I Saw Her' – were included in the prestigious *Nine Lives* retrospective box set, released in 2006 by Rhino Entertainment.

70 Plant got the chance to jam with the respected Malian guitarist Ali Farka Toure at the Festival. He told the *BBC*: "There is contemporary reflection of life here. There are heroes but these are the same heroes that were here at the time of all revolution and all political and sociological change."

71 Interestingly for eager fans, the album was released in a 'Special Edition' format with a bonus-disc that featured a 44 minute interview with Robert Plant, conducted by the revered British journalist Nigel Williamson; however, it only sold via the popular US retail company Best Buy. Coupled with the latter version, another 'Special Edition' of the album was issued in France a couple of months later with several live bonus songs that were recorded at Studio 104 in Paris on June 9. It sold via Plant's official website with proceeds going to a charity organisation called Turtle Will which aids native people in African countries. A few Led Zeppelin songs were included, namely, 'Black Dog', 'When The Levee Breaks', 'Gallows Pole' and 'Whole Lotta Love'.

72 In 2007, the album was reissued in remastered and expanded form by Rhino Entertainment. This latest version includes the bonus tracks 'Red, White And Blue', 'All The Money In The World', 'Shine It All Around (Girls Remix)' 'Tin Pan Valley (Girls Remix)' and 'The Enchanter (Unkle Reconstruction)'.

73 Somewhere amongst Plant's fully booked touring schedule he found time to lay down his vocals on a cover version of The Buzzcocks' 'Ever Fallen In Love (With Someone You Shouldn't've)?' for a John Peel tribute CD which was released in November.

74 Not forgetting he did manage to arrange a new line-up of The Honeydrippers to play a benefit gig in Kidderminster on December 23 and at a club in Dudley in January.

75 Jimmy Page's anti-hero Aleister Crowley – who died in obscurity and relative poverty in Hastings in 1947 – also found a new fan base within the hippie generation of the 1960s. New believers followed some of Crowley's fundamental beliefs such as free sex and the ability to find pleasure from pushing through the boundaries of pain.

76 The *Led Zeppelin and JRR Tolkien Relations Page* (*www.geocities.com/Athens/2406*) has some interesting and bewildering theories!

Editor's Note: The duo, Page & Plant, is referred to with an ampersand, to differentiate from the numerous narrative mentions of Robert Plant and Jimmy Page.

Visit our website at *www.impbooks.com*
for more information on our full list of titles, including books on:

Bruce Dickinson, Bernard Sumner, Slash, Damon Albarn,
MC5, Dave Grohl, Muse, The Streets, Johnny Marr,
Green Day, Ian Hunter, Mick Ronson,
David Bowie, The Killers, My Chemical Romance,
System Of A Down, The Prodigy and many more.